Alterity Politics

Alterity Politics

Ethics and Performative Subjectivity

Jeffrey T. Nealon

Duke University Press · Durham and London, 1998

© 1998 Duke University Press
All rights reserved
Printed in the United States of America on acid-free paper ∞
Typeset in Trump Mediaeval by Tseng Information Systems, Inc.
Library of Congress Cataloging-in-Publication Data appear
on the last printed page of this book.

For Barbara Nealon-Sanderson (1951–1989)
and Lorraine Jean Nealon (1928–1995)

Contents

Acknowledgments

Not surprisingly, this book owes itself to a series of relations with others. In and around State College, the site where the bulk of it was written, it owes its largest debt to that deployment of intensities known as Rich Doyle. Likewise, Caren Irr will see the material force of her thought reflected on virtually every page. And Sherry Brennan has been, from beginning to end, what Levinas would call this book's primary "provocation"—its most consistent critic as well as its biggest supporter.

The Cultural Studies Group at Penn State—especially Celeste Fraser Delgado, Steve Ellis, Henry Giroux, Billy Joe Harris, Susan Harris, Doug Holt, Iyun Osagie, Shari Roberts, Francesca Royster, and Evan Watkins—served as both a catalyst and a sounding board for much of this work. In addition, Don Bialostosky, John Sallis, and Sandy Schwartz provided valuable insight at critical moments.

Along the way, many other friends and colleagues have contributed more than they will ever know toward the development of this project. In State College: Amy Greenberg, Alphonso Lingis, Charles

Scott, and Susan Schoenbohm. At the 1993 NEH Seminar on Ethics and Aesthetics in Berkeley: John McGowan, Alan Schrift, Judith Butler, and Charles Altieri. In Chicago: those expert welcomers of the other, Pascale-Anne Brault and Michael Naas; on the international circuit: John Protevi. Elizabeth Grosz and Steven Shaviro produced crucial interventions around my reading of Deleuze; and, in a book that is at least partially about originary debts, I should note that Paul Davies's reading of Levinas laid the initial groundwork for much of this work.

During this writing I enjoyed crucial support from the Penn State Liberal Arts Research and Graduate Studies Office and the Department of English. The gift of time should never be taken lightly or without acknowledgment. Nor should the gift of cold, hard cash: Don Bialostosky, the Head of the English Department, and Ray Lombra, Associate Dean of Research and Graduate Studies, generously supported permissions costs for the art work in chapter 5.

This book is dedicated to my sister and my mother, the people who first taught me what a difference a little difference could make.

Preface

And while the intended liberatory aims of feminist and queer performativity are laudable, performative theory tends to be flawed by its disregard for ethical questions. —Lynne Huffer, "Luce *et Veritas:* Toward an Ethics of Performance"

Oddly enough, the trajectory of this text on ethics leads away from the recognizably ethical questions treated in the opening chapters (subjectivity, community, dialogics) toward more ethically unfamiliar notions like response to the inhuman, the chiasmus, exemplarity, anger, and becoming-other. So perhaps a hesitation, a word or two about the emergence of this book, is in order. It began as a project concerning Emmanuel Levinas's work and what his texts could add to the recent resurgence of ethics in literary and cultural studies. I was and am especially interested in Levinas's one-way movement of performative subjectivity: the ethical subject in Levinas does not ever merely return to or coincide with itself; rather, it is nothing other than exterior *response* to the other. And concomitantly, Levinasian ethics does not rest in a series of rules to be followed, but rather in inexorable and constant exposure to alterity. Ethical response is the production of social relations, rather than the tracing of preexisting ethical templates.

However, the more I read Levinas, the more certain questions began to haunt me. How could the human other constitute the ultimate horizon of this ethical response? How does or can this Levinasian discourse handle politics and questions of power? What of the piety that seems to lurk not too far beneath the surface of Levinas's texts? It became clear to me that this couldn't be a book merely about Levinas, especially if I wished to explore the thing that made Levinas so interesting to me in the first place: the metonymic linking of cultural sites of emergence, the materialization of ethical sites and responses.

It was the unlikely imbrication of Levinas's discourse with Judith Butler's work on performative identity and the subjections of sex and gender that offered the bridge between questions about ethical response and questions about political and social power—a link between questions of *alterity* and questions of *politics*. Levinasians of a certain stripe will, no doubt, find this an illegitimate linkage, a collapsing of ethics *into* politics. As Lynne Huffer writes, for example, Butler's "performativity elides the possibility of an ethical relation" (21) because it replaces Levinas's face-to-face relation with a merely political mask-to-mask relation. On the other hand, theorists of social and cultural power (especially feminists) often cringe before Levinas's seeming neglect of social questions and his frequent deployment of a patriarchal theological discourse. Nevertheless, it is precisely a linkage of obligation and concrete response that I am interested in bringing to the contemporary discussion concerning ethics, and it is such a site-specific imbrication of "practice" and "theory" ("performativity" and "ethics") that came to orient the emergence of this book. Predictably, following the itinerary of this response also led me to pose certain questions to Butler's work, which I do primarily through a consideration of Gilles Deleuze and Félix Guattari's texts.

Of course, alongside the theoretical itinerary of the book is an equally crucial performative engagement with specific sites of cultural production (the work of William Burroughs, Amiri Baraka, Andy Warhol) and the social formation of subjects (identity politics, multiculturalism, the "angry white male"). In what I take to be an ethical movement, this text traces an itinerary outward from my own limited understanding of ethics and responsibility, a movement that does not and cannot return to the cultural discourses of ethics as I know or knew them. If it does nothing else, this text attempts to remain turned toward alterity. It certainly doesn't comprise a new ethics, but rather tries to remain oriented toward what Charles Scott calls *The Question of Ethics:* "Learning to name things anew, to become alert to exclusions and to forgotten aspects in a people's history, to overhear what is usually drowned out by the predominant values, to rethink what is ordinarily taken for granted, to find out how to hold itself in question: these are aspects of the thought of the question of ethics" (7–8).

Alterity Politics

Introduction · Alterity Politics:
Toward an Ethics without Lack

Others are anxious to get to know you better.
—Empress of China fortune cookie

These days, it seems that everybody loves "the other." University pro-
fessors and corporate CEOs alike proclaim the importance of diversity;
even Arby's fast-food restaurant reminds us that "Different is Good."
Of course, once one tries to specify what "the other" means within a
particular context (once a specific other or difference is named by a
discourse), a flurry of anxious criticism ensues: for example, in recent
literary and cultural studies, first-wave feminism has been accused of
heterosexism and indifference to race; a certain Marxism is accused
of ignoring gender and the specificity of non-Western cultures when
it defines otherness in terms of economic class; some postcolonial
discourses are chastised for indulging in Eurocentric theorizing rather
than attending to the lived exclusions of diasporic lives; deconstructive discourses are faulted for ignoring any concrete others, while
Habermasian communicative rationality is charged with anthropomorphism. The list inexorably goes on.

Judith Butler thematizes this problem concisely in *Gender Trouble:* theories of identity and alterity "that elaborate predicates of color, sexuality, ethnicity, class, and able-bodiedness invariably close with an *embarrassed 'etc.'* at the end of the list. Through this horizontal trajectory of adjectives, these positions strive to encompass a situated subject, but invariably fail to be complete. This failure, however, is instructive: what political impetus is to be derived from the *exasperated 'etc.'* that so often occurs at the end of such lines?" (143; my italics). There is a certain way in which this book is nothing other than a series of engagements with this quotation and the myriad problems with which it confronts us: Why is it so difficult to "situate" and respond to a set of specific others—ethically, politically, or theoretically—and what does the difficulty of doing so teach us about identity politics and the possibility of what I call an alterity politics? Can this "failure" of sameness be rethematized as an affirmation of difference? What possibilities are there for concrete responses that do not merely or finally reduce otherness to a subset of the same, to a subset of an inquiring subject's identity? These are the questions that I will most consistently return to in the course of this book. If *identity politics* is an attempt to thematize the other in terms of its similarities with the self, I am interested here in constructing an ethical *alterity politics* that considers identity as beholden and responsive first and foremost to the other.

There is, of course, a theoretical or ethical component to the word "politics" as it is used in formulations like "identity politics" or "alterity politics," and I should make it clear from the outset that I use the word in a fairly narrow sense as a negotiation that takes place in what might still loosely be called a *polis,* situated at a particular space or place. This book is not about alterity per se nor about politics per se, but about the imbrication of the two. It is in fact this imbrication of the theoretical and the social that gives force and definition to my sense of *ethics.* As a mode of inquiry, ethics necessarily concerns itself both with general theoretical structures and specific concrete responses; indeed, one might argue that its ability to bring together the theoretical and political is one of the reasons ethics has reemerged so centrally in recent critical discourse. Any interesting or useful ethics is precisely a politics of the other, a linkage of theoretical necessity with concrete response. Finally, it is only in such concrete ethical response that "alterity" and "politics" are imbricated, and as such it is this response—this *performative responsibility*—that I will take as my primary topic as well as my mode of inquiry throughout this book.

Here in the introduction, I investigate the ways in which the elusive "etc." of identity politics is linked in much current discourse to the notion of identity's "failure." I begin here because, on a larger scale, thematizing alterity as *other than a lack or failure of plenitude* is the principal vector connecting the seemingly odd assemblage of material treated in this book. In the end, it is this refusal of lack—the refusal to thematize difference in terms of the possibility or impossibility of sameness—that ties together the disparate figures and topics engaged in this work.

The Failures of Identity Politics

Of course, no discourse of otherness can hope to map the entire conflicted terrain of alterity in the postmodern world(s), where totalizing theories have fallen out of favor for very good theoretical and practical reasons. History continually reminds us that such totalizing theoretical and political systems are dangerous for marginal groups, and hence constitute the wrong place to start thinking about a multiculturalist politics of the other. However, although the postmodern inability or unwillingness to produce an all-encompassing theory of otherness has been an enabling factor for the multiculturalist project at large, the inability to locate and attend to a series of specific others has not, it seems, proven to be similarly empowering. In fact, this inability to treat multiple subject positions—the inability to attend to more than one specific alterity at a time—has come to be the dominant critique of so-called identity politics.[1]

The well-known failures of identity politics—its disintegration into partisan bickering, its inability to forge links among subaltern groups, its tendency to situate others while resisting its own situatedness—are often treated (by both its proponents and its critics) as a symptom of Butler's "embarrassed 'etc.' ":[2] identity politics as a project is doomed to fail because every specific identity likewise fails to be complete, falls short of some kind of plenitude. The specific "I" that lacks wholeness is symptomatic of a generalized "we" that lacks wholeness, and vice versa. In an attempt to redescribe or reencounter this seeming "failure" of identity, theorized reinscriptions of identity politics—ones that eschew simple appeals to the asocial authenticity of subjective experience—argue that any particular identity is actually predicated upon (and thereby inextricable from) the differences that form Butler's "horizontal trajectory of adjectives." As William Connolly argues in *Identity/Difference*, for example, "Identity requires difference in order to be, and it converts difference into otherness in order to secure its own self-certainty" (64). If we've learned anything at all from the so-called linguistic turn in the human sciences, we've learned that any state of sameness actually *requires* difference in order to structure itself. Identity is structured like a language: we can only recognize the so-called plenitude of a particular identity insofar as it differentiates itself from (and thereby necessarily contains a trace of) the ostensible nonplenitude of difference. Like Saussure's famous characterization of language, subjective identity knows only "differences *without positive terms*" (*Course*, 120; italics in original).

This realization that difference structures sameness comprises what we might call the theoretical success of multiculturalism. The sense that there are no simply positive terms in postmodern life has certainly led to liberating effects, among them what Connolly calls an increasing "appreciation of difference" (*Identity/Difference*, 167). As he writes, identity's necessary dependence on difference has kept open a space for the other: "When this bond through differentiation is acknowledged, the moral demand for an all-embracing identity grounded in the truth of a fixed moral code loses some of the power it exercised over the self" (167). In other words, the success of a poststructuralist-multiculturalist identity politics lies in its recognizing the structuring space of otherness; this recognition has in turn shown the way for further concrete deployments of toleration and respect, "enabling the self to bestow value upon the alter-identity it contests" (167).

However, this redescribed theoretical and practical realization of alterity's necessity is not only identity politics' success, but also paradoxically its failure: identity politics' *theoretical success* (the realization that difference grounds sameness) belies its inevitable *social or political failure*. As the sad facts of the daily headlines and radio talk-show programs attest, people aren't walking through the open door of respect and recognition in large numbers. The theoretical recognition of our common intersubjective ground somehow hasn't abrogated the social problems of identity politics. For social theorists, this is perhaps not surprising: no "theory" can guarantee harmonious societies, and in fact, the contemporary linguistic-turn philosophies of difference—where intersubjectivity is based on the paradigm of linguistic response, the necessity of difference in structuring the same— seem merely another version of the Hegelian master/slave dialectic of recognition that has been familiar to social theorists for nearly two hundred years. As Axel Honneth reminds us, Hegel is the great thinker of intersubjectivity, insisting as he does on the "interlocking of individuation and recognition," where "every individual is dependent on the possibility of constant reassurance by the Other" (189). Because none of us can be Hegelian masters or Saussurean positive terms, we are all cousins to Hegel's bondsman or Saussure's differences, tied to a system of social recognition for our intersubjective desires, meanings, and identities.

In both social and linguistic accounts of identity formation, then, the very notion of intersubjective ground is based on a certain *failure or lack:* I can't have everything—I lack completeness; I cannot be a "positive term"—so I live in/with the solace of others, who likewise lack such wholeness. As M. M. Bakhtin phrases this dilemma in his early work on ethics, *Art and Answerability,* "I turn to the outside of myself and surrender myself to the mercy of *the other.* . . . I know that in the other as well there is the same insanity of not coinciding (in principle) with himself, the same unconsummatedness of life" (128). The intersubjective community is a community of lack in which each person or group is compelled to give up the hopeless project of totalization for the attainable mini-totality of social recognition. Such a political community of the "we" finds its commonality in difference defined as a lack of sameness; in response to this situation, interest groups within such a community of difference band together under identity markers to supplement this (un)founding lack.

Perhaps, though, one could argue that the subjective differences of identity markers—Bakhtin's "unconsummated life" or Butler's "embarrassed 'etc.'"—are better understood as a postmodern celebratory *excess* of identities rather than a nostalgic, modernist lament for the *lack* of common identity. On this line of reasoning, because each "I" is open-ended and excessive, I cannot simply conflate myself with the other, but I am nevertheless bound to an intersubjective realm where we each negotiate our ever-shifting social identity. As Amarpal Dhaliwal argues, perhaps "(re)conceptualizing identity as a process" of excessive self-creation offers a way out of the recriminatory traps of identity politics: perhaps "identity," in other words, "should be posed as continually changing, changeable, and not as a fixed endpoint to be ultimately achieved" (84).

Paradoxically, it is here we might note that the seeming *excess* of perception that accrues to the intersubjective, self-overcoming "I" remains a certain kind of *lack:* the excessive I remains an identity that lacks wholeness or complete control over its circumstances, so it must continually reinvent itself to cope with changing circumstances. As Bakhtin writes of his social theory of intersubjective dialogics, although "the interrelationship of *'I*–the *other'* is not convertible for me in lived life in any concrete way" (*Art,* 23 n), for me the other nevertheless exists in the same intersubjective dialogic space and faces similar human tasks; like the "I," "the other . . . cannot complete himself by himself" (24). I need the other to realize myself and vice versa; our mutual *excess* of perception and restless adventure of desire is made possible by our mutual recognition of an essential *lack* of wholeness. Bakhtin continues: "what is lacking, moreover, is precisely *external* unity and continuity; a human being experiencing life in the category of his own *I* is incapable of gathering himself into an outward whole that would be even relatively finished. . . . In this sense, one can speak of human being's absolute need for the other, for the other's seeing, remembering, gathering and unifying self-activity—the only self-activity capable of producing his outwardly finished personality" (35–36). As in Lacanian theories of expropriation from the real into the symbolic, intersubjective identity theories like Bakhtin's maintain a notion of excess that is subtended by a prior notion of lack. Bakhtin maintains, "Correlative with this excess, there is a certain deficiency" (23 n); or, as Slavoj Žižek puts it with a bit more chiasmic flair, "We come across identity when predicates fail. Identity is the surplus which cannot be captured by predicates" (*For They Know Not,* 36). My excessive subjectivity, in other words, is "incapable of gathering" itself into a whole, and in turn I recognize that each of us shares this excessive lack of wholeness, which can be rethematized in social terms as the subject's need for recognition in an otherwise groundless social landscape. In the end, whether it is thematized as nostalgia for wholeness or a celebration of possibility, "human being's absolute need for the other" remains a function of shared human lack or incompleteness. And, as Michael Holquist writes of Bakhtin's identity-based dialogics, "a first implication of recognizing that we are all unique is the paradoxical result that we are *therefore* fated to need the other if we are to consummate our selves" ("Architectonics," xxv).

For all its gains, such a contemporary intersubjective or multiculturalist reinscription of identity politics remains unable to deal with the other *as* other; it continues to thematize differences among persons, groups, and discourses in terms of (the impossibility of their) sameness. Each group or identity wants to rule the field, but it can't, so every group and individual must share this lack, mourn collectively for what each can't have. In turn, however, it is precisely this lack or expropriation that bolsters the recriminatory politics of resentment that has plagued and continues to plague identity politics. Connolly argues that the recognition of otherness within the self should have opened a distinctly ethico-political space of acknowledgment: "to acknowledge a variety of contingent elements in the formation of identity is to take a significant step toward increasing tolerance for a range of antinomies in oneself" (*Identity/Difference*, 178). However, if this need for recognition and intersubjectivity hasn't exactly cashed out in an increasing tolerance of alterity, at this point we might simply want to ask, why not? Why hasn't the postmodern realization of difference's necessity led to an increased social respect and tolerance?

This is obviously an extremely complicated question, but we might haltingly begin to address it by pointing out that because intersubjective theories argue that we *need* each other for recognition and happiness, such theories continue to harbor a regulatory ideal of complete subjective freedom, which is actually *freedom from recognition, freedom from difference itself*.[3] It is not necessarily surprising, then, that *needing* the other often shows itself as *resenting* the other. As Wendy Brown argues, insofar as it measures subjective injury in terms of exclusion from a kind of white male normativity of self-determination, a politics of identity inexorably harbors the ideal along with a resentment toward it; she contends that, "like all resentments, [identity politics] retains the real or imagined holdings of its reviled subject — in this case, bourgeois male privileges — as objects of desire" ("Wounded," 394). Brown goes on to argue that because identity politics' productive moment consists in the "politicization of *exclusion* from an ostensible universal" (398), it thereby remains "a protest that reinstalls the humanist ideal — and a specific white, middle-class, masculinist expression of this ideal — insofar as it premises itself on exclusion from it" (398). Finally, identity politics suggests, we need the other because we've all been excluded from the privileges of an ideal or autonomous self.

Such need is, however, a recipe for continued subjective control. As Emmanuel Levinas writes, at first people are happy for their needs: they need others, food, and so on, what Levinas calls "independence through dependence" (*Totality*, 115). These happy needs, however, only point to a time when need can finally be overcome in fulfillment.

He maintains: "need is the primary movement of the same. To be sure, need is also a dependence with regard to the other, but it is a dependence across time, a dependence that is not an instantaneous betraying of the same but a suspension or postponement of dependence, and thus the possibility to break, by labor and by economy, the very thrust of the alterity upon which need depends" (116). As Levinas suggests, the exterior dependence to which need inexorably points is kept at bay by the subject's positing a future time when need's purpose will have been comprehended or its grasp broken by fulfillment. In other words, a regulatory freedom from alterity watches over the lack that forces the subject—resentfully—into an economy of mutual recognition. In this way, the interior subject's *need* for the other actually shelters it from alterity. As Levinas argues, "Needs are in my power; they constitute me as the same and not as dependent on the other" (116).

We do, however, need to go slowly here. As Brown insists, such a critique of identity politics does not wish to treat social needs or exclusions from privilege as trivial or unreal, but rather to point out that the horizon of expropriation (which identity politics depends upon) reduces rather than heightens attention to the specificities of interpellation and identity production. For example, the much ballyhooed return of the angry white male in American political discourse (which I discuss at length in chapter 7) has its phantasmatic roots in the majority of such men's very real exclusion from a white, middle-class male ideal of power and privilege. When Norm from Scranton calls Rush Limbaugh to complain of his expropriation, he appeals to the same sense of need, exclusion, and frustration that drives more obviously righteous claims to discrimination. However, the telling point in this return of the angry white male is that a discourse of identity's lack—failure to attain the ideal—tends to level all identity "failures" onto the same plane, and thereby to homogenize the very specific traumas that accrue to a particular subjectivity. Norm's anger, though very real, is simply not of the same order as other brands of social interpellation. Likewise, discriminations based on age, weight, race, style of dress, and physical challenge are obviously not of the same category, and getting a lousy table in a restaurant is not in any meaningful way akin to being denied employment, even if both events take place for to the same discriminatory reason. At its strongest, however, an identity politics of exclusion attempts to conflate these specific injuries around the common theme of lack or expropriation: any specific lack or failure becomes a symptom of a more generalized lack;

likewise, what we have in common is that we all lack in some way. We meet upon the common ground of intersubjective impasse.

One could, of course, reinscribe this impasse as the ethical or political itself. One could argue, as Žižek does, that due to the subject's founding expropriation, it necessarily "bears an indelible mark of failure and the Ought—and thereby its inherent *ethical* character" (*For They Know Not*, 110). Likewise, in *Hegemony and Socialist Strategy*, Ernesto Laclau and Chantal Mouffe rethematize the political precisely as an ethico-political confrontation with a necessary impossibility or failure. As they write of their post-Marxism, "Let us avoid any temptation to go back to the 'origins.' Let us simply pierce a moment in time and try to detect the presence of that void which the logic of hegemony will attempt to fill" (8).

Perhaps the most compelling ethico-politics of lack is Homi K. Bhabha's postcolonial theorizing of the "DissemiNation" in his essay of the same name. For Bhabha, the modern nation fills the void created by modernity's expropriation of the subject from earlier forms of social organization. He argues, "The nation fills the void left in the uprooting of communities and kin, and turns that loss into the language of metaphor" (291). What Bhabha calls the "double-time of the nation" (294)—a doubling that tries to suture "out of the many one" (294)—is the dual time of national metaphor, an attempt to carry over and teach a sense of identification (community and kin) that is always interrupted by what he calls the "performative" impossibility of such a "pedagogical" carrying over. The plenitude or wholeness of national time is, according to Bhabha, necessarily interrupted by an "*anterior* default of a presence" (305); there is, in other words, a void or alterity that marks the impossible founding of the nation, an irrepressible absence or lack of wholeness that lies beneath the performative suture "We the people."[4]

In Bhabha's "DissemiNation," one might say that the exclusionary violence of the "colonial" always interrupts the attempt to configure the "postcolonial." As he explains, the plenitude or "pluralism of the national sign, where difference returns as the same, is contested by the signifier's 'loss of identity' that inscribes the narrative of the people in the ambivalent, 'double' writing of the performative and the pedagogical" (305). At the postcolonial site of the modern nation, there is always this alterior interruption—this originary, disseminated void or "loss of identity" before the performative founding of the nation's seemingly seamless origin. This originary lack creates "always the distracting presence of another temporality that disturbs the contemporaneity of the national present" (295). Bhabha calls this interruption a "repetition of that minus in the origin" (306), and for Bhabha this "minus" or lack becomes the necessary site of ethical and political resistance within the always already conflicted postcolonial nation.

Thus the homogeneity—or, in Laclau and Mouffe's parlance, the hegemony—of "the people" must be thought in this double time: the time of the nation, the people, and the same becomes the time of difference's exclusion, a presence constantly interrupted by the alterity of an impossibility or void at the origin. Bhabha sums up this site of postcolonial resistance:

> the performative introduces a temporality of the "in-between" through the "gap" or "emptiness" of the signifier that punctuates linguistic difference. The boundary that marks the nation's selfhood interrupts the self-generating time of national production with a space of representation that threatens binary division with its difference. The barred Nation It/Self, alienated from its eternal self-generation, becomes a liminal form of social representation, a space that is *internally* marked by cultural difference and the heterogeneous histories of contending peoples, antagonistic authorities, and tense cultural locations. (299)

Bhabha here insists that the nation's "other" is always already an internal question; the other is at the heart of any attempt to constitute sameness. Because absence both founds and unfounds identity, any "gap" in the nation's self-definition becomes a privileged site for locating ethical resistence, and for a political rearticulation of national and subjective identity.

Although I find Bhabha's politics of originary lack and resistance to be compelling, I wonder whether it doesn't remain predicated on the possibility of some kind of wholeness or plenitude. The specificity of any individual or group in Bhabha's "DissemiNation" is related originally to the specificity of an absence: identity is first and foremost the site or cite of a certain *lack*, and this subjective lack mirrors the founding lack of the nation—thereby, on Bhabha's reading, highlighting contest and difference within a groundless, divided social sphere.

However, just as identity politics harbors normativity in its notions of injurious exclusion, I wonder whether Bhabha's notion of a society of lack—as well as Žižek's and Laclau and Mouffe's, admittedly in different ways—doesn't protect a kind of normative plenitude, if only as that which can never be accomplished. In other words, the primary relation—to oneself and to the other—remains an imaginary relation of expropriation: revelation comes from incompleteness, lack, slippage. But to term this noncenter of the social or the subject a "failure" presupposes the normativity of some state that is somehow not constituted by these interpellative social conditions, a state where the nation or the subject would or could be undivided. In a discourse like Bhabha's, which strives to highlight the constitutive social conditions of the postcolonial subject's emergence, it seems odd to talk in terms of failure or lack, insofar as Bhabha's analysis, as one of its founding premises, would want to expose the promise of complete subjective freedom as an ideological or transcendental chimera founded by and in hegemonic national narratives. In other words, in taking into account the social interpellations of the national subject, it seems that one would be obliged to account for *not-free* as otherwise than a *lack or failure of freedom*.

The difficulty inherent in a politics of lack, then, is that difference is thought symptomatically, in terms of its relation to an originary, normative lack or plenitude. As I will argue in various ways in this book, such a notion of difference-as-lack underestimates the *productive* qualities of alterity.[5] Throughout this book I suggest that identity and difference are not *an effect* of an originary loss or plenitude, but rather that identity and difference, though they certainly are located in specific chains of effects, likewise *produce effects*. Certainly, the politics of lack is also concerned first and foremost with producing effects; as Bhabha rightly points out, one of the effects such failure can produce is resistance and skepticism concerning the supposed wholeness put forth in hegemonic national narratives. However, it seems that resentment, rather than collective resistance, has been the preeminent social effect of the politics of lack. And perhaps this resentment is itself a symptom of a larger problem with an identity politics of collective lack: subjectivity thought as lack seems inexorably to separate the subject from what it can do; it thematizes the subject as an effect (a noun) rather than an effectivity (an action).

If the subject is nothing other than a symptom of a founding lack, its primary mode of agency is then directed toward making up for that lack: the dominant effects it produces are futile attempts to suture an originary gap. As Žižek maintains, such a subject can, at its best, learn to enjoy its symptom, come to grips with the "humble consent that 'all is NOT rational,' that the moment of contingent antagonism is irreducible, that notional Necessity itself hangs on and is 'embedded' in an encompassing contingency" (*For They Know Not*, 169). Although this insight about irreducible contingency is perhaps itself irreducible, the explanation of such contingency offered here seems to recuperate a fairly familiar and problematic transcendentalist horizon: the reason X failed is because everything fails. As Žižek contends, "Reflection, to be sure, ultimately always fails" (86), so the founding moment of expropriation recurs in all the subject's subsequent productions.

Perhaps all "postmoderns" can agree that reflection, like any other subjective action or response, is not in control of its outcomes; but this hardly seems to signal or necessitate its "failure." Why not say that reflection, to be sure, always produces effects far beyond the ones intended? This is clearly what Žižek means when he talks of Hegelian-Lacanian failure; as he writes, "essence" is "the name for the impossibility that hinders the constitution of a full identity-with-itself" (*For They Know Not*, 37): to say that reflection fails is to say that it produces more than it can control because it lacks a stable ground. However, to thematize this excessive production of effects as a hindrance or failure, and then to read that failure as an allegory of the inexorable process of loss, seems to cover over the important affirmative qualities of alterity or difference. Certainly, the subject is an effect, but it is an effect that produces all kinds of other effects, and these effects are not merely recuperable within the process of mourning for a lack. In other words, it seems that understanding difference in terms of allegorical expropriation—as the constant discovery of lack—underestimates the hazardous productivity of difference's specificity.

As long as identity is not thematized as a hazardous performative *act*—a verb rather than an noun, a multiple becoming rather than a monological symptom, a deployment of force rather than an assured process of mourning, a subjection that calls for(th) response rather than the revelation of an assured lack of wholeness—it seems destined to remain a locus for resentment, naming itself always in terms of its expropriation from an ideal that it can't ever hope, and doesn't even wish, to attain. As Gilles Deleuze polemically maintains, "Those who bear the negative know not what they do" (*Difference*, 55); in other words, whereas its proponents take the process of loss and mourning to be an ethical expropriation of the subject, for Deleuze this process is actually the assured movement of a resentful subjectivity. Those who tarry with the negative, he suggests, know all too well what they do: they know that totalization will fail, the subject will be frustrated, promises will inexorably be broken. And it is precisely because of this *success*—because lack surreptitiously returns the horizon of wholeness to the subject—that ethics, like cultural and sexual difference, must be reinscribed outside the realm of loss, lack, or failure.[6] It is, at least, in the name of such a project that this book will proceed.

Promises, Promises

Hegel, that great thinker of identity as lack, long ago ruined introductions for all of us: proper discourse, he insists in the preface to the *Phenomenology of Spirit*, should do or perform something, not merely offer promises of work to come. As Hegel shows us, and a host of psychoanalytically inflected speech-act theory confirms, prefacing promises are invariably broken because the later materialization of the promised deed will always produce a remainder. The deed will always exceed (and thereby fall short of simply fulfilling) the original promise. In the prefatory promise, we confront yet again the excess-that-is-lack.

Of course, this creates a problem for me, insofar as I've already made a number of promises here: to thematize a relation with the other that does not merely return to the same, to discuss the general state of ethics and performative subjectivity in recent theoretical discourse, to work out a notion of difference as other than lack or failure of sameness. To take up these promises adequately, then, I will also have to proceed according to a different performative logic of the promise, one that does not merely return to the assured inevitability of the broken promise or the negative assurance of lack or slippage. To move beyond the assured negativity of failure, I will need to enact a logic of the promise that is not phrased in exclusively negative terms, a promise other than one that is constantly being broken.

That being the case, perhaps we can agree from the outset that promises can only be fulfilled or broken by other promises: acts call for other, future acts, not some state of plenitude or lack in which further acts would either be unnecessary or futile. Such a positive logic of the promise puts a sharper point on the sense of ethical response that permeates this text: throughout, I will argue not that response to alterity is called for(th) because subjects and the political spaces they inhabit are invariably incomplete, but rather that response is necessitated in and from a positive or "performative" logic of alterity. As Jacques Derrida writes, a promise "is a singular promise. Its performance does not promise, literally, to *say* in the constative sense, but again to '*do.*' It promises another 'performative,' and the content of the promise is determined, like its form, by the possibility of that other" (*Truth*, 3). A response, Derrida argues, is always a "response in deed, at work rather in the series of strategic negotiations. . . . response does not respond to a problem or question, it responds to the other—for the other" ("At This Very Moment," 17). Response to the other, this book will argue, is finally about action, about producing deeds and negotiations, not about mourning for a loss or lack.

Of course, this architectonic of response invariably begs difficult questions concerning to whom or what one responds, and how one enacts that response. As Charles Altieri argues, perhaps such a "stance yields too quickly to the allure of an ungraspable otherness, without sufficiently elaborating possibilities for identification and judgment" (321 n). For Altieri, and a host of other critics, because "responsiveness per se does not show where responsibility lies in conflict situations" (220), such an ethics remains a contentless generality, without the political force to ensure respect for the other. Such responsibility remains an inevitably broken promise.

Aliteri presents a serious challenge to a performative alterity politics of response, but I will try to take up both this *critique* and the *enactment* of responsibility in the performance of specific analyses. To take up these questions on a merely metatheoretical level would only serve to confirm Altieri's worst suspicions. Suffice it to say at this point, that there are good theoretical and political reasons *not* to restrict response from before the fact; there are, in other words, good reasons not to name or know beforehand those or that to which one owes ethical response, as I try to show in chapter 3, treating Burroughs and Levinas. Hopefully, the myriad and shifting subject matters of the following chapters will exemplify—though in chapter 5 that word itself becomes complicated in my treatment of ethics and exemplarity in Van Gogh and Warhol—the kind of response that is called for in and by our groundless postmodern landscape.

Rather than representing a bug in the programming, I take this text's multiple sites of intervention to be a positive, if not essential, feature of a performative ethics, which must embody a site-specific "drift" that is necessary to the outward, affirmative movement of responsibility. Specifically, chapter 1 introduces the notion of "performativity," heavily influenced by Judith Butler, that I will deploy throughout the book. Chapter 2 discusses Bakhtin's and Levinas's differing understandings of dialogic ethics. Chapter 4 revisits the question of lack as ethical expropriation in Žižek, Butler, and Paul de Man, and chapter 6 performs a Deleuzian reading of race and ethical becoming-other in Amiri Baraka and Ishmael Reed. Chapter 7 focuses many of the book's energies and arguments through a performative diagnosis of a specific political subject position, the North American "angry white male." The conclusion revisits many of the themes of this introduction by taking up the question of ethical choice and the performative affirmation of alterity.

Certainly, these remain mere promises, but as Derrida reminds us, "a promise must promise to be kept, that is, not to remain 'spiritual' or 'abstract,' but to produce events, new effective forms of action, practice, [and] organization" (*Specters*, 89). In the end, it is not a necessary failure or the resentment of a broken promise that drives alterity politics; rather, it is the positive promise and concretization of different actions, practices, and organizations that orient and give force to an alterity politics of response.

1 · *Today; or, Between Emergence and Possibility: Foucault, Derrida, and Butler on Performative Identity*

What difference does today introduce with respect to yesterday?
—Michel Foucault, "What Is Enlightenment?"

While Jacques Derrida and Michel Foucault continue to exercise wide-ranging influences on cultural and literary theory, it would seem that the book is closed on the specific relations between Derrida's work and Foucault's. As Derrida writes in a recent essay on Foucault, the sometimes acrimonious debate ended with Foucault's death.[1] In retrospect, however, it seems clear that the acrimony of the debate has covered over more productive reflection on the possible intersections between their work. Perhaps such reflection is only becoming possible today, as the polemics of yesterday fade into the background. Here, I'd like to suggest that one such productive way of (re)articulating the *differend* between Foucault's work and Derrida's would be to take very seriously Foucault's emphasis on material conditions of *emergence* (on the question of *today*) in seeming contradistinction to the deconstructive emphasis on conditions of *possibility* or *impossibility* (the question of the *origin* or the *future*). As Foucault insists, he's primarily interested in a "history of the present"; not the *arché* or the *telos*, but rather the *emergence* and *transformation* of origins and ends. As he writes, his projects are in this way akin to Kant's: "*not seeking to understand the present on the basis of a totality or of a future* achievement," but rather "looking for a difference: What difference does *today* introduce with respect to *yesterday?*" ("What Is Enlightenment?" 34; my italics).

Even in his most recognizably "philosophical" or methodological work—that is, in *The Archaeology of Knowledge* and its analysis of the "statement"—Foucault remains skeptical of any discourse that engages itself with conditions of possibility: as he contends in the *Archaeology*, "for statements it is not a condition of possibility but a law of coexistence" (116). If nothing else, this Foucauldian insistence on the emergence and coexistence of statements (and his concomitant emphasis on the genealogical sites of chance, materiality, and discontinuity) may offer a slightly more sober way of understanding the dispute with Derrida than is offered in Foucault's rather vitriolic response to Derrida's reading of *The History of Madness*. In addition, though, I'm hoping that examining and reinscribing this debate (specifically in terms of Judith Butler's recent work on performative identity) has something to tell us, in a Foucauldian vein, about *today*.

But first, yesterday: Foucault's 1971 essay "Nietzsche, Genealogy, History" is very clear concerning the stakes of this distinction between conditions of emergence and conditions of possibility. For Foucault, Nietzsche allows us to disrupt the specious privilege of metaphysical originality when he poses the question of origin not in strictly transcendentalist terms—not as *Ursprung*—but rather in "genealogical" terms. Nietzsche challenges us to rethink origin in two specific ways: first, as *Herkunft* (stock or descent; the chance, discontinuous history of what Foucault calls "the body—and everything that touches it: diet, climate, and soil" [83]); second, Nietzsche asks us to think origin as *Entstehung*, which Foucault glosses as emergence or event, "the moment of [force's] arising" (83) that "designates a place of confrontation" (84). By insisting on this distinction between conditions of possibility and conditions of emergence, Foucault's reading of Nietzsche continually highlights the genealogical principle, which holds that "What is found at the historical beginning of things is not the inviolable identity of their origin; it is the dissension of other things. It is disparity" (79). Genealogy consistently "opposes itself to the search for 'origins' " (77); that is, it opposes itself to the search for conditions of possibility, to the continuous or discontinuous exposure of the *Ursprung*'s historico-transcendental traces in philosophy and in the human sciences.

It is in this context that we might again recall or reexamine Foucault's objections to Derrida in the *Archaeology* (though note that Derrida is never named directly in the text). According to Foucault, even if one emphasizes a radically discontinuous notion of conditions of possibility, a certain kind of pernicious transcendentalism nevertheless

> can be purified in the problematic of a trace, which, prior to all speech, is the opening of inscription, the gap of deferred time; it is always the historico-transcendental theme that is reinvested. A theme [from which] enunciative analysis tries to free itself. In order to restore statements to their pure dispersion. . . . . In order to consider them in their discontinuity, without having to relate them . . . to a more fundamental opening or difference. In order to seize their very irruption, at the place and at the moment at which it occurred. (121)

At least provisionally, Foucault posits his emphasis on conditions of emergence (the "very irruption at the place and at the moment at which it occurred") as a wedge to interrupt the smooth disciplinary movement from objects to their governing laws of possible inscription. Although deconstruction would seem to have performed just such a shift of emphasis—from the question of what something is in itself to the examination of how it is configured, haunted, and transformed by its others—Foucault nonetheless asks after the ways in which such a deconstructive movement surreptitiously protects or projects the "transcendental" space of the "trace" or the "opening of inscription."

For Foucault, perhaps we could say that it is the *direction or orientation* of Derrida's analyses that consistently runs the risk of re-instituting a kind of metaphysical privilege by gesturing toward some notion of the quasi-transcendental origin and/or the uncertain future engendered by it. And, concomitantly, Foucault seems to understand deconstructive analysis as nothing other than the monotonous exposure of an originary "gap of deferred time" (*écart du temps différé*), the endless staging and iteration of the slippage engendered by *différance* as a condition of (im)possibility. Here, according to Foucault, both the origin and the future remain shrouded, an "enigmatic, silent remainder" (*Archaeology*, 112), and the present remains nothing more than "a series of traces" (107).

As something of an aside, it would perhaps be easier to understand Foucault's infamous charge that deconstruction, thus understood, comprises "a historically well-determined little pedagogy" ("My Body," 27) if we recall Nietzsche's comments on Wagner's Hegelianism: "German youths understood him. The two words 'infinite' and 'meaning' were really sufficient: they induced a state of incomparable well-being in young men" (*Case*, 178). In the end, it is this incomparably reassuring feeling of infinitely problematized transcendental symbolism that Foucault reads all over Derrida's work on iterability and conditions of (im)possibility; and it is precisely this kind of reassurance—one could perhaps say the reassurance of the deferred future—that Foucault is out to disrupt in all of his work on conflicted conditions of emergence.[2]

All of this is, I suppose, familiar territory for readers of Derrida and Foucault, as are the potential defenses and counterarguments on both sides. But, here I'd rather not continue to revisit these arguments in an attempt to recover or reopen a philosophical debate; in lieu of that, I'll just go on record as saying that, for me, Foucault's is a too hasty reading of Derrida.[3] So instead of reopening the debate between Foucault and Derrida, I'd like to follow what I take to be a Foucauldian line and shift ground slightly to examine a way that they are productively being thought together. Specifically, I'd like to discuss how they are thought or brought together in Judith Butler's recent work on performative identity. Although reading Butler in this way certainly ignores any number of other important horizons within her work (her sustained engagements with feminism, psychoanalysis, queer theory, etc.), I hope to show that through her interventions on the question of performativity, we can see how Derrida's seeming emphasis on conditions of possibility is precisely a kind of confrontation with conditions of emergence and coexistence, and, likewise, we can see that Foucault as a thinker of emergence is no apologist for a kind of "social constructionism." In other words, in attempting to follow Foucault, I'm somewhat less interested in rehearsing a philosophical debate than I am in the question of *today*, in the conflicted sites where this philosophical debate has reemerged and is being reinscribed.

Judith Butler and "Performative" Identity

Almost universally understood—or, as it were, *mis*understood—as a theorist of identity as ironic yet power-laden theatrical perform*ance,* Butler, in her 1993 *Bodies That Matter,* asks us to reconsider her work on gender and compulsory heterosexuality in terms of Derrida's analysis of perform*ative* iterability in his "Signature Event Context."[4] Given Butler's project (recall *Gender Trouble*'s subtitle, "Feminism and the *Subversion of Identity*"), her engagement with Derrida's work is muted when compared to her more sustained and fore-grounded engagement with Foucauldian questions concerning power and the disciplinary interpellation of bodies.[5] On further reflection, though, Butler's interest in a Derridean intervention is easy enough to understand: if meaning and identity are always context-bound—if, as Derrida maintains, there is nothing outside the (con)text—then any particular meaning or identity carries with it the necessary, struc-tural possibility of its own subversion by other recontextualizations or reinscriptions. In other words, it is from within the very logic of contextual meaning that it becomes (im)possible for there to be a meta-context, a context outside of or not subject to the law of con-text. And from this, the possibility of *subversion* (as reinscription of existing contexts) is engendered.

   As Derrida points out in "Signature," J. L. Austin's *How to Do Things with Words* shows us that all supposed "constative" utter-ances—which, as Jonathan Culler writes, pretend merely to "describe a state of affairs" (112)—are in fact already "performative" utterances, "which are not true or false and which actually perform the action to which they refer" (Culler, 112). All "constative" meaning is not merely referenced from a preexisting storehouse of decided truisms, but is actually brought about in and through a series of "performative" ac-tions—statements and restatements that redeploy and reestablish the performative force of truth in differing contexts. As Culler points out, "Austin reversed his predecessors' hierarchical opposition by show-ing that constatives were a special case of performatives" (119–20). As Derrida shows in taking Austin a step further, precisely because Austin maintains that all meaning is in this way beholden to action (rather than vice versa), all meanings are then essentially haunted by the possibility of subversive rearticulation—by the performative structure of signification itself.

   However, for Butler's purposes it is important also to recall Derrida's insistence that this possibility of subversion from within the horizon of contextual meaning is *not* brought about by a positive or negative polysemia (as Foucault seems to understand the "transcendentalist" upshot of Derrida's work). Subversion is not, in other words, made efficacious because each subject or word is uniquely lacking or excessive, and therefore marked by an irreducibly rich individuality that explodes context and lives outside its laws; rather, the reinscriptive possibility of subversion from within is a matter of the *structure* of the mark, what Derrida calls "the structure of the remnant or of iteration" ("Living On," 81). The "crisis" of meaning or identity, then, is not an accident nor a simple impossibility (neither a transcendental *lack* nor a *plenitude* of meaning, to be understood neither in terms of the *absolute past* nor in terms of the *deferred future*); rather, this supposed crisis is a consequence of what Derrida calls "the positive possibility and 'internal' structure of . . . language, . . . the possibility of extraction and of citational grafting which belongs to the structure of every mark, spoken or written" ("Signature," 319–20).

The upshot of all this in Butler's reading is that what we might somewhat hastily call the law of material context—the specific emergence or situation that decides determinate meaning—always produces the possibility of another context, insofar as any word in any discourse is subject to "extraction" from one context and "citational grafting" onto or into another.

Certainly, concepts such as agency, responsibility, and intention do not merely vanish here, but they do lose their absolute privilege. Derrida writes, "In this typology, the category intention will not disappear; it will have its place, but from this place it will no longer be able to govern the entire chain and the entire system of utterances" ("Signature," 326). As Butler reinscribes this Derridean notion into the realm of gender identity and production, following the logic of performatives, "the question of *agency* is [then] reformulated as a question of how signification and resignification work" (*Gender*, 144).

In *Gender Trouble*, Butler reshapes these Derridean notions of iterability, contextuality, and performative response to examine the cultural significance of gender once it is unmoored from the determining essentialist context of "sex." As for Derrida the performative law of contextual iterability always simultaneously produces the possibility (indeed, the *necessity*) of so-called deviant contexts, for Butler the cultural interpellations of gender (what she calls the "girling of the girl") necessarily carry with them more than mere contextual determinations of identity: "the rules governing signification not only restrict, but enable the assertion of alternative domains of cultural intelligibility" (*Gender*, 145). For Butler, as for Derrida, to say that subjective agency is "performative" is *not* to say that agency doesn't exist or that all agency is merely an ironic perform*ance*; rather, it is to say that agency is necessarily a matter of *response* to already given codes. The perform*ative* subject does not and cannot merely found its own conditions or its own identity; at the same time, however, this subject is not merely determined in some lockstep way. Butler argues, "the subject is not *determined* by the rules through which it is generated because signification is *not a founding act, but rather a regulated process of repetition*" (145). So, for Butler the question of the subject is not fruitfully posed in a binary matrix: the age-old nature-or-nurture question, "Does the subject determine or is it determined by its context?", will get you nowhere. Insofar as we cannot create and master the distance between ourselves and the codes that interpellate us, "it is only *within* the practices of repetitive signifying that a subversion of identity becomes possible" (145). Thus, the *emergence* of social agency is rethought through Butler's engagement with the *possibility* of reinscriptive response.

However, we have to hesitate here and note that, on what might, however ironically, be called a "classical" Derridean reading, Butler's "question of how signification and resignification work" would stubbornly remain a kind of metaphysical question about conditions of possibility. For example, the conclusion of Derrida's analysis in "Signature Event Context" is a familiar one for his readers: "The condition of possibility for these [performative] effects is simultaneously, once again, the condition of their impossibility, of the impossibility of their rigorous purity" (328). If performatives do indeed give rise to constatives rather than vice versa, the conditions of possibility for constative effects—nouns, stable identities, knowledges—are simultaneously the conditions of such states' impossibility. If constatives are made possible only through performative effects, then true constatives are, strictly speaking, impossible. Here, the discontinuous origin of performativity seems to give way to the uncertain future of reinscription; the impossibility of absolute grounding gives way to the impossibility of closure. And this is precisely where the question posed by Foucault—Why the ever so slight privilege of conditions of *possibility* rather than conditions of *emergence?*—becomes most crucial, especially for a project like Butler's.

Indeed, the turn away from conditions of possibility in Foucault very much captures the ethos of Butler's work on gender and shares certain obsessions with it: for Butler, "gender" cannot be reduced to or ruled by a prediscursive notion of "sex," in the same way that for Foucault statements cannot be reduced to or explained by the conditions of possibility that are said to govern them; those conditions are themselves statements, discursive formations that are the *product* of reinscriptive power relations rather than the *origin* of such relations.[6] So for Butler, the so-called "'gender core' is thus produced by the regulation of attributes along culturally established lines of coherence" (*Gender*, 24). In other words, the production of a so-called natural sex identity is an "effect of the apparatus of cultural construction designated by gender" (7), one that enforces compulsory heterosexuality. Conditions of possibility, then, are effects of conditions of emergence rather than vice versa. However, Butler's point, as I take it, is not so much that sex comes after gender rather than before it (a simple reversal of transcendental privilege), but that sexes, genders, and the practices that enforce the relations among them are effects of interpellating discursive formations. This would seem to be precisely the place in Butler's work where she would be obliged to abandon a Derridean analysis of *possibility* and turn to a more Foucauldian vocabulary of *emergence*. Emergence, in other words, would need to step into the space of possibility.

But, paradoxically, I'd suggest that it is here, where they seem farthest apart, that Derrida and Foucault are thought together in Butler's notion of performative identity. Certainly for Derrida, iterability as the possibility of repetition does function as a condition of (im)possibility: a performative statement has to hold in several contexts if it is to be meaningful, but those conditions of possibility—iterability over a number of contexts—necessarily inscribe the possibility of one more context onto or into any chain. These conditions of *possibility* send the chain of substitutions reeling into the future, where they will always have to be *materially* reinscribed and negotiated. Therefore, rather than securing closure, these conditions secure exactly the opposite: the necessary, structural openness to other material contexts; rather than securing an originary philosophical monotony, Derrida's analyses bring us back constantly to the question of conflicted emergence. The question of the future seems precisely to be the question of *material (re)emergence*, what Derrida calls the emergence of "monstrosity." In short, if for Derrida the general conditions of a speech act's ability to be successful in any context are at the same time the terms of its inexorable inability to saturate (and therefore remain strictly within) a particular context, then it is paradoxically here that we would be obliged to note that Derrida's interest is not solely in a philosophical question about conditions of possibility or the ineffability of the future.

Rather, Derrida is interested in looking at how contextual conditions emerge and are decided in specific material situations of performative emergence and reinscription. Perhaps this offers us a way to understand Derrida's own oft-repeated performative, "Deconstruction is a situation." Or, as he contends, "Deconstruction is neither a theory nor a philosophy. It is neither a school nor a method. It is not even a discourse, nor an act, nor a practice. It is what happens, what is happening today in what they call society, politics, diplomacy, economics, historical reality, and so on and so forth. Deconstruction is the case" ("Some Statements," 85).[7] Given this insistence on emergence within sociohistorical context—on "what is happening *today*"—perhaps Derrida cannot be so easily collapsed into a thinking of the discontinuous origin and ineffable future, monotonously exposed by a rarified analysis. Though, at the same time, one can almost hear a Foucauldian question emerging from the anonymous murmur, a question concerning the seemingly totalized conditions of the statement, "Deconstruction is the case."

Though I suppose he would be hard-pressed to agree, it seems that Foucault's analysis of the statement in the *Archaeology* is strikingly similar to Derrida's analysis of the contextual performative. In fact, one could gloss Derrida on the undecidability of text by quoting Foucault on the network of statements:

> A statement always has margins peopled by other statements. These margins are not what is usually meant by "context"—real or verbal—that is, all the situational or linguistic elements, taken together, that motivate a formulation and determine its meaning. They are distinct from such a "context" precisely in so far as they make it possible. . . . There is no statement in general, no free, independent statement; but a statement always belongs to a series or whole, always plays a role among other statements, deriving support from them and distinguishing itself from them: it is always part of a network of statements. (*Archaeology*, 97–98, 99; translation slightly modified)

Here, it seems that Foucault revisits any number of seemingly Derridean themes. There is no historical extra-text precisely because such a supposed anchoring context is the *product* rather than the determining *condition* of historicity, of what Derrida calls the "textual" field. There is no statement in general, but always a series or network of statements, and studying these statements entails patiently tracking their reinscriptive deployment of force, the ways in which they derive support and distinguish themselves from other statements. This constitutes what Foucault, in an interesting imbrication of emergence and possibility, calls the "historical *a priori*."[8]

However, differences—and substantial ones—remain. For Foucault, the emphasis or upshot of his analysis, its force and directionality, is different: the crucial Foucauldian object of analysis is the specific emergence of a series of exclusions that form a context, "a specific history that does not refer back to the laws of an alien development" (*Archaeology*, 127). Of course, any context or statement is theoretically open to reinscription, but Foucault is interested in tracking historical determinations through examining the exclusions necessary to create a specific "meaningful" context (e.g., the institutional and discursive operations that have to be performed to secure a meaningful context for the category or statement "madman" or "ill man" or "woman"). So for Foucault, the question is not so much a matter of futurity and the material *possibility* or *necessity* of reinscription, but the specificity of the context as it emerges. Of course, on any but the least generous reading, it seems clear that Derrida is not merely interested in futurity, but is likewise insistent on the necessary violence that configures and transforms contexts.[9]

Still, Derrida and Foucault might be said to agree on at least this much: the reinscription of the statement or the speech act in another context each time (re)decides and (re)positions the referent of a discursive act. Both agree that "meaning" or "identity" is not a fixed relation (not simply a matter of referencing conditions of possibility), but is produced by a reappearance (the performative conditions of emergence).[10] In neither case, then, is it some tautological metaphysical or originary "law" that decides; rather, it is the specificity of a material reaction or reinscription, and I think that Butler's work shows us how Foucault and Derrida can be thought together precisely in terms of such a movement of production and subversion from within. On these terms, and without merely collapsing their projects into one another, Derrida certainly could be read against Foucault's "transcendentalist" reading of him. Perhaps the proper name for deconstruction, as Rodolphe Gasché has argued, is radical empiricism (see "God, for Example," 63). And, if this is the case, it would seem to open a door to enlist Derrida in the service of a certain materialist analysis.

However, this conclusion, especially stated as such (as a *conclusion*), runs the risk of trading a hazardous debate (Foucault versus Derrida) for a simple platitude, the now familiar refrain heard in virtually any humanities job interview: "everything (gender, race, nation, subject, etc.) is socially constructed." Much to what I think would have been his chagrin, Foucault's Nietzschean insistence on conditions of emergence seems to have been translated from a challenge to think and respond otherwise into a rote conclusion. Foucault's complex and supple imbrication of the questions of emergence and possibility has, it seems, been left behind in much recent work in North American humanities, work that rather monotonously goes about demonstrating cultural discontinuity and social construction in its analyses. And even the "empiricist" reading of Derrida risks bolstering this institutional project. Foucault specifically warns against this fetishizing of discontinuity in the human sciences: "My problem was not at all to say, '*Voilà*, long live discontinuity, we are in the discontinuous and a good thing too,' but to pose the question, 'How is it that at certain moments and in certain orders of knowledge, there are these sudden take-offs, these hastenings of evolution, these transformations which fail to correspond to the calm, continuist image that is normally accredited?' (*Power/Knowledge*, 112). Nevertheless, with the conclusion that everything is socially constructed from discontinuous patterns of emergence, Foucault's fears about the "pedagogical" dangers of Derrida's discourse turn on his own; to paraphrase Nietzsche, perhaps today a fat phrase ("social construction") has replaced a thin question mark.[11]

This, I think, is where Butler's intervention is again crucial. In *Bodies That Matter*, Butler asks us to take a step back from this platitudinous understanding that "everything is socially constructed" and move toward an examination of the specific foreclosures or exclusions by which identities are secured; also, and perhaps more important for my argument here and throughout this book, Butler foregrounds the question of resistance precisely by performatively reinscribing the insights of Foucault and Derrida. She investigates or demonstrates how resistance happens, how it is engendered and made concrete through the structuring emergence of the subject that is foreclosure itself. Performative foreclosure, in other words, becomes the hinge by which Butler thinks possibility and emergence together. As she maintains, "Thinking the body as constructed demands a rethinking of the meaning of construction itself" (*Bodies*, xi). Thinking about emergence entails thinking about possibility, and this insistence on the imbri-

cation of the material and theoretical—the actual and the possible—
within bodily agency is precisely the reason why performativity comprises a privileged thread to open and keep open the question of ethics
and ethical response.

For Butler, although it is certainly important and productive to
think Foucault and Derrida together by pointing out that "sex is a
social construction" that emerges and is subverted through iterable
performatives and practices, it is another matter altogether to account
for the ways in which "remainder" subjectivities are actually produced in specific historico-cultural situations *as* abjected, produced
as by-products of the violent exclusions that secure normative identities. Butler writes in the service of that project:

> there is an "outside" to what is constructed by discourse, but
> this is not an absolute "outside," an ontological thereness that
> exceeds or counters the boundaries of discourse; as a constitutive
> "outside," it is that which can only be thought—when it can—
> in relation to that discourse, at and as its most tenuous borders.
> The debate between constructivism and essentialism thus misses
> the point of deconstruction altogether, for the point has never
> been that "everything is discursively constructed"; that point . . .
> refuses the constitutive force of exclusion, erasure, violent fore-
> closure, abjection, and its disruptive return within the very terms
> of discursive legitimacy. (*Bodies*, 8)

The upshot of Butler's notion of performativity, in other words, is
not that everything is structure*d*, but rather that everything is dependent on structure*s*—linguistic, institutional, and political structures
that are cited and recited in any specific case; and, she argues, it is
precisely an attention to the material specificity of the "constitutive
'outside' " in any particular case that would allow us to respond to and
reinscribe the multiple exclusions that make one identity possible or
livable, while making other identities impossible or unlivable. The
social constructionism debate, in other words, needs to pay attention
to the *material specificity of the restrictions* that make possible the
construction and maintenance of a particular normativity.

Given this distinctly ethical logic of foreclosure, any attempt to deal
solely with conditions of emergence at the expense of conditions of
possibility (or vice versa) is doomed to a certain productive haunting—
I hesitate to say "failure." In fact, given where the humanities have
arrived in recent years (at the seemingly totalized conclusion that

everything is a social construction), perhaps *today* a confrontation with conditions of possibility offers any number of important and productive caveats, not the least of which might be a wariness about the dangers of a normative anthropomorphism and its unmarked privilege within "social constructionism." Butler writes about the debate surrounding the social construction of gender:

> The "activity" of this gendering cannot, strictly speaking, be a human act or expression, a willful appropriation, and it is certainly *not* a question of taking on a mask; it is the matrix through which all willing first becomes possible, its enabling cultural contradiction. In this sense, the *matrix of gender relations is prior to the emergence of the "human."* . . . The construction of the human is a differential operation that produces the more and the less "human," the inhuman, the humanly unthinkable. These excluded sites come to bound the "human" as its constitutive outside, and to haunt those boundaries as the persistent possibility of their disruption and rearticulation. (*Bodies*, 8)

It is perhaps as this hesitating confrontation with something other than the human and its privileges that one might be able to recover a productive discourse about "conditions of possibility"; and it is certainly worth noting that both Foucault and Derrida share Butler's hesitation before categories that have yet to emerge as ethically compelling, a certain *material* commitment or response to what is not-yet: the affirmation of emergence itself, the affirmation of *today* that entails a metonymic ethical link to the necessary emergences of the future.

In the end, if we're obliged to do justice to—to *decide* about—the topic of emergence and possibility in Derrida and Foucault, I'd be tempted to say that what both separates and brings them together is not an affinity or difference in arguments or themes, but rather a kind of mood or Heideggerian *Stimmung* in their work: both work to keep thinking at some kind of limit, and both are consistently oriented toward that limit in their work. It may, however, be enough to say that Derrida is interested in and oriented toward that limit primarily as *possibility*; his work is engaged in opening, enabling, and even *protecting* the possibility of grafting something other onto or into philosophy.[12] And whereas Foucault is certainly interested in and dependent upon that possible grafting, the mood of his work and its orientation seems to be more in the direction of the graft itself: in describing what emerges in the space of possibility, what specific forces attempt to take hold of those spaces.

Perhaps one could say that, in the end, Butler's performative imbrication of Foucault and Derrida is ethically compelling precisely because it is an attempt to enact a thinking of today and tomorrow, interpellation and reinscription, action and ethics, politics and alterity. In any case, it is toward such a multiple imbrication that this book will remain focused as it visits multiple sites of contestation and reinscription, organized around the questions of ethics and performative identity.

2 · The Ethics of Dialogue: Bakhtin's Answerability and Levinas's Responsibility

Communication with the other can be transcendent only as a dangerous life, a fine risk to be run. —Emmanuel Levinas, *Otherwise than Being*

The reemergence of subjective agency as a crucial category in recent literary and cultural studies can be seen as a direct response to the decentering of the subject enacted by the first wave of poststructuralism. Poststructuralists of all stripes are increasingly being pressed to engage the question of ethical agency "after" the subject.[1] At the same time, however, a certain critique of the humanist or Enlightenment subject remains firmly in place. Although there is a great deal of sympathy for rethinking notions of subjectivity in the current theoretical field, no one wants anything to do with the appropriating instrumental rationality of the bourgeois subject. In fact, virtually all critical camps—groups as diverse as Habermasians, feminists, postcolonial theorists, Marxists, Deleuzians, African Americanists, deconstructors, Lacanians, queer theorists, and pragmatists—remain aligned in their attempts to critique a subjectivity that inexorably goes about reducing the other to the categories of the self. Any ethical system that understands the other as simply "like the self" will be unable to respond adequately to the other's uniqueness and singularity; indeed, such a reduction amounts to a kind of subjective colonialism, where all the other's desires are reduced to the desires of the "home country," the self.

Perhaps a touchstone for this critique of the subject is Max Horkheimer and Theodor Adorno's excursus on the *Odyssey* in *Dialectic of Enlightenment.* Recall their argument that Odysseus, ancient "figure of the protagonist compelled to wander," is in fact "a prototype of the bourgeois individual" (43). It is important to recall, as Horkheimer and Adorno remind us time and again, that the Enlightenment subject does not seek static knowledge or simple completeness, but rather seeks precisely the opposite: to escape from the stasis of nature or myth through the knowledge-gathering adventures of experience. The instrumental subject actually seeks out hazard, constantly risks confrontation with otherness; finally, the subject risks death in order to conquer its potentially crippling power, in order to bring the fear of death—the ultimate alterity—under subjective control. As Horkheimer and Adorno contend, this notion of "the self does not constitute the fixed antithesis to adventure, but in its rigidity molds itself only by way of that antithesis: being an entity only in the diversity of that which denies all unity. . . . Odysseus loses himself in order to find himself" (47–8). The Enlightenment subject, contrary to the caricature one often sees of it, finally doesn't want or seek a monologic unity: to possess such stasis is merely to be enthralled in the face of nature or myth, to have one's life determined by something other.

So the Enlightenment subject, "in order to find himself," turns *not inward* to the tautological unity of the cogito, but rather *outward* to the diversity of the other(s); such a subject "loses himself" in order to secure the higher dynamism of an evolving, adventuring appropriation that can confront and conquer ever newer forms of otherness. Such a subject has learned to make use of the other, and finds itself only by means of the other. The bourgeois subject, one might say, profits from its investment in the other; it gets a return for its risk. Finally, it is this imperialist brand of bourgeois or instrumental subjectivity— which often goes by the proper name Hegel—that is questioned in virtually all accounts of contemporary ethics: the static stability of the Cartesian cogito's "I think, therefore I am," though certainly isolated from others, is not necessarily ethically dangerous; but the Hegelian subject, whose formula might be expressed as "I desire (to appropriate), therefore I am," presents a much greater ethical challenge.[2]

Of course, to recall the renewed emphasis on agency with which we began this chapter, Horkheimer and Adorno's critique of the subject doesn't mean that subjectivity can be or is abandoned altogether in the construction of a postmodern ethics. Certainly, concrete action in intersubjective realms remains crucial to any ethical system, and such action seems to demand a subject position, a specific site where ethical conduct can be called for and rendered. Ethical platitudes are worth little unless they translate into material actions and obligations among subjects in specific contexts. In short, it seems that ethics can't live with the subject, but can't live without it either.

In response to this difficult problem, postmodern thinkers have increasingly turned to a dialogic, intersubjective understanding of ethics. Dialogic intersubjectivity, understood in terms of an impassioned play of voices, has displaced the dominant modernist and existentialist metaphor of the monadic subject and its plaintive demand for social recognition and submission from the other. As Dorothy Hale writes, "Voice has become the metaphor that best accommodates the conflicting desires of critics and theorists who want to have their cultural subject and de-essentialize it too" (445). Voice can "de-essentialize" ethics precisely because it also highlights an emphasis on "response": "voicing" an opinion, for example, is not the same as "holding" an opinion. "Voice" becomes such an attractive concept because it is not tied essentially to one point of view; rather, one must learn to *find* one's own voice and to *hear* the voice of the other within a common social context. It is precisely in the movements of seeking, listening, and answering that an intersubjective ethics of response might be born. And this points to the distinctly *ethical* character of dialogics: if social space is understood as a rich dialogue of voices rather than a fight for recognition and domination, then the other is not necessarily a menacing or hostile force. The dialogue of multiple voices has become a powerful metaphor for a social space wherein, as Michael Gardiner puts it, "otherness is no longer considered foreign or threatening" ("Alterity," 140).

If dialogue is the name for this social imbrication of voice and response, it seems the perfect middle ground to articulate a non-appropriative ethical subject position. Zygmunt Bauman asserts in *Postmodern Ethics*, "A postmodern ethics would be one that readmits the Other as a neighbor, . . . an ethics that recasts the Other as the crucial character in the process through which the moral self comes into its own" (84). Indeed, a dialogic understanding of subjectivity would seem to offer a subject position that, pace Horkheimer and Adorno's bourgeois subject, "readmits the Other as a neighbor," as a "crucial character" in the development of the responding "moral self." Perhaps ethical responsibility is first and foremost the ability to respond, and if we're looking for such a postmodern dialogic ethics that takes full account of our obligation to respond to the other, Bauman proclaims that the search is over: "Levinas's is the postmodern ethics" (84). What Levinas calls his ethics "of responsibility, that is, of sociality" (*Otherwise*, 26), offers us a way to rethink the response that the subject owes to the other in the dialogue of "sociality."

Although Levinas's work is becoming more well-known, it may be appropriate briefly to introduce the unfamiliar reader to his ethical and philosophical itinerary. Levinas is perhaps best known for his work on the primacy of "the other." According to Levinas, it is not abstract systems of obligation that give a thickness to human ethical life; rather, ethics is born and maintained through the necessity of *performative response* to the other person, and such a responsiveness (which he calls "responsibility") comes necessarily *before* the solidification of any theoretical rules or political norms of ethical conduct. In this way, Levinas asks us to consider the primacy of "nonphilosophical" experience; that is, he continually calls attention to the primacy of an experience of sociality or otherness that comes before any philosophical understanding or reification of our respective subject positions. Levinas has many names for this "nonphilosophical" encounter (proximity, vulnerability, sociality, responsibility, saying), but perhaps the most famous Levinasian trope for this experience is the dialogic "face-to-face" encounter with the other. As Levinas maintains, the face-to-face "situation is an experience in the strongest sense of the term: a contact with a reality that does not fit into any a priori idea, which overflows all of them. . . . A face is pure experience, conceptless experience" ("Philosophy," 59). In Levinas's work, such an "experience" of the other exceeds all my categories of knowledge and understanding. As Gardiner explains in "Alterity and Ethics," the Levinasian relation between self and other "cannot [simply] be translated into rational, conceptual thought, for this would destroy the unmotivated, spontaneous character of the encounter" (131). But, at the same time, there is an obligation to respond built into the very situation of the face-to-face encounter, insofar as the experience of the other person is also a concrete, social phenomenon. We must respond to the social fact of otherness in the way that we must respond to the experiential fact that fire burns flesh and food nourishes it; such response does not simply—or even primarily—find its origin in the subject's "choice."

It seems that Levinas leaves us, then, in an odd position: there are no preexisting ethical grammars by which I might respond adequately to the other, and yet I must respond nevertheless. Finally, Levinas reworks this seeming paradox by insisting that the self "always already" responds to the other in saying or doing anything at all (even ignoring or dismissing the other is, after all, a kind of response). Levinas argues that because the ineluctable experience of the other is the founding of selfhood, "I" am never anything but that *response* to the other. Whatever my "self" might be is always beholden to the other, not vice versa. In the end, Levinas will give the name "ethics" to "this calling into question of my spontaneity by the presence of the other" (*Totality*, 43).

In this chapter, I'd like to explore the responsibility called for in Levinas's ethics in the light of another discourse that takes the other to be a "crucial character" in the dialogic, performative formation of the self: M. M. Bakhtin's ethics of "answerability."[3] At first, this may seem like an odd pairing insofar as Bakhtin's formidable reputation has not been built primarily as an ethicist. However, with the translation into English of his early writings and increasing evidence of his theological interests, Bakhtin's dialogics is becoming recontextualized as a powerful *ethical* discourse.[4] Gary Saul Morson and Caryl Emerson, for example, point out that consideration of Bakhtin's "unfinished or unpublished manuscripts dating from the 1910s and early 1920s"—translated as *Art and Answerability* and *Toward a Philosophy of the Act*—would "seem likely to alter our sense of Bakhtin, primarily by calling attention to the centrality of ethics in his thought" (*Rethinking*, 2). Indeed, as Paul de Man argues, it is through recognizing Bakhtin's stress on alterity or "exotopy that, finally, a larger philosophical claim can be made for Bakhtin not just as a technician of literary discourse but as a thinker or metaphysician whose name can be considered next to those of Husserl, Heidegger, or . . . Levinas" ("Dialogue," 110).[5]

It is Bakhtin's and Levinas's mutual insistence on the subject's irreducible engagement with otherness that has brought them so centrally into the contemporary dialogue concerning ethical subjectivity: confronted by an excessive alterity, the subject *must* perform a response. As Augusto Ponzio elaborates and expands, "What unites especially Bakhtin and Levinas is their both having identified otherness within the sphere of the self, which does not lead to its assimilation, but quite on the contrary, gives rise to a constitutive impediment to the integrity and closure of self" (6). Both thinkers deploy some notion of unassimilable excess as a bulwark against the reification of otherness that they, like Horkheimer and Adorno, read in the Hegelian dialectic. Both Bakhtin and Levinas insist that ethics exists in an open and ongoing obligation to respond to the other, rather than a static march toward some philosophical end or conclusion.

As Bakhtin elaborates in *Problems of Dostoevsky's Poetics*, dialogics "must not be understood as the dialectical evolution of the spirit" (26). For Bakhtin, as for Levinas, a dialectical understanding of subjectivity inexorably privileges sameness over difference, thereby reducing the encounter with otherness, in Bakhtin's words, "to a philosophical monologue unfolding dialectically. The unified, dialectically evolving spirit, understood in Hegelian terms, can give rise to nothing but a philosophical monologue. And the soil of monistic idealism is the least likely place for a plurality of unmerged consciousness to blossom" (26; compare Levinas, *Totality*, 36–38). It is precisely this excessive or infinite "plurality of unmerged consciousness" that both Bakhtin and Levinas wish to rescue from the "monistic idealism" of Hegelian dialectics, and both attempt to do so by insisting on an irreducible element in human contact, an element in face-to-face or dialogic encounters that cannot simply be sublated at a higher level. Levinas claims, "with the appearance of the human—and this is my entire philosophy—there is something more important than my life, and that is the life of the other" ("Paradox," 172).[6] The specificity of this surplus in human dialogue remains crucial to both Bakhtin and Levinas because it keeps the otherwise monadic subject open to the outside; such an excess necessitates that the self is never merely an appropriation machine, but always open—performatively responding or answering—to the other.

In the most basic terms, then, Bakhtin and Levinas share the powerful ethical conviction that contact with the human other cannot simply be reified into a moment or movement of appropriation. Bakhtin maintains, "there always remains an unrealized surplus of humanness" (*Dialogic*, 37) in the dialogic encounter with others, and it is precisely this surplus that is the groundless ethical ground for both Bakhtin's "answerability" and Levinas's "responsibility." As Levinas writes, social dialogue "has to be conceived as a responsibility for the other; it might be called humanity, or subjectivity, or self" (*Otherwise*,

46). For Levinas, to live and speak in a society is always already to be responding to concrete others; again, he insists that the movement of response—responsibility—toward the human other comes prior to the static theoretical or moral realm of prescriptive ethics. Bakhtin elaborates a similar sentiment in terms of answerability: "it is of course necessary to take the performed act *not* as a fact contemplated from outside or thought of theoretically, but to take it from within, in its answerability. This answerability of the actually performed act is the taking-into-account in it of all the factors—a taking-into-account of its sense-validity as well as of its factual performance in all its concrete historicity and individuality" (*Toward*, 28). Here Bakhtin, like Levinas, asks us to think and respond to the other not abstractly or theoretically, but "from within" a dialogic situation, "in all its concrete historicity and individuality." As Bakhtin concisely sums up this common ground with Levinas, "theoretical philosophy cannot pretend to being a first philosophy" (*Toward*, 19; compare Levinas, *Totality* 42–48). Both thinkers begin by insisting that universal or philosophical constatives are always beholden to site-specific performatives.

For both Bakhtin and Levinas, then, it is *ethics*—answerability or responsibility—that is literally first philosophy: response to the concrete other comes first, before the thematics of abstract ontology. In short, it is the radically social and nonontological nature of both Bakhtin's and Levinas's discourses that makes them so appealing to contemporary critics who, as Hale put it, want to have their ethical subject position and de-essentialize it too. As Gardiner writes, "each of them argues that ethics is constitutively linked to corporeality, the direct experience of 'lived' time and place, and our affective and meaningful relations with concrete others" ("Alterity," 122). Both Bakhtin and Levinas link ethical dialogue to the bewildering specificity of others and social contexts, rather than to the monologizing generality of ethical rules.

Dialogic ethics, then, seems to offer a way out of the dead end of identity politics by offering instead a socially grounded and compelling notion of ethics that does not resort to the ontological schemes of abstract Kantian obligation. An ethics of answerability or responsibility offers a way to understand specific differences and enact specific ethical commitments, without falling back on the totalizing gestures of a universalizing, rule- or norm-governed structure. In both Levinas and Bakhtin, one responds or answers first and foremost to the social other, rather than responding to or through an abstract system of ethical rules to be followed; likewise, both thinkers insist that a response to the other that merely applies such a set of neutral or abstract principles is no ethical response at all. Thereby, they open up a productive horizon to rethink the social interaction of self and other in our groundless postmodern landscape.

However, substantial differences remain between Levinas and Bakhtin, and these differences are worth examining at some length because of the light they shed on contemporary attempts to construct an ethics for the postmodern subject. As I argued at the outset of this book, nearly every contemporary critical camp agrees that there is an irreducible excess to postmodern life—an "embarrassed 'etc.'" at the heart of identity—and any ethico-political treatment of otherness would need somehow to take this excess into account. Levinas and Bakhtin are so crucial to this debate because they offer us a way to think that excess or "etc." *as* the ethical specificity of the other, who always exceeds and questions the categories of the self. However, the most crucial of the *differences* between Bakhtin and Levinas also revolves around this notion of excess that gives a uniqueness or irreducibility to human ethical life. Finally, examining this difference between Bakhtin and Levinas will offer another angle of intervention into the current debates, especially the social constructionism versus essentialism controversy, surrounding the ethical subject.

Subjectivity and Irreducibility

As I argue above, Levinas and Bakhtin offer us a way to understand subjective irreducibility as the groundless ground of a postmodern ethics of response. However, they not only come together but also part company at this irreducibility—specifically over the question of *where* or *to whom* this irreducible or unique excess accrues. For Levinas, this excess (which he calls "infinity") is the irreducible specificity of the other that traces and calls for the responsibility of the self; as Levinas states, "the other is unique" ("Paradox," 174) and I am infinitely substitutable. As he clarifies in *Otherwise than Being*, "there is *nothing* that is named *I*; the I is said by him that speaks. . . . Here uniqueness means the impossibility of slipping away and being replaced. . . . This uniqueness not assumed, not subsumed, is traumatic; it is an election in persecution" (56). For Levinas, "I" is merely a substitutable linguistic placeholder: I am the entity that says "here I am" in response to the other. Hence, in the encounter between me and the other, "identity" (as stable or developing personhood) accrues to neither party. Levinas continues, "Uniqueness is without identity. Not an identity, it is beyond consciousness, which is in itself and for itself. For it is already a substitution for the other" (57). My singularity or subjectivity, in other words, is given as a function of the other's unique and irreducible infinity; I can expect no gain from a confrontation with this otherness, but rather only the serial epiphany of my subjectivity as everywhere beholden to the other. What I find out from experience is the "traumatic" fact that the other is always there already, and hence any act I perform is necessarily conditioned by—Levinas would say *owed to*—the other. It is, then, before the other's infinity that I am subject(ed), and therefore to the other that I always owe my response.

To put it somewhat less poetically, in Levinas the seemingly "originary" impulses to think, act, or resist do not find their genealogy in me, and hence these abilities cannot be read as my unique features or strengths. My abilities to think, act, and resist are literally *from* and *for* the other. As Levinas concisely puts it, in his thinking, "It is not I who resist the system; . . . it is the other" (*Totality*, 40); it is not I who am irreducible and infinite—it is not I who am always there—but the other. Insofar as a determinate I cannot have a simple relation with the irreducible infinite, any relation with the other necessarily constitutes what Levinas calls an "irreducible relation," a relation with the other that does not finally accrue or return to the I.[7]

For Levinas, then, it is not a matter of some abstract notion of infinity that offers subjective access to greater self-knowledge or to the world—as it is, for example, in the relation between *Dasein* and Being in Heidegger's phenomenology—but rather a matter of subjects literally created through an encounter with the other: "It is as though persecution by another were at the bottom of solidarity with another" (*Otherwise*, 102). For Levinas, I come into being only as subjected to a social network of signification or substitution for-the-other: "The notions of access to being, representation, and thematization . . . presuppose sensibility, and thus proximity, vulnerability and signifyingness" (68). For Levinas, being able to think or respond in concrete contexts presupposes a necessary subjection before the infinite alterity of the other; response presupposes that one is first open to the other, in a social space or "proximity" that is characterized by "vulnerability" or inexorable exposure. As Jacques Derrida clarifies in an essay on Levinas, "Without that responsibility there would be no language" ("At This Very Moment," 23): without there first being openness to the other—in Levinas's terminology, "sensibility, and thus proximity, vulnerability and signifyingness"—there would be no communication or dialogue. The response that one offers to the other in dialogue, then, always carries a trace of this "passivity," this ethical responsibility *prior* to response that interrupts from before the fact my subjective uniqueness or plenitude.

My subjection in the face-to-face is, however, also my solidarity with the other. Subjectivity is produced only insofar as any I is simultaneously what Levinas calls a "hostage," subject to a very specific proximal/social relation or founding debt, but at the same time infinitely replaceable: "In substitution my being that belongs to me and not to another is undone, and it is through this substitution that I am not 'another,' but me. The self in a being is exactly the not-being-able-to-slip-away-from an assignation that does not aim at any generality. . . . Subjectivity is being hostage (*Otherwise*, 127). Through subjection to or in a network of preexisting social "substitution," a specific named subject comes into being as "the not-being-able-to-slip-away-from an assignation." Levinasian subjectivity, however, is not an Oedipal alienation from a prior wholeness which then forces the I to choose among a series of avatars within a network of synchronic signification; rather, subjectivity is the diachronic social *production* of identity in the *subjection* of the face-to-face. This serial nature of substitution accrues a debt that any subject owes to the other: even in its seeming uniqueness, the subject-as-hostage (the I not chosen by a subject but produced by the other's infinity) is always replaceable within a social realm characterized by the performative subjection of identities without alienation or lack.[8] In the end, Levinas insists that "It is not the insufficiency of the I that prevents totalization, but the infinity of the other" (*Totality*, 80).

In Bakhtin, on the other hand, it is the I—the self—that harbors lack and produces excess, and it is the other who is infinitely substitutable in the drama of this revelation. As Bakhtin contends in *Art and Answerability*, "The other human being exists for me entirely *in* the object and his *I* is only an object for me. . . . I am incapable of fitting all of myself into an object, for I exceed any object as the active *subiectum* of it" (38). For Bakhtin, unlike Levinas, I am the source and guarantor of excess, and as such it is to *me* that the irreducibility of the human accrues. As Bakhtin writes, the "ever-present *excess* of my seeing, knowing, and possessing in relation to any other human being is founded on the uniqueness and irreplaceability of my place in the world. For only I—the one-and-only I—occupy in a given set of circumstances this particular place at this particular time; all other human beings are situated outside me" (23). For Bakhtin, it remains the "irreplaceabl[e]" I who is the source of singularity and excess; it is not the other but "the one-and-only I" who resists systemization and guarantees continued openness and response. He elaborates: "in order to live and act, I need to be unconsummated, I need to be open for myself. . . . I have to be, for myself, someone who is axiologically yet-to-be, someone who does not coincide with his already existing makeup" (13).

We should, however, hesitate here for a moment, and point out that Bakhtin's "I-for-myself" is only one category within the tripartite structure of Bakhtinian selfhood. As Morson and Emerson point out in *Mikhail Bakhtin: Creation of a Prosaics*, Bakhtin "deals with the self in three related categories. First there is the I-for-myself (how my self looks and feels to my own consciousness), and then two categories of outsideness and otherness, I-for-others (how my self appears to those outside it) and the reverse, the other-for-me (how outsiders appear to my self)" (180). It is from within this tripartite structure that we can see Bakhtin's most persuasive argument for the structural necessity of otherness: I cannot perceive myself, and hence the I-for-myself is constantly in a state of flux. Among the three selves that comprise subjectivity, only the I-for-others and the other-for-me can enjoy any kind of stability, and therefore it is only within the categories of outsideness that the I-for-myself has any hope of realizing or stabilizing itself. The I-for-myself is, in other words, inexorably dependent on the others.

Oddly enough, then, it seems that the I-for-myself is *both* utterly helpless *and* uncontestedly primary within the Bakhtinian categories of selfhood. As Morson and Emerson make clear, "*first* there is the I-for-myself . . . and *then* two categories of outsideness or otherness." Although the Bakhtinian I-for-myself is always intimately and inextricably associated with the I-for-others and the other-for-me, I think it is fair to say that, unlike Levinas's discourse, Bakhtin's work is *not* primarily concerned with the privilege or specificity of the other per se; rather, Bakhtin seems concerned with otherness primarily insofar as it is related to the openness and creativity of what Morson and Emerson call "the primary actor, the I-for-myself" (*Creation*, 188). In other words, the categories of outsideness seem interesting or necessary in Bakhtin precisely insofar as they have something to offer to the unconsummated fluidity that is the I-for-myself.

To use his most suggestive metaphor, the Bakhtinian subject's encounter with the other is based on aesthetic models, where I am the author and the other is my character—someone with whom I relate and experiment, someone who opens me to the potentialities that are "axiologically yet-to-be." As Michael Holquist elaborates in "The Architectonics of Answerability," "I consummate—or give finished form to—another. It is this fact that induces Bakhtin to make one of his bolder hypotheses: to treat the activity of perception as the structure of authoring. I give shape *both* to others and to my self as an author gives shape to his heroes" (xxx). The hero or the other, then, is in some sense a version of the author—a version of me—but still remains absolutely irreducible to that author, remains in fact the marker of the author's openness to his or her own excessive, eventful self-overcoming in dialogue with the other. Holquist argues that, for Bakhtin, "I am an event, the event of constantly responding to utterances from the different worlds I pass through" (*Dialogism*, 48); and in the eyes of the author, his or her text is precisely one of these passing worlds in which he or she is a voice situated among a carnival of many others.

Explained in this way, however, Bakhtinian subjectivity would seem to be hard-pressed to answer Horkheimer and Adorno's critique of the wandering Enlightenment subject. Bakhtin's "I" seems to be quite Odyssean, passing from adventure to adventure, "consummating" others while scrupulously keeping itself from being consummated; in fact, it seems the constant consummation of others that keeps the Bakhtinian self open, or at least allows the self dialogically to recognize its own nonconsummation. Like Odysseus, the Bakhtinian subject returns home from experience each time and finds itself changed and enriched, more open to its own possibilities as it travels through different worlds of otherness. It seems that the Bakhtinian subject encounters otherness primarily as a reassurance of its own developing, shifting sameness; the self encounters the other as a way of enhancing its own sense of multiplicity.

In other words, although the Bakhtinian confrontation with the other opens a "zone of freedom and open-endedness" (*Problems* 297), the possibilities of this zone accrue solely to a kind of voracious I. Bakhtin maintains, "the closer the image to the zone *I-for-myself*, the less there is object-like and finalized in it, the more it becomes an image of personality, free and open-ended" (297). Here, Bakhtin's realm of the other seems hopelessly inauthentic ("object-like and finalized"), whereas the realm of the I remains the sole locus of possibility and authenticity.[9] The "personality, free and open-ended," that emerges from dialogic encounter to dialogic encounter seems to mirror Horkheimer and Adorno's Hegelian bourgeois subject, greedily protecting its unique centrifugal personhood—its vast potential—from the centripetal forces of alterity, from "all that is externalizing and false" (Bakhtin, *Problems*, 294).

Of course, those sympathetic to Bakhtin have been quick to pick up on this seemingly troublesome point of convergence. Graham Pechey insists, for example, that "Bakhtin's notion of the 'personality' has nothing whatever to do with the monadic individual of bourgeois individualism" (26). In fact, for Pechey, Bakhtin remains best understood in terms of the "post-Hegelian revolt against the category of totality" (30). Holquist concurs, arguing that Bakhtinian "otherness is not merely a [Hegelian] dialectical alienation on its way to sublation that will endow it with a unifying identity in higher consciousness. On the contrary: in dialogism consciousness *is* otherness" (*Dialogism*, 18). However, though Holquist maintains that "consciousness *is* otherness" in Bakhtin, at the same time he asserts that "the position of the observer is fundamental" (21); likewise, Pechey maintains that "a radical reading [of Bakhtin] needs to affirm rather than apologize for this emphasis on the subject" (28).

For a Bakhtinian, this otherness where the self remains primary can seem like a troubling paradox only if one is *not* thinking dialogically. As Holquist argues, this seeming oxymoron—the privilege of self in an inescapable field of otherness—is simple enough to explain: the Bakhtinian "'self' is dialogic, a *relation*" (*Dialogism*, 19). Given the necessity of this structural dialogism in Bakhtin, Holquist concludes that the primacy of the self "must not be misinterpreted as yet another Romantic claim for the primacy of the absolute subject: self for Bakhtin is a cognitive necessity, not a mystified privilege" (22).[10] In other words, the Bakhtinian self, primary or not, must structure itself in terms of otherness: its self, its language, and its identity are socially constructed. Tzvetan Todorov puts it with characteristic brevity: "Instead of a 'dialectics of nature,' Bakhtin puts forward a 'dialogics of culture'" (104).

The upshot of all this is that Bakhtinian subjectivity can be, in Holquist's words, nothing other than "the differential relation between a center and all that is not center. . . . It is important from the outset, then, that 'center' in Bakhtin's thought be understood for what it is: a relative rather than absolute term, and, as such, one with no claim to absolute privilege" (*Dialogism*, 18). Like the I of

Hegelian transcendental privilege, the Bakhtinian I remains at the center of a discourse; however, both that center and that discourse are for Bakhtin inherently relative rather than driven by a transcendental Hegelian telos, subject to cultural change and modification rather than a static and monological march toward the end of absolute spirit. As Pechey concurs and sums up, this ever-shifting subject is Bakhtin's crucial "means of resisting Hegel's total absorption of the world in the absolute self-knowledge of Spirit, his abolition of a multiform objectivity in a uniform subjectivity" (24). On this reading, Bakhtinian multiform subjectivity escapes charges of totalization because such a subject is "always relative and never absolute" (29).

Leaving aside for the moment the chiasmic performativity of the phrase "always relative and never absolute," for both Holquist and Pechey the defense of dialogics against the charge of totalizing Hegelian subjective imperialism lies in the fact that Bakhtinian otherness and selfhood are relationally or socially constructed. In fact, it is precisely this insistence on social interaction that many contemporary critics find so appealing in Bakhtin. The Bakhtinian self structurally *needs* otherness, and is cheerfully, rather than resentfully, open to it. As Caryl Emerson puts it, the other in Bakhtin is not an alien menace, but "a friendly other, a living factor in the attempts of the *I* toward self-definition" (in Bakhtin, *Problems*, 302 n). In a dialogic system, neither self nor other can live independently; though the self may be privileged, it can never be complete. As Holquist writes, once we realize with Bakhtin that "I cannot *perceive* my self," we then necessarily "grasp how far removed the self is from any privilege" (*Dialogism*, 26) and open the door to a dialogic ethics based on welcoming the other as partner rather than using or resenting him or her.[11]

As compelling as this line of reasoning may be, it doesn't seem to answer the critique of the voracious Enlightenment subject with which we began. As Horkheimer and Adorno make clear, such an appropriating subjectivity wants nothing to do with static self-perception: its "privilege," pace Holquist, is nothing other than its unstable mobility, its perception of itself as open to possibility.[12] It is after all Hegel, the supposedly monologic target of so much Bakhtinian dialogic critique, who admonishes us in *Phenomenology of Spirit* that "philosophy must beware of the wish to be edifying" (6); the Hegelian subject "is indeed never at rest but always engaged in moving forward" (6), finding "self-identity in otherness" (33). In fact, in the *Phenomenology* the Hegelian desiring subject finally learns only one thing: it "comes to know by experience that its essence is neither in the object nor in the 'I'" (62), but rather in a relational process that Hegel calls "mediation": the *becoming-other* that has to be taken back" (11), the movement outside the self that must return to and enrich the self.[13]

As Hegel explains dialectical mediation, "consciousness simultaneously *distinguishes* itself from something, and at the same time *relates* itself to it, or, as it is said, this something exists *for* consciousness" (52). Thus, to say that a "relational" understanding of subjectivity essentially challenges Hegel would seem to be a serious underestimation of Hegelian discourse. Likewise, one can't get off the Hegelian hook by saying that the I in Hegel is static, transcendental, or monologic; the consciousness that is the "hero" of the *Phenomenology* is in constant joust with the authorial consciousness that narrates the hero's struggles.[14] As Hegel maintains, "The I, or becoming in general, [is] this meditation" (11) on both the social and philosophical level.

To put it another way (and in terminology we encountered above), in Hegel the dialectical relation between self and other is "always relative" and changing, "never absolute" and fixed. Like Bakhtin, Hegel wants no traffic with static truths. In fact, the entire *Phenomenology* is a diatribe against such supposed truths: "disparity . . . is itself still directly present in the True as such. . . . Dogmatism . . . is nothing else but the opinion that the True exists in a proposition which is a fixed result" (23). At his most Bakhtinian, Hegel will assert that "The True is thus the Bacchanalian revel in which no member is not drunk" (27). In the end, the only "Truth" to be found in Hegel is the fallible process of mediation among subjects, not the fixed, static platitudes of a bygone philosophical era. As he insists, "it should be noted that current opinion itself has already come to view the scientific regime bequeathed by mathematics as quite *old-fashioned*—with its explanations, divisions, axioms, sets of theorems, its proofs, principles, deductions, and conclusions from them. Even if its unfitness is not clearly understood, little or no use is any longer made of it; and though not condemned outright, no one likes it very much" (28). Any static notion of "Truth" for Hegel is already "quite *old-fashioned*" in 1807; indeed, if we want access to truth, the only path is dialogical rather than monological—dealing with social specificities rather than metaphysical or mathematical abstractions. It is, then, only through dynamic, dialectical means that one can come to "conclusions" that are not mere tautologies, not imposed axiologically from some transcendental or mathematical space above the conflicted surface of a culture. Such a movement of subjective Enlightenment, as Horkheimer and Adorno show, is always dynamic *process*, never an absolute *conclusion*.

Through this seeming digression into Hegel's *Phenomenology*, I am not primarily interested in arguing that his texts can or should be read in more or less Bakhtinian ways (or vice versa), but that, despite the protestation of Bakhtinians, the supposedly liberating social or ethical effects of Bakhtinian dialogics aren't so easily separable from the supposedly totalizing effects of Hegelian dialectics. Likewise, no matter what discourse is producing them, the effects of thorough-going subjective privilege, whether transcendental or social, aren't easily recuperable from Horkheimer and Adorno's indictment of the bourgeois subject. In other words, it is precisely the privilege of a de-veloping, diversified subjectivity that constitutes the *critique* of the Enlightenment subject (which goes about reassuring itself through the adventures of alterity); so a process-oriented, diversified Bakhtinian subject could hardly be the unproblematic *answer* to that critique. When one counters, as Mathew Roberts does, that Bakhtin's relation with the other "is precisely *enriching*, not privative" (124), perhaps we see the problem most clearly: the subject's assurances of its own "enriching" through contact with the other actually constitutes what Horkheimer and Adorno locate as its "privative" dimension, so it is difficult to hear this notion of excessive subjective possibility as a cri-tique of the bourgeois subject. The contingency of the Enlightenment subject is its royal road to greater freedom; the contingent subject is not confined to mastering one object or set of objects.

Likewise, the deployment of a certain kind of trickle-down theory of subjectivity—if it's good for me, it's good for the other—seems rather suspect in Bakhtin. Even in the Dostoevsky book, where Bakh-tin seems to grant a clear autonomy to the hero (making the hero more than just a consummated function of the author), the hero's position nevertheless remains thematized in terms of (and thereby subordinated to) the seeming generosity of the author or the I. Bakh-tin contends, "the new artistic position of the author with regard to the hero in Dostoevsky's polyphonic novel is a *fully realized and thoroughly consistent dialogic position*, one that affirms the indepen-dence, internal freedom, unfinalizability and indeterminacy of the hero. For the author the hero is not 'he' and not 'I' but a fully valid 'thou,' that is another and other autonomous 'I.'" (*Problems*, 63). De-spite appearances of a certain generosity, the hero here nevertheless remains consummated by the author; but the twist is that the hero is consummated as autonomous, granted the status as "a fully valid 'thou'" by the generosity of the dispensing I. In the end, the hero's autonomy serves for Bakhtin as "the position enabling a person to interpret and evaluate his own self and his surrounding reality" (47). In short, the other—even as he or she is granted autonomy—always remains subject to the categories of the self. As Bakhtin maintains, I sacrifice myself before the other "to enable me, by way of self-abasement before him, to liberate myself from that possible influence exerted by his valuing position outside me and the possibilities associated with this position (to be unafraid of the opinion of others, to overcome my fear of shame)" (Art, 142). Finally, I generously open myself to the others in order to overcome them, to conquer and consummate their external opinions of me.[15]

At its best, the other in Bakhtin remains just like me: independent, internally free, unfinalizable, and indeterminate. As Pechey optimistically writes, "when everyone is absolutely an author no one is absolutely in authority" (28). I can, then, live with or alongside the other, but each of our gazes remains fixed on and directed toward the regulatory function of our own privative possibility.[16] In the end, what is important is authoring my text: the story of my "independence, internal freedom, unfinalizability and indeterminacy." Admittedly, for that sense of my existential mission to be fully realized, I must also grant these qualities to the other. The emphasis remains, however, on the author's "own self"—on my mission in a world of otherness. Bakhtin writes, "In a human being there is always something that only he himself can reveal, in a free act of self-consciousness and discourse, something that does not submit to an externalizing secondhand definition" (Problems, 58; italics in original). Within such an overarching project of subjective fulfillment or self-revelation, the other remains my enemy even though (or more precisely because) I need him or her to fulfill my dialogic destiny; it is from the "externalizing secondhand definition" of the other that I must wrest my own authentic selfhood. As Bakhtin puts it, "As long as a person is alive he lives by the fact that he is not yet finalized. . . . [M]an is free, and can therefore violate any regulating norms which might be thrust upon him. Dostoevsky's hero always seeks to destroy that framework of other people's words about him that might finalize and deaden him" (59). In Bakhtin, the outward dialogic or relational movement of subjectivity, however seemingly generous, remains regulated by a thoroughgoing privilege of enriching self-privilege: the richness of the subject in its personal destiny lives by creatively transfiguring the inauthentic chatter of *"other people's words."*[17] In terms of the critique of subjective totality with which we began, Bakhtin's discourse remains a symptom rather than a critical intervention.[18]

Social Construction Again

In a larger sense, and more crucially for current discussions of otherness, I am also interested in arguing that one can't merely rely on some notion of "social construction" to wipe out or mitigate charges of "essentialism." As Michael Taussig points out in *Mimesis and Alterity*, to argue that something is "socially constructed" has somehow come to mean that the thing is bereft of privilege, benign or enriching rather than menacing or privative ("essentialist"). However, this claim seems difficult to sustain on actual examination. No one believes, for example, that draconian criminal sentencing statutes in the United States are "essential"; they are clearly the construction of a society at a specific time in response to a particular law-and-order hysteria. Judges and prosecutors have no "absolute" privilege. However, that doesn't make these laws any less socially privileging or change the effects that these mere social constructions have upon those subject to them. As Frantz Fanon poignantly notes, none of his liberal white "friends" believed in anything so crude as essentialized black identity, but the *effects* of his blackness in their eyes continued to be the same, whether essential or socially conceived: " 'But of course, come in, sir, there is no colour prejudice among us. . . . Quite, the Negro is a man like ourselves. . . . It is not because he is black that he is less intelligent than we are' " (113; Fanon's ellipses).

Social constructionism has developed its own rote ontology, its own strategic essentialism represented concisely in Pechey's phrase "always relative and never absolute." However, the fact of social construction (its inability to escape a certain metaphysics or absolutism—that fact that it *is* a fact) seems to open up more questions than it answers. Taussig phrases the problem in terms of recent cultural studies work:

> When it was enthusiastically pointed out within memory of our present Academy that race or gender or nation . . . were so many social constructions, inventions, and representations, a window

was opened, an invitation to begin the critical project of analysis and cultural reconstruction was offered. And one still feels its
power even though what was nothing more than an invitation, a
preamble to an investigation, has, by and large, been converted
instead into a conclusion—e.g., "sex is a social construction,"
"race is a social construction," "the nation is an invention," and
so forth. . . . To adopt Hegel, the beginnings of knowledge were
made to pass for actual knowing. (xvi)

As Taussig argues, when the beginnings of knowledge—the insight
that things are constructed—passes for the end of knowledge, it leaves
us without a wedge by which to examine the privileges of construction itself, its *ethical consequences or effects.* Essentialism is clearly
inadequate, a hiding place for a social construction that wants to
avoid scrutiny. But, Taussig argues, merely to attribute some sort of
positive or revolutionary vector to social construction seems equally
misguided.[19] To say "performative" or "ethical" is *not* merely to say
"socially constructed."

Again, we need to recall that this announcement—everywhere
there is social construction—was brought to you by the very Enlightenment that we are now trying to flee: the Enlightened subject
wants nothing other than to escape from the essentialism of natural
consciousness into the space of social knowledge and freedom, into
self-consciousness. Whether this is seen as an "essential" or "social"
process seems to me less important than examining the *effects* of the
process itself. Indeed, even if one were to agree with Bakhtinians that
there is a transcendental telos to the Hegelian dialectical system, isn't
that telos constructed from his discussions of experience? Wouldn't
one still have to deal with the ethical questions of thematizing the
other always in terms of the same, regardless of whether that reduction were sanctioned "essentially" or "socially"? Isn't such scrutiny
especially pressing when one holds that the essential is nothing other
than a subset of the social?

In the end, the social constructionism versus essentialism argument seems an attempt to settle, rather than open up, a number of
difficult and complex questions. At its best, social constructionism is
deployed in the current theoretical field as an attempt to reopen or
save a notion of agency from the stone determinism of essentialist
narratives; but we might note that with the bath water of determinism
also goes the baby of a certain ethical *necessity.* To put it another way,

with the return to ethical agency and subjective possibility, we seem to lose the importance of *subjection:* the subject is constructed, to be sure, but that construction can never be simply (or even primarily) in the service of the subject's free, enriching *choice.*

It is here, I think, that Levinas's discourse of subjection before the other becomes crucial. Levinas's notion of subjection is not a ham-fisted determinism, where subjection merely creates slaves or automatons. Rather, for Levinas subjection necessarily happens in response itself, in responding to the other by saying I: performative responsibility is subjectivity itself. As he maintains, responding to an other is not a perform*ance,* choosing to take on a mask or imaginatively to inhabit the other's place; response "is not a confusion with another, which would be a way of resting in an avatar, but incessant signification, a restlessness for the other. . . . This responsibility is like a cellular irritability" (*Otherwise,* 143). For Levinas, I am irreducibly open to the other, restless for the other, engaged in "incessant signification," which is not a series of performances or "a way of resting in an avatar," but rather is the concrete necessity of response to the other. In other words, the subject's (in)ability to escape the law (of substitution, of social construction, of ideological interpellation) likewise calls it to respond: I first am marked, interpellated, subject to something other than myself before I respond, and a trace of that marking inhabits all of my responses.

Subjective agency certainly remains in such a model; however, the I cannot, once and for all, free itself from the external laws—the specificities of social proximity and contact with the other—to which it is subject. As Levinas writes, such a "response answers, before any understanding, for a debt contracted before any freedom and before any consciousness and any present. . . . Subjectivity, prior to or beyond the free and the non-free, obliged with regard to the neighbor, is the breaking point where essence is exceeded by the infinite" (*Otherwise,* 12). At this breaking point, where the "essence" of the self is transgressed and subtended by the "infinite" other, response is called forth. Responsibility is, then, before and beyond the free and the not-free; it comes *before* any notion of freedom or bondage, and as such it is the groundless ground of human subjectivity, inexorably open to the approach of the other. As Levinas puts it, "Saying is communication, to be sure, but as a condition for all communication, as exposure" (48). Again, paradoxically, it is precisely this subjected predicament (where there is no outside or ground, and I am thereby called to respond) that makes possible the articulation of my identity—which is, of course, never "mine"; it is, rather, a "saying" that consistently *exposes* me to the network of serial substitution out of which the I emerges.

There is, in other words, neither a determinism nor a nihilism in Levinasian responsibility; there is agency, but there is always something prior, a hesitation, a marking or inscription that necessarily makes subjective agency a *re*marking or *re*inscription of existing sociolinguistic codes. And an emphasis on this responsible remarking or reinscription may offer us a way to rethink the social construction-ism debate. This emphasis calls our attention to the *specificities* of certain kinds of *subjection:* what makes us unique is not our personal qualities (the ways we can rise above other people's definitions of us) but precisely the qualities of our subjections. Perhaps what we require is not an *identity politics* of who we are, but an *alterity politics* of how we've come to be who we are: not the answerability of Bakhtinian subjective privilege, but the Levinasian responsibility engendered by the other. The social constructionism debate, in other words, needs to pay more attention to the specificity of the subjections or restrictions that make possible the construction and maintenance of any particular subjectivity. It is outside the self that we need to look for the conditions of agency, responsibility, and ethical subjectivity. And the self that says or signifies its subjectivity before the other never merely returns to itself.

In the end, Levinas insists, responsibility is and has to be anti-Odyssean: a one-way movement outward, an irrecoverable exteriority. Saying expropriates the subject because it carries a trace of the mark of subjection. He writes, "Responsibility, the signification which is non-indifference, goes one way, from me to the other" (*Otherwise*, 138). And this, it seems to me, is the crucial intervention that he performs for a rethinking of the ethical subject: to speak—to say I—is to be always already subjected, to be always already responding to and before the other. Certainly, this is true in some measure for Bakhtin also, but in a Bakhtinian universe, "I always have a loophole. . . . The *other* is intimately associated with the world; *I* am intimately associated with my inner, world-exceeding self-activity" (*Art*, 40). For Bakhtin, it is my freedom that is at stake in the dialogue of the social; and in the end, the Bakhtinian other is complete, whereas I transcend consummation through my "inner, world-exceeding self-activity." In Bakhtin's work, the risks of infinity and answerability accrue finally to the self; the hesitating subjections and responses of performativity give way to a model of subjectivity as appropriating performance. In Levinas, however, infinity and responsibility are always located in a place or space other than my subjectivity, and as such Levinas begins to perform a gesture that we could call an ethics or politics of the other. Perhaps this is the "fine risk" that Levinas points to in our epigraph: not the risk of subjective Bakhtinian adventure, which succeeds in enriching the subject even when it fails, but rather the higher risk of response as unrecoverable exposure to the other.

The metaphysical desire . . . desires beyond everything that can simply
complete it. It is like goodness—the Desired does not fulfill it, but deepens
it. . . . [Desire] nourishes itself, one might say, with its hunger.
—Emmanuel Levinas, *Totality and Infinity*

Junk yields a basic formula of "evil" virus: *The Algebra of Need.* The face
of "evil" is always the face of total need. A dope fiend is a man in total need
of dope. Beyond a certain frequency need knows absolutely no limit or
control. . . . I never had enough junk—no one ever does.
—William Burroughs, *Naked Lunch*

The antidrug slogan "Just say no!" is an odd response indeed. Say no
to what or to whom? Say no to a threat, to something that will draw
you too far outside yourself. Say no because you want to say yes. Say
no because, somewhere outside yourself, you know that this "you"
owes a debt to the yes, the openness to alterity that is foreclosed in
the proper construction of subjectivity. Of course, "just say no" never
says no solely to a person—to a dealer or a user; rather, you "just say

no" to the yes itself, a yes that is not human but is perhaps the ground of human response. This constant reminder to "just say no," then, is always haunted by a trace of the yes. As William Burroughs asks in *Naked Lunch*, "In the words of total need, *'Wouldn't you?'* Yes you would" (xi).

In *Crack Wars: Literature, Addiction, Mania*, Avital Ronell argues that the logics of drug addiction can hardly be separated from the discourse of alterity. In the exterior or alterior space of addiction, she writes, "You find yourself incontrovertibly obligated: something occurs prior to owing, and more fundamental still than that of which any trace of empirical guilt can give an account. This relation—to whom? to what?—is no more and no less than your liability—what you owe before you think, understand, or give; that is, what you owe from the very fact that you exist" (57). Ronell is, of course, no simple apologist for a Romantic celebration of drug use; as she maintains, "it is as preposterous to be 'for' drugs as it is to take up a position 'against' drugs" (50), but it is the case that the logics of intoxication, as well as the kinds of desire that one can read in spaces of addiction, are inexorably tied up with current critical vocabularies of alterity and identity: as we have seen in previous chapters, postmodern thinkers have increasingly come to understand alterity as a debt that can never be repaid, a difference that constitutes sameness, the incontrovertibility of a continuing obligation to someone or something "other."

Of course, the leisurely space of recreational drug use most often can and does serve to produce isolated reveries that cut the subject off from alterity, and we should be careful not to conflate drug *use* with *addiction*. However, the serial iteration of episodes of intoxication—what one might clinically or etymologically call "addiction," literally being delivered over to an other—brings on another set of considerations.[1] For example, as William Burroughs characterizes the junk equation in our second epigraph, it necessarily begins in an economy of simple need over which the subject exercises a kind of determinative imperialism: junkies want to be inside, to protect and extend the privilege of the same; they want the pure, interior subjectivity of the junk stupor—with "metabolism approaching Absolute ZERO" (*Naked Lunch*, xvii)—to keep at bay the outside, the other.

But that economy of finite need and subjective imperialism quickly shows an economy of desire, an infinite economy of "total need" that breaks the interiority of mere need. In *Naked Lunch*, Burroughs writes, in the voice of the smug, bourgeois "Opium 'Smoker'":

How low the other junkies are whereas WE—WE have this tent
and this lamp and this tent and this lamp and this tent and nice
and warm in here nice and warm nice and IN HERE and nice and
OUTSIDE ITS COLD. . . . ITS COLD OUTSIDE where the dross eaters
and the needle boys won't last two years not six months hardly
won't last stumble bum around and there is no class in them. . . .
But WE SIT HERE and never increase the DOSE . . . never—never
increase the dose never except TONIGHT is a SPECIAL OCCASION
with all the dross eaters and needle boys out there in the cold.
(xviii; ellipses in original)

Here, the junkies' increasing need for junk shows a finite economy of
subjective determination turning into an infinite economy of inexorable exposure to the outside: "But WE SIT HERE and never increase
the DOSE . . . never—never increase the dose never except TONIGHT."
The junkies' need draws the junkies outside, despite themselves, from
their warm tent to the place of "all the dross eaters and needle boys
out there in the cold." According to Burroughs, the junk user, as he or
she necessarily increases dosage, is drawn inexorably from the warm
protective interior (the fulfilled need) of use to the cold exterior of
addiction—the revelation of "total need" beyond any possible satisfaction. Burroughs writes about his addiction, "suddenly, my habit
began to jump and jump. Forty, sixty grains a day. And it still was
not enough" (xiii). Addiction, it seems, inexorably mutates from a
question of fulfilling need to something else: something other, finally,
than a question with an answer; something other than a need that
could be serviced by a person, object, or substance.

In other words, addiction takes need to the point where it is no
longer thematizable as subjective lack; as need becomes addiction,
the junkie is no longer within the horizon of subjective control or
intention. Burroughs contends in *Junky*, "You don't decide to be an
addict. . . . Junk is not, like alcohol or weed, a means to increased en-
joyment of life. Junk is not a kick. It is a way of life" (xv–xvi). "Junk"
opens onto an unrecoverable exteriority beyond need, an economy
that we might call infinite or "metaphysical" desire, following Levinas's use of the term in our first epigraph.[2] For Levinas, the desire at
play in the face-to-face encounter with the other cannot be confused
with a simple need; rather, it is a "*sens unique*," an unrecoverable
movement outward, a one-way direction: a "movement of the Same
towards the Other which never returns to the Same" ("Meaning,"

91). And, as Burroughs's Sailor reminds us in *Naked Lunch*, there may be no better description of addiction: "Junk is a one-way street. No U-turn. You can't go back no more" (186). However, within Burroughs's exterior movement, we will have to encounter an other other than the Levinasian widow, stranger, or orphan—an other, finally, that is other to the human and the privileges of the human that the philosophical discourse of ethics, including Levinasian ethics, all too often takes for granted. An inhuman other: an other that is other even to the irreducible alterity that one encounters in the dialogic or face-to-face encounters we looked at in the previous chapter. This chapter will try to track what happens when Levinas's humanism of the other person comes face-to-face with junk, the other of *anthropos* traced in Burroughs's "the face of 'evil' [that] is always the face of total need."

Levinas in Rehab

For Levinas, to be sure, drug intoxication is far from an experience of alterity. In fact, he maintains that "the strange place of illusion, intoxication, [and] artificial paradises" can best be understood as an attempt to withdraw from contact with and responsibility for the other: "The relaxation in intoxication is a semblance of distance and irresponsibility. It is a suppression of fraternity, or a murder of the brother" (*Otherwise*, 192 n). According to Levinas, such intoxication brings only a greater intensification of the subject's interiority, a refusal of "fraternity" as exterior substitution for the other.

In fact, intoxication or junk addiction brings to the subject only the disappearance of the world and the concomitant submersion in the terrifying chaos of what Levinas calls the *il y a* ("there is"), a radical givenness without direction that is similar in some ways to Sartre's experience of "nausea."[3] As Levinas describes the *il y a*, "the Being which we become aware of when the world disappears is not a person or a thing, or the sum total of persons and things; it is the fact that one is, the fact that *there is*" (*Existence*, 21). For Levinas, the *there is* is the indeterminate, anonymous rustling of being qua being. Adriaan Peperzak comments in *To the Other* that the *il y a* is "an indeterminate, shapeless, colorless, chaotic and dangerous 'rumbling and rustling.' The confrontation with its anonymous forces generates neither light nor freedom but rather terror as a loss of selfhood. Immersion in the lawless chaos of 'there is' would be equivalent to the absorption by a depersonalized realm of pure materiality" (18).

A phenomenological-methodological link between his earliest and latest texts, the *il y a* is an unsettling fellow traveler for the entirety of Levinas's career. Curiously, the *il y a* performs a kind of dual function in his texts: as Peperzak's summary makes clear, the first function is the ruining or interruption of a self that would think itself in tune with the harmonious gift of being. In the expropriating experience of the *il y a* (a "depersonalized realm of pure materiality"), being is indifferent to the subject. The *il y a* is the anonymous murmur that precedes and outlasts any particular subject. Levinas writes, "Being is essentially alien [*étranger*] and strikes against us. We undergo its suffocating embrace like the night, but it does not respond to us" (*Existence*, 23). In order, then, for an ethical subject to come into being at all, such a subject must not only undergo the experience of being as the *il y a*, he or she must go a step further and *escape* from it. Peperzak continues, "With regard to this 'Being,' the first task and desire [of the ethical subject] is to escape or 'evade' it. The source of true light, meaning, and truth can only be found in something 'other' than (this) Being" (18). The horror of the *il y a* finally turns the subject toward the other.

Against the Heideggerian injunction in *Being and Time* to live up to the challenge of being's gift of possibility, Levinas offers a thematization of being as radical *impossibility*: for Levinas, existence or being is the terrifying absurdity named by the *il y a*, and this indolent anonymity functions to disrupt the generosity and possibility named by Heidegger's *es gibt* ("there is" or "it gives"). For Levinas, existence is a burden to be overcome rather than a fate to be resolutely carried out; the existent is "fatigued by the future" (*Existence*, 29) rather than invigorated by a Heideggerian "ecstacy *toward the end*" (*Existence*, 19).[4] To be an ethical Heideggerian *Dasein*, one must live one's life authentically in the generous light of being's possibility, an ontological multiplicity revealed by the ownmost possibility of one's own death.[5] According to Levinas's reading of Heidegger, at its ethical best any particular *Dasein* can live *with* or *alongside* another *Dasein*, each authentically related to his or her own ownmost possibility. Ethics, if it exists at all, rests not in *Dasein*'s relation to others but in the authenticity and resoluteness of its relation to its own death as possibility — and by synecdoche, the relation to being's generosity. In Levinas's version of Heidegger, then, the relation with others is necessarily inauthentic, always subordinated to *Dasein*'s authentic relation with neutral, anonymous Being-as-possibility.[6]

For Levinas, on the other hand, if one is to be an ethical subject, he or she must *escape* the dark, anonymous rumbling of being; for there

to be a subjectivity responsive to the other, there must be a hypostasis
that lifts the subject out of its wallowing in the solipsistic raw materiality of the *il y a*. Out of the *there is* of anonymous being, there
must rise a *here I am (me voici)* that nonetheless retains the trace of
the hesitation and debt—what Levinas will call the "passivity"—characteristic of the *il y a*'s impossibility. As he maintains, hypostasis is
subject-production, the introduction of space or place into the anonymous murmur of being: "to be conscious is to be torn away from the
there is" (*Existence*, 60).

Subjectivity is torn away from the anonymity of the *there is* by
a responding to the other that is not reducible to any simple rule-
governed or universalizing code; the ethical subject is, in other words,
a responding, site-specific performative that is irreducible to an ontological or transhistorical substantive. Levinas writes, "the body [is] the
very advent of consciousness. It is nowise a thing—not only because
a soul inhabits it, but because its being belongs to the order of events
and not to that of substantives. It is not posited; it is a position. It is
not situated in a space given beforehand; it is the irruption in anonymous being of localization itself. . . . [The body as subjectivity] does
not express an event; it is itself this event" (*Existence*, 71,72). This is
perhaps the most concise statement of Levinas's understanding of a
subjectivity that rises out of the *il y a* through hypostasis: the subject comes about through a performative response to the call of the
other, through the bodily taking up of a "position," "the irruption in
anonymous being of localization itself." Here the subject is brought
into being through a radically specific performative event or saying;
but it will be a strange "being" indeed, insofar as being is generally
understood to be synonymous with a generalizable, substantive said.

Of course, the Levinasian subject is a kind of substantive; it has to
have a body—a place and a voice—in order to respond concretely to the
other. It cannot merely languish in and among a network of possible
responses. Rather, the subject is an active, responding substantiation:
"it is a pure verb. . . . The function of a verb does not consist in naming, but in producing language" (*Existence*, 82). He goes on to explain:

> We are looking for the very apparition of the substantive. To
> designate this apparition we have taken up the term *hyposta-
> sis* which, in the history of philosophy, designated the event by
> which the act expressed by a verb became a being designated
> by a substantive. Hypostasis . . . signifies the suspension of the

anonymous *there is,* the apparition of a private domain, of a noun
[or name, *nom*]. . . . Consciousness, position, the present, the "I,"
are not initially—although they are finally—existents. They are
events by which the unnameable verb *to be* turns into substantives. They are hypostasis. (82–83)

The performative hypostasis is the birth of subjectivity, but the ethical
network of substitution or signification that a subject arises from—
this network of performative responses that must precede, even if it is
finally inadequate to, any particular response—also necessarily makes
that hypostatic subject a noncoincident one, open to alterity. The subject that arises in the hypostasis is not a simple substantive or noun,
even though it necessarily becomes one through a trick of syntax.
Levinas writes, "One can then not define a subject by identity, since
identity covers over the event of the identification of the subject" (87).
Identity, even when all is said and done, is not something that the
subject *has;* identity is, rather, the "event of the identification" that I
am, and this "originary" hypostatic "event" is (re)enacted or traced in
the subject's continuing performative responses to the call of alterity.

Hence, it is the preoriginary debt that any subject owes to this prior
network of substitution-for-the-other that keeps subjectivity open,
keeps the saying of performative ethical subjectivity irreducible to the
simple said of ontology. Levinas will call this a network of "fraternity"
or "responsibility, that is, of sociality, an order to which finite truth—
being and consciousness—is subordinate" (*Otherwise,* 26). Sociality,
as substitution of potential identities in a serial network of performative subjectivity, both makes identity and response possible and at
the same time makes it impossible for any identity to remain monadic, static, and unresponsive. The subject always already responds
in the movement from the anonymous "one" to the hypostatic "me";
the subject responds in the very subjection of identity, the very act of
speaking.

However, this hypostasis is *not* simply or primarily the intentional
act of a subject; it is, rather, subjection in and through the face-to-face
encounter with the other person. As Levinas insists, "the localization
of consciousness is not subjective; it is the subjectivization of the
subject" (*Existence,* 69). Thus, "here I am" rises out of the *there is* as
an accusative, where I am the object rather than the subject of the
statement, where I am responding to a call from the face of the other.
Jan de Greef explains that "for Levinas the movement [of subjectivity]

does not go from me to the other but from the other to me. . . .
Here I am (me voici)—the uncondition of the hostage—can only be
said in response to an 'appeal' or a 'preliminary citation.' Convocation
precedes invocation" (166). It is to-the-other that one responds in the
hypostasis that lifts the subject out of the *il y a;* the face of the other,
and its call for response-as-subjection, is the only thing that can break
the subject's imprisonment in the anonymous *il y a* and open the
space of continuing response to alterity. Levinas sums up the project
of his *Existence and Existents:* "it sets out to approach the idea of
Being in general in its impersonality so as to then be able to analyze
the notion of the present and of position, in which a being, a subject,
an existent, arises in impersonal Being, through a hypostasis" (19). As
the evasion of the "impersonal being" that is the *il y a,* hypostasis (as
the concrete performative response to the face or voice of the other
person) is the birth of the ethical Levinasian subject.

Such a subjection before the other makes or produces a subject at
the same time that it unmakes any chance for that subject to remain an alienated or free monad. As Levinas argues, "The subject
is inseparable from this appeal or this election, which cannot be de-
clined" (*Otherwise,* 53), so the subject cannot be thematized in terms
of alienation from some prior state of wholeness. In Levinasian subjectivity, there is an originary interpellating appeal of expropriation,
not an originary loss of the ability to appropriate. Identity and alterity,
rethought as performative response, are fueled by the infinity of substitution, not by the lack and desire for reappropriation that characterizes the evacuated Lacanian subject. And this Levinasian responding
signification or substitution leaves the subject inexorably responsive
to the founding debt of alterity: "Signification is the-one-for-the-other
which characterizes an identity that does not coincide with itself"
(*Otherwise,* 70). There is, in other words, no subject unbound from
other because the process of subject formation (the production of *a*
subject) takes place in and through this common social network of
iterable substitution. In the terms Levinas uses most insistently in
Otherwise than Being, identity is a performative "saying" that is irreducible to a constative "said." Insofar as substitution or signification
literally makes and unmakes the subject in the performative project
of saying "here I am," such an ethical entity—both subject of and subject to alterity—is literally otherwise than being, other-wise than an
ontological, synchronic, or substantive identity.[7] The "saying" is *beyond* essence because it makes the "said" of essence possible without

ever being merely reducible to it; just as infinite metaphysical desire subtends and traverses mere subjective need, the performative ethical saying is before and beyond the said.[8]

The Junk Con

If we return to Burroughs and the question of drugs, then, it seems fairly clear why intoxication or addiction is not akin to ethical subjectivity for Levinas: because intoxication is a wallowing in the terrifying materiality of the *il y a*'s "impersonal being," a state where the call or face of the other counts for nothing. Strictly speaking, there can be no response to alterity—no saying, substitution, or signification—from an entity immersed in anonymous being: in the *il y a*, an ethical subject has yet to arise through a hypostasis. Perhaps we could take, as a concrete example of such anonymous immersion without ethical response, Burroughs's narration of his last year of addiction in North Africa:[9]

> I lived in one room in the Native Quarter of Tangier. I had not taken a bath in a year nor changed my clothes or removed them except to stick a needle every hour in the fibrous grey wooden flesh of terminal addiction. . . . I did absolutely nothing. I could look at the end of my shoe for eight hours. I was only roused to action when the hourglass of junk ran out. If a friend came to visit—and they rarely did since who or what was left to visit—I sat there not caring that he had entered my field of vision—a grey screen always blanker and fainter—and not caring when he walked out of it. If he died on the spot I would have sat there looking at my shoe waiting to go through his pockets. Wouldn't you? (*Naked Lunch*, xiii)

Surely this is a portrait of drug use beyond the production of pleasure or nostalgia for it; rather, this is a portrait of addiction as the horror of immersion in the *il y a*, where the addict does "absolutely nothing," save an interminable staring at anonymous objects, wallowing in a state of sheer materiality.[10]

From a Levinasian point of view, however, more disturbing than Burroughs's portrait of the "bare fact of presence" (*Existence*, 65) in the interminability of addiction is the accompanying renunciation of a relation with the other: "If a friend came to visit . . . I sat there not caring that he had entered my field of vision . . . and not caring when he walked out of it." And even more horrific than the mere ignoring of the other is the callous disregard shown by the addict for the other's very being: "If he died on the spot I would have sat there looking at my shoe waiting to go through his pockets. Wouldn't you?" There is little for any ethical system to admire in these lines, and they seem particularly to bear upon Levinas's concerns about a subjectivity for-the-other: here Burroughs's junkie is inexorably and completely for-himself; even the death of the other would not disrupt the interiority of the same. In fact, the death of the other would have meaning only insofar as it could feed the privilege of sameness—as long as the other had some cash in his or her pockets to feed the junkie's habit.

However, the approval or condemnation of such behavior is not the location of the ethical in this scene, for Levinas as well as for Burroughs. That which calls for response here is, rather, Burroughs's insistent and strategically placed question "Wouldn't you?" I would suggest that the callous disregard shown here is, on another reading, a kind of absolute exposure, an exposure more absolute and limitless than the Levinasian relations "welcoming" that it would seem one owes to the neighbor or the friend. "Wouldn't you?" calls me to nonreciprocal substitution-for-the-other, interpellates me through a saying that is irreducible to a said. Such a saying calls not for moral judgment, but for ethical response to my irreducible exposure to the other.

It is crucial, I think, to forestall any reading of Burroughs's "Wouldn't you?" that would endorse a kind of perspectival notion of alterity, where "Wouldn't you?" would be read as asking or demanding each reasonable participant in a community to see issues through the eyes of the other.[11] For Burroughs as well as for Levinas, that kind of subjective imperialism is not the solution but rather the problem of control itself, what Burroughs calls "sending" as "one-way telepathic control" (148) projected from "I" to "you." If, as Burroughs writes, "*Naked Lunch* is a blueprint, a How-To Book" (203), perhaps it calls for a kind of hesitation before the other, a responding otherwise: "How-To extend levels of experience by opening the door at the end of a long hall. . . . Doors that open only in *Silence*. . . . *Naked Lunch* demands Silence from The Reader. Otherwise he is taking his own pulse" (203; ellipses in original). Such a Burroughsian "Silence" is not a simple *lack* of response (how can one read without responding, without attention?); rather, it is the hesitation before response—an attention that does not merely project itself as the theme and center of any encounter, does not merely take its own pulse. There is, in other words, a gap or "Silence" between the other and myself, and that gap is precisely my inexorable exposure to the other, that which comes before what "I" think or "I" do.

Indeed, in Levinasian terms the "welcoming" of the face of the other is precisely this inexorable exposure before a decision: the yes before a no (or a known), saying before a said, the openness or "sensibility" of the body-as-face that precedes any experience of knowing. These are all what Levinas calls "my pre-originary *susceptiveness*" (*Otherwise*, 122).[12] As he elaborates, "Sensibility, all the passivity of saying, cannot be reduced to an experience that a subject would have of it, even if it makes possible such an experience. An exposure to the other, it is signification, is signification itself, the one-for-the-other to the point of substitution, but a substitution in separation, that is, responsibility" (54). According to Levinas, the openness to the other—sensibility, saying, signification—cannot finally be reduced to an "experience" of the other; that would be to suture a subjective void, to reduce the saying of the other to the said of the same, and to collapse the subjective "separation" necessary for Levinasian "responsibility." The other, then, must be attended to not in terms of my experience but in terms of my substitution and separation; not in terms of my project but in terms of my subjection.

That being the case, it seems that one can frown on Burroughs's portrait of addiction as "unethical" only by reducing it to an "experience" of addiction that leads to an utter disregard for the ethics of response. But Burroughs's Levinasian insistence on the consequences of total need as absolute exposure would seem to oblige us to attend to this episode differently—not in terms of the obviously unacceptable ethical behavior represented by Burroughs's junkie, but rather in terms of the condition of absolute exposure that is prior to any ethical action: the question of substitution for-the-other. In other words, the instructive moment here is not the one in which the junkie might rummage through the dead friend's pockets, but the moment when that relation is thematized in terms of an absolute exposure that makes such an action possible, if not inexorable: "Wouldn't you?"

The desiring junkie-subject is never a "said," never a complete or alienated synchronic monad. He or she is constantly in performative process; the junkie-subject "nourishes itself, one might say, with its hunger" (*Totality*, 34). The "I" that is the junkie is characterized by a "saying" that constantly keeps the junk-addled subject in touch with its subjection to the other: if the Reagan-Bush drug slogan "Just say no!" seems to put forth a certain faith in intentionality and the choosing monadic subject (when it clearly evidences the opposite), Burroughs's insistence on the junkie's question, "Wouldn't you?", inexorably directs us outside ourselves, to that somewhere between, before, or beyond the same and the other. Finally, and perhaps to the chagrin of Levinas, I'd like to suggest that the radically exterior Levinasian ethical subject is always a junkie, moving constantly outside itself in the diachronic movement of desire, a responding, substitutable hostage to and for the other.

Perhaps this opens a certain moral question, but moralizing about junk can begin only when one reads the junkie's inability to "just say no" as a subjective weakness. Levinas, who clearly has no interest in such a moralizing ethics, offers us a way to read Burroughs's episode in wholly other terms. On a Levinasian reading, the problem with junk—as with the *il y a* so closely related to it—is not the absence or evasion of self or destiny; the problem is, rather, the absence or evasion of the other or response. As Levinas claims, the concept of "evasion," so precious to those who would moralize about drugs sapping the subject's will, already presupposes an unrestrained freedom of the will: "Every idea of evasion, as every idea of malediction weighing on a destiny, already presupposes the ego constituted on the basis of the self and already free" (*Otherwise*, 195 n). Whereas the antidrug crusader sees addiction as a fall from or evasion of will, Levinas asks us to read addiction as the continuation or logical extension of an almost pure imperialist will, an extension perhaps of the Nietzschean will-to-power that would rather will nothingness than not will at all.[13]

For the "just say no" moralistic version of drug rehabilitation, the dependency of the addict needs to be exposed and broken so the subject can be free again. If there were a Levinasian rehab, it might proceed in exactly the opposite way: by exposing the dream of subjective freedom as a symptom of addiction rather than a cure for it. Such a "cure" might hope to produce not a sutured subject, free again to shape its own destiny, but rather "an ego awakened from its imperialist dream, its transcendental imperialism, awakened to itself, a patience as a subjection to everything" (*Otherwise*, 164). For a Levinasian ethical subject to come into being, it is clear that "the *there is* is needed" (164). However, in Levinas the *there is* functions not as the drug counselor's negative portrait of an unfree self, but as a kind of deliverance of the self from its dreams of subjective imperialism. Such a deliverance calls for a hy-

postasis that lifts the subject out of the *il y a* into responsibility, out of
the interiority of self into the face-to-face as "the impossibility of slipping away, absolute susceptibility, gravity without any frivolity" (128).

Can I tug on your coat for a minute?

Finally, though, this leaves us with any number of unanswered
questions and potentially unhappy resonances between Levinas's discourse and the moralizing ethics that he rejects. First, there is the
question of will. Levinas offers an interesting rejoinder to those who
would read the junkie as will-less, but when he argues that intoxication is evasion—"slipping away" from responsibility, away from a
"gravity without any frivolity"—and as such is in fact an act of will, he
returns full circle to a very traditional discourse on drugs, a discourse
perhaps more sinister than the discourse of subjective weakness. For
Levinas, it seems that intoxication is a brand of turpitude, a willful renunciation of citizenship and responsibility, "murder of the brother."
Certainly, a thematization of the drug user as a passive dupe is inadequate, but Levinas's portrait of the willful druggie may prove to be
even more troubling. Both thematizations seem to avoid the question
of desire as it is embodied in intoxicants, in something other to or
other than the human subject and its will.

This problem of the will is related to Levinas's insistence on "overcoming" or evading the *il y a.* It seems that the overcoming of the
il y a in ethical face-to-face subjectivity is an avoidance of the very
thing that interrupts and keeps open this relation without relation. In
other words, Levinas's analysis seems to beg the question of how we
can protect the face-to-face's authentic ethical disruption (calling the
subject to respond) from the *il y a*'s seemingly inauthentic disruption
(sinking the subject into anonymous fascination).

This doubling of disruptions is especially puzzling because the *il
y a*—as unethical disruption—seems to be in a position of almost
absolute proximity to the material network of ethical substitution out
of which arises a specific "passive" ethical subjectification. Levinas
writes, "The oneself cannot form itself; it is already formed with absolute passivity. . . . The recurrence of the oneself refers to the hither
side of the present in which every identity identified in the said is constituted" (*Otherwise,* 104–5). This "hither side of the present" (*en deçà
du présent*) is the debt that ontology owes to the undeniable prox-

imity or approach of the other, the inexorable upshot of something
on *this* side of the transcendental hinter world.[14] This transcendent
(but not *transcendental*)[15] "something" on the hither side—the legacy
of phenomenology in Levinas's thought—has various names in various Levinasian contexts: desire, the other, substitution, the face, the
body, signification, sensibility, recurrence, saying, passivity, the one-
for-the-other. This is not, as it would seem at first, a confusion on
Levinas's part, an inability to keep his terminology straight. It is,
rather, central to his project: signification, as substitution for the
other, calls for a specific response in each situation. Just as, for example, in Derrida's work the economy of *pharmakon* is not the same
as the problem of *supplément* (each is a radically specific response to
a particular textual situation), the constant shifting of terminology in
Levinas is crucial to the larger "logic" of his thinking.

There remains, however, something of a "good cop, bad cop" sce-
nario in Levinas's thematization of such a preoriginary discourse.[16]
Fraternity and responsibility are the preoriginary good cop: holding
me accountable to the other and the others, they function as a debt
that must be returned to time and again. The *il y a*, on the other
hand, is the preoriginary bad cop: exiling me to a solipsistic prison
without visitors, it is a horror that must be overcome if I am to be
an ethical subject. Certainly, either way there would have to be a
hypostasis to bring the subject from the preoriginary network into
a specific position in or at a particular site; whether thematized as
benign or menacing, the preoriginary network of fraternity or the *il
y a* is not itself response, even though (or more precisely *because*) it
makes response possible. The response that is "saying" in Levinas is
an act, first and foremost; as Jean-François Lyotard puts it in his essay
on "Levinas's Logic," it is a doing before understanding (125).

Levinas posits a preoriginary network—a prescriptive call before
denotative understanding—to keep open the (im)possibility of further or other responses. Such a network is structurally necessary in
his text to account for the subject's not coinciding with itself, but
in terms other than alienation, loss, or lack; Levinas's discourse can
separate itself from the existentialist or psychoanalytic thematization
of the other as my enemy only if there is a preoriginary expropriation,
such that there can be no simple alienation as a separation or fall
from wholeness. Certainly both the revelation of the trace of fraternity and immersion in the *il y a* perform this preoriginary function
of ruining and opening out the interiority of the monadic subject. A

question remains, however, concerning whether Levinas can protect his discourse of fraternity from the *il y a*, and what the consequences of such a protection might be.

Levinas's reasons for insisting on the primacy of human fraternity and contact are easy enough to understand: as we have seen, in an attempt to save something like *Mitsein* in Heidegger from the monadic interiority of *Dasein*'s fascination with "anonymous" death and being as possibility, Levinas introduces the ethical as the exterior irreducibility of human contact in the face-to-face (in *Otherwise*, the animated ethical saying that is irreducible to the neutrality of the ontological said). Indeed, it is this irreducible exposure to the other that I attempted to use in chapter 2 as a wedge to question the privilege of the humanist subject in Bakhtin's discourse. But the ethical in Levinas, we should note, also remains thematized strictly in humanist terms: the *face* and the *voice*.

Burroughs allows us to pose an essential question to Levinas: What happens when one encounters, within the world rather than in the realm of being, the "face" of the inhuman (as junk) and the "voice" that makes voice (im)possible (as an anonymous serial network of subjective substitutions)? If Levinas's problem with Heidegger is that *Dasein*'s relation with being and the other is posed in terms of *possibility* rather than *impossibility*, one has to wonder then about Levinas's own evasion of the radical impossibility named by the *il y a*, about the work done in his own discourse by the face and the voice. In other words, Levinas's posing of the other in terms of the face and the voice may surreptitiously work to evade the "experience" of the impossible that is alterity measured on other than human terms.

To unpack this question, we could perhaps turn back to Burroughs, specifically, his "Christ and the Museum of Extinct Species," a story that, among other things, points to the ways in which extinction haunts existents. The domination of "man" has brought about the extinction of its other, animals, but this extinction haunts "man" as "man" experiences its closure; and "man" is constantly kept in touch with the extinction of animals (with its others) by the virus of language: "What does your virus do with enemies? It makes enemies into itself. . . . Consider the history of disease: it is as old as life. Soon as something gets alive, there is something there waiting to disease it. Put yourself in virus's shoes, and wouldn't you?" (272, 268). Of course, "Wouldn't you?" is the junkie's question from *Naked Lunch*, the question of the "inhuman" junkie posed to the human society,

the question that should merely reveal the need of the junkie—who
seemingly justifies himself or herself with this response—but that
also reveals the structure of infinite desire grounding all mere need.

This, finally, returns us to the quotation marks around the "'evil'
virus" in the quotation from Burroughs that serves as one of this
essay's epigraphs: junk is an "evil" to human culture, to thinking and
action, because it is quite literally inhuman, that which carries the
other of *anthropos:* "junk" brings the denial of logos, the sapping of
the will, the introduction of impossibility, and the ruining of community. Given his constant emphasis on demystification, we should be
suspicious of any place in Burroughs's text where he seems to be moralizing; it seems that the liminal states that "junk" gestures toward
make its ham-fisted identification as merely "evil" impossible, insofar
as these states quite literally name the exterior fields of alterity in
which any particular opposition must configure itself.

"Junk" forces us to confront the face of that which is wholly other—
other even to the other person. And it is also here that one can call
attention to Burroughs's continuing fascination with the "virus"; as
Benway introduces the concept to the Burroughs oeuvre in *Naked
Lunch*, "It is thought that the virus is a degeneration from a more
complex life form. It may at one time have been capable of independent life. Now it has fallen to the borderline between living and dead
matter. It can exhibit living qualities only in a host, by using the life
of another—the renunciation of life itself, a *falling* towards inorganic,
inflexible machine, towards dead matter" (122). The virus, famously
related to language in Burroughs, carries or introduces the alterity-
based temporality of the postmodern subject, which "may at one time
have been capable of independent life. Now it has fallen to the borderline between living and dead matter": between the individual and the
"parasitic" network of iterable performative substitution from which
it arises.

Insofar as Levinas teaches us that the individual is nothing other—
but nothing less—than a hypostasis within the shifting categories of
substitution for-the-other, his own account of subjectivity as such
an iterable substitution would seem to create problems for the privileging of the category "human." Levinas himself warns us "not to
make a drama out of a tautology" (*Existence*, 87), not to mistake
the hypostasis of subjectivity for an originary category of supposed
discovery or self-revelation. Both Levinas and Burroughs force us to
acknowledge that the parasitic network of substitution, which seems

merely to feed on the plenitude of human identity, in fact makes the plenitude of that identity (im)possible in the first place.[17] But this very logic of the iterable network of performative identity would seem to pose essential questions to Levinas's thematization of identity and alterity by questioning his insistence on what he calls the "priority" of the "human face"[18] and voice (and concomitant evasion of "junk" as radical material iterability). Despite Levinas's well-taken criticisms concerning ontology's fetishizing of "anonymous" being, it may be that the wholly other is traced in other than human beings. That (im)possibility, at least, needs to be taken into account; and the attempt to analyze such an (im)possibility in terms of Burroughs's thematization of "junk" helps to draw Levinasian ethical desire outside the human, where it is not supposed to travel.

In the end, it seems to me that Levinas attempts to exile the very thing that makes his discourse so unique and compelling: the irreducibility of the confrontation with the wholly other. In his insistence that the subject must overcome the crippling hesitation of the *il y a* to respond to the other, Levinas offers us an important rejoinder to those ethical systems that would be content to rest in generalizations and pieties. Levinas insists instead on an ethics of response to the neighboring other in the light of justice for the others. But when Levinas argues that one is subjected solely by other humans in the face-to-face encounter, he elides any number of important ethical considerations. First is the role of inhuman systems, substances, economies, drives, and practices in shaping the hypostatic response that is both the self and the other. Certainly Levinas teaches us that the subject is never a monad: it is always beholden to the other in its subjection; it is always a hostage. But if subjective response is a saying, the material networks of languages and practices available to the subject in and through its subjection need to be taken into account. The subject's daily confrontation with interpellating inhuman systems is, it would seem, just as formative as his or her daily confrontation with the humans that people these systems.

As Levinas insists, contact with something anonymous, such as work, is not of the same order as contact with coworkers. People overflow the roles they are assigned within such systems; Larry in Accounting is *more* than Larry in Accounting. What we do at work or have for lunch today sinks into anonymity, whereas in our face-to-face meetings—on break from our tasks, over cigarettes and coffee— Larry somehow isn't simply consumed or forgotten. If we attend to his difference as difference, Larry can't sink into anonymity. Burroughs, however, teaches us also to ask after the lunch, cigarettes, and coffee, which may not disappear into anonymity quite so quickly. Neither, he might add, should the spaces in which we work and the systems that parse out such space, and therefore frame many of our daily face-to-face encounters. These "inhuman" considerations likewise call for response.

Certainly, Levinas recognizes this when he brings the third into the drama of the face-to-face. As he writes of social justice, "If proximity ordered to me only the other alone, there would not have been any problem" (in Peperzak, 180 n). But the others confront me also in the face-to-face with the other, and demand that the "self-suffcent 'I-Thou'" relation be extended to the others in a relation of justice. Here Levinas—responding, always, to Heidegger—is careful not to pose the relation of social justice with the others as a falling away from some state of authenticity: "It is not that there first would be the face, and then the being it manifests or expresses would concern himself with justice; the epiphany of the face qua face opens humanity" (Totality, 213). Whereas the face-to-face has a certain quasi-phenomenological priority in Levinas—there has to be the specificity of bodily *contact* and response if one is to avoid mere pious generalizations—the face-to-face in turn opens more than the closed loop of my responsibility for you: insofar as "the face qua face opens humanity," my responsibility for the others is inscribed in my very responsibility for you. The specific other and the social-historical realm of others cannot be separated in the revelation of the face-to-face.[19]

But even in his thematization of justice, there nevertheless remains the trace of Levinas's most pervasive ethical exclusion, an absolute privilege of the same that lives on in this discourse of the other: "justice" in Levinas—infinite response in the here and now—remains synonymous with "humanity"; justice is owed to the others who are as human as the other. The face-to-face extends my responsibility to all who possess a face; the saying of my response to the other human's voice extends to all other humans' voices. I must respond to—and am the "brother" of—only that which has a voice and a face. But what about the face of systems, the face of total need confronted in intoxicants, or the face of animals? Levinas responds:

> I cannot say at what moment you have the right to be called "face." The human face is completely different and only after-wards do we discover the face of an animal. I don't know if a

snake has a face. . . . I do not know at what moment the human appears, but what I want to emphasize is that the human breaks with pure being, which is always a persistence in being. . . . [W]ith the appearance of the human—and this is my entire philosophy— there is something more important than my life, and that is the life of the other. ("Paradox," 171–72)[20]

In thematizing response solely in terms of the human face and voice, it would seem that Levinas leaves untouched the oldest and perhaps most sinister unexamined privilege of the same: *anthropos,* and only *anthropos,* has *logos;* and as such, *anthropos* responds not to the barbarous or the inanimate, but only to those who qualify for the privileges of "humanity," only to those deemed to possess a face, only to those recognized to be living in the *logos.*[21] Certainly, as the history of anticolonial and feminist movements have taught us, those who we now believe unproblematically to possess a "face" and a "voice" weren't always granted such privilege, and present struggles continue to remind us that the racist's or homophobe's first refuge is a distinction between a privileged humanity and its supposed others.

In addition, we might ask about those ethical calls of the future from "beings" that we cannot now even imagine, ethical calls that Donna Haraway categorizes under the heading of the "cyborg [which] appears in myth precisely where the boundary between human and animal is transgressed" (152). Certainly, the historical and theoretical similarities that Haraway draws among the discourses surrounding her title subjects, *Simians, Cyborgs, and Women,* should force us to ask after and hold open categories that have not yet been recognized as ethically compelling. The "human," in other words, may name the latest, if certainly not the last, attempt to circumscribe a constitutive boundary around ethical response. Of course, the permeability of this boundary is traced in nearly all the crucial socio-ethical questions of today. From abortion to cryogenics to cybernetics, from animal research to gene therapy to cloning, we see the ethical necessity surrounding the disruption and rearticulation of any stable sense or site we might offer to define (human) life itself. And any strong or useful sense of ethics would seem to entail that ethical response is not limited from before the fact.

In the end, Levinas's insistence on the "human" as sole category of ethical response further protects and extends the imperialism of Western subjectivity, what Butler calls, in another context, an "imperialist humanism that works through unmarked privilege" (*Bodies,*

118). Despite the Levinasian advances toward a nonontological ethics of response as substitution for the other, Levinas nevertheless also extends the privilege of "man," which, as Haraway reminds us, is quite literally the "the one who is not animal, barbarian or woman" (156).[22] And to quote selectively from Levinas's citation of Pascal, "*That* is how the usurpation of the whole world began": with the protection of the category "human" from its others.[23]

4 · *Enjoy Your Chiasmus! Ethics, Failure, and the Performative in Žižek and de Man*

Reflection, to be sure, ultimately always fails.
—Slavoj Žižek on Hegel, *For They Know Not What They Do*

To live is to read, or rather [to] commit again and again the failure
to read which is the human lot.
—J. Hillis Miller on de Man, *Ethics of Reading*

Since the law must be repeated to remain an authoritative law,
the law perpetually reinstitutes the possibility of its own failure.
—Judith Butler on Lacan, *Bodies That Matter*

If, as we have seen in the previous chapters, humanist appropriation
is an ethical problem in Bakhtinian or Levinasian notions of performative subjectivity, then showing the inexorable failure, disruption,
and/or contingency of that humanism would seem to be an important first step in the ethical humbling of the subject. One could, in
other words, interrupt the over-hasty privilege of the human subject
in performative ethics by insisting that the subject exists only in and
through a network of inevitable expropriation. Where Bakhtin sees

the friendly other or Levinas responds to the human face or voice, the subject could confront instead a chiasmus, an absolute impossibility, an unrecoverable alienation or disruption. Such a confrontation might inaugurate an inquiry wherein, as Paul de Man writes, "ethics has nothing to do with the will (thwarted or free) of a subject, nor *a fortiori*, with a relationship between subjects" (*Allegories*, 206).

In the process of confronting such an expropriating alterity, the subject would be forced to confront performative identity as other than a kind of privilege; rather, as Slavoj Žižek writes, the subject would be compelled to rethink "identity itself as a name for a certain radical impossibility" (*For They Know Not*, 37). Such a subject, Žižek writes, "bears an indelible mark of failure and the Ought—and thereby its inherent *ethical* character" (110). As Žižek continues in *Enjoy Your Symptom!*, "failure" could then be thematized as the principal wedge by which the subject is inexorably kept open to otherness: "identity becomes 'authoritarian,'" he writes, "the moment we overlook, in a kind of illusory perspective, that it is nothing but the inscription of pure *difference*, of a *lack*" (91; my italics).

I'd like to continue the dialogic style of the preceding chapters by focusing initially on two theorists who thematize ethics as a confrontation with irreducible failure or lack: Slavoj Žižek and Paul de Man. Like this text's previous pairing of Levinas with Bakhtin and Burroughs, Žižek and de Man would seem to be a very odd couple indeed: Žižek, a Slovenian theorist trying to reinvigorate Lacan's links to Hegel through film theory, would seem to have very little in common with the much maligned Belgian father of American deconstruction.[1] Both, however, come together as proponents of a certain kind of relentless negative critique, a critique that, both Žižek and de Man insist, can nevertheless lead to a certain insight. Both are interested, as de Man puts it, in the "negative, apparently destructive labor that led to what could legitimately be called insight" (*Blindness*, 103). Both thereby inherit and radicalize a Hegelian legacy, where the only possible path to reach a truth is to go by way of an irreducible detour, what de Man calls "the negative road of exposing an error" (*Allegories*, 16).[2] Žižek gestures toward the oddly "positive" moment of such a "negative" critique in his account of Lacan and Derrida in *Tarrying with the Negative*: "Lacan accepts the 'deconstructionist' motif of radical contingency, but turns this motif against itself, using it to assert his commitment to Truth *as contingent*" (4).

Following Žižek's cue, perhaps the similarities shared by Žižek and de Man can come into initial focus by examining their (strikingly similar) critiques of Jacques Derrida's work. Of course Žižek is, for the most part, skeptical of deconstruction, while de Man is best known as a deconstructor; but they overlap when Žižek and de Man take up Derrida's (mis)reading of the authors closest to their respective critical hearts: for Žižek, Derrida misreads both Lacan and Hegel; de Man takes Derrida to task for his reading of Rousseau. Though on the surface there is nothing particularly surprising or revelatory about such a conjunction—theorists particularly invested in certain authors should be expected to defend their readings against rival interpretations—more to the point is the specific *kind* or *style* of critique that both Žižek and de Man launch at Derrida.

First, both accuse Derrida of using the insights gained by reading an author more or less unconsciously or blindly as a kind of critical stick, initially taken from the author under consideration, and then used to beat him.[3] In addition, and more important for my purposes, both de Man and Žižek seem to understand "deconstruction" as the ongoing exposure or demonstration of failure or contingency. For both thinkers, it is precisely this inevitability of contingency or failure that Derrida deploys against his rivals, the critical stick that he borrows from Rousseau, Hegel, and Lacan, and then turns on them. Both Žižek and de Man attempt to show how Derrida remains blind to the work of the negative—and hence blind to a certain "deconstruction"—already at play in these discourses.

It would be tempting to take this circuit of (mis)readings to yet another metalevel, and argue that both de Man and Žižek in turn misread Derrida—and more specifically the ethics of deconstructive performativity—precisely around this question of reading's or identity's inevitable failure. Deconstruction, one might argue, is a *critique* rather than a *demonstration* of the inevitability of failure.[4]

Rather than police that road, however, I prefer to concentrate here not so much on the supposed adequacy or accuracy of either de Man's or Žižek's reading of Derrida, but instead cut to the chase by working out a series of what I take to be ethical questions about the oddly reassuring "success" of lack-driven discourses—about the "success through failure" of de Man's literary criticism or Žižek's psychoanalysis of popular culture. Finally, I will argue, contra de Man and Žižek, that the productive ethical moment in performative subjectivity consists not solely or even primarily in an *exposure* of or response to *failure's inevitability*, but rather in an ethical critique of the subjective reassurance and resentment that comes from tarrying with the negative.

De Man and Žižek on Derrida

De Man writes that Derrida's now famous analysis of Rousseau in *Of Grammatology* boils down to "Derrida deconstructing a pseudo-Rousseau by means of insights that could have been gained from the 'real' Rousseau" (*Blindness*, 140). According to de Man, when Derrida demonstrates the failure of representation to ground the plenitude of presence in Rousseau's text, he is in effect using Rousseau's *very point* (that there is no simple plenitude of meaning) to critique Rousseau. As de Man insists, Rousseau knows about this necessity beforehand: his notion of "representation" fails "not, as Derrida suggests, because Rousseau wants the meaning of the sign" (*Blindness*, 127), but precisely because Rousseau knows that meaning is inseparable from failure, that the necessary and unavoidably rhetorical dimensions of language ("culture") will constantly undo any access to a supposedly pure meaning ("nature").

Specifically, de Man argues that "Contrary to Derrida's assertion, Rousseau's theory of representation is not directed toward meaning as presence and plenitude but toward meaning as void" (127). So Rousseau in fact (pre)figures and one-ups deconstruction's project of exposing "meaning as void": "Derrida's theory of *écriture* corresponds closely to Rousseau's statement on the figural nature of the language of passion. . . . [B]oth are in fact saying the same thing" (137–38). Rousseau's text, in other words, is *down* with the void, and as such it doesn't need Derrida to point out the priority of figurality or the necessity of contingency, displacement, and the disruption of meaning. As de Man sums up his analysis, "Rousseau's text has no blind spots: it accounts at all moments for its own rhetorical mode. Derrida misconstrues as blindness what is instead a transposition from the literal to the figural level of discourse" (139). Finally, "There is no need to deconstruct Rousseau" (139) precisely because Rousseau's text is nothing other than an allegory of its own failure to move from the rhetorical to the literal;[5] such a "deconstruction" is already performed in and by Rousseau.

Žižek argues a similar thesis concerning Derrida and Lacan. For Žižek, Derrida's deconstruction of Lacan's reading of Poe's "Purloined Letter" turns on a Derridean question concerning contingency, a question posed in the face of Lacan's surety that a letter always reaches its destination. As Žižek contends, Derrida's question "exhibits what we could call a primordial response of common sense: what if a letter does *not* reach its destination? Isn't it always possible for a letter to go astray?" (*Enjoy*, 9). Žižek goes on to suggest, however, that Derrida's *critique* of Lacan—"Isn't it always possible for a letter to go astray?"— misses the very point of Lacan's analysis: for Lacan, the letter always arrives *not* because of an iron teleological determinism, but rather because of the irreducibility of contingency. Žižek asserts, "If, however, the Lacanian theory insists categorically that a letter *does* always arrive at its destination, it is not because of an unshakable belief in teleology, in the power of a message to reach its preordained goal" (9). What "always arrives," in other words, is contingency and expropriation (failure), *not* the surety of an attained conclusion or end (success). Žižek writes of the letter's arrival:

> far from realizing a predestined telos, this moment marks the intrusion of a radical openness in which every ideal support of our existence is suspended. This moment is the moment of death and sublimation . . . ; it materializes the pure Nothingness of the hole, the void in the Other (the symbolic order), the void designated, in Lacan, by the German word *das Ding*, the Thing, the pure substance of enjoyment resisting symbolization. . . . When the letter arrives at its destination, the stain spoiling the picture is not abolished, effaced: what we are forced to grasp is, on the contrary, the fact that the real "message," the real letter awaiting us is the stain itself. (8)

Because what inexorably arrives in Lacan's reading is not a reassuring end but interruption or contingency ("the void"), Žižek argues that Derrida's critique or question—"Hey, what about contingency?"— "is therefore simply beside the point" (12): Derrida presupposes that Lacan is arguing something he's not. In fact, Derrida's critique only reinforces Lacan's point about the necessity of misrecognition. Ironically, then, Derrida's misreading of Lacan is further *proof* that the letter always arrives at its destination, just as for de Man, Derrida's misreading of Rousseau can actually be rendered in and by the terms of Rousseau's own rhetoricity.

To use de Man's vocabulary to redeploy Žižek's response to Derrida, the deconstructive "insight" into irreducible contingency in Lacan is made possible by Derrida's "blindness" to Lacan's having already articulated the insight. As de Man maintains, "Critics' moments of greatest blindness with regard to their own critical assumptions are also the moments at which they achieve their greatest insight" (*Blind-*

ness, 109). So, for both de Man and Žižek one does indeed gain some
insight through deconstructive reading or misreading: one confronts
the endlessly demonstrable necessity of totalization's failure. In the
end, then, de Man and Žižek are critical not so much of what they
take to be Derrida's *conclusion* (that failure is inevitable), but rather
they both criticize his unwillingness or inability to thematize the fact
that this "insight" is always already made possible by the "blindness"
of the work of the negative.

And as de Man sums up, it is precisely the inevitability of this
impossibility that makes insight's blindness truly radical and disrup-
tive: "Neither does Rousseau hold up any hope that one could ever
escape from the regressive process of misunderstanding that he describes" (*Blindness*, 140). As Žižek inflects this insight in Lacanian
terms, "Lacan's point is not that full self-consciousness is impossible
since something always eludes the grasp of my conscious ego. Instead,
it is the far more paradoxical thesis that *this decentered hard kernel
which eludes my grasp is ultimately self-consciousness itself*" (*Tarrying*, 66). For both de Man and Žižek, then, the irreducibility of failure
is not *merely* a negative insight: the point, in other words, is not that
meaning or subjectivity is simply impossible; rather, the upshot of
negative critique is the "insight" or "the far more paradoxical thesis"
that *impossibility is meaning or subjectivity*.[6] The "ethical" force attached to this point is precisely that subjective contingency or failure
is not an accidental or passing phase on the way to a higher knowledge or stable identity.

In the end, the de Manian reader or Žižekian subject is inexorably
expropriated by the blindness of its insight; it is forced to confront, as
Žižek writes, that "identity is always impossible, inherently *hindered*
its constitutive gap is always already sutured by some supplementary
feature—yet one should add that identity 'itself' is ultimately nothing
but a name for such a supplementary feature which 'sticks out' and
suspends the essential quality of the domain whose identity it constitutes" (*Enjoy*, 89). The totalizing reader or the appropriating subject
inexorably confronts the negative, "an irreducible lack which forever
prevents it from achieving full self-identity" (*Tarrying*, 26). And ethics
is born(e) in or by this expropriation of the subject, this tarrying with
the negative: ethics is born(e) in the "insight" that identity is whole
only insofar as it is radically suspended, incomplete, lacking wholeness.

So, what is the upshot of this ethical expropriation for performative subjectivity? First, it is worth noting that the confrontation with impossibility thematized by de Man and Žižek is familiar for readers of speech-act theory and performative identity. In a performative theory of identity, the subject's failure to escape the law (of iteration, of social construction, of ideological interpellation) likewise calls it to respond: in other words, you first are marked—interpellated, subject to something other than yourself—before you can remark your identity. You are, for example, gendered before you can remark or remake your gender roles. There certainly is subjective agency in such a model. However, the subject cannot, once and for all, free itself from these external laws to which it is subject; it cannot finally create and master the distance between itself and these societal and metaphysical codes. And paradoxically, it is this predicament (where there is no outside or ground, but the subject is nonetheless called to respond) that makes possible the reinscription of identity.

And perhaps this helps us to understand how, as Butler insists, "performative" identity is not merely reducible to understanding identity as a theatrical "performance." Because the subject is the product of specific constraining normative frames, it cannot simply choose its gender as actors pick parts in plays; but, at the same time, because these compulsory normative frames never merely determine a subject without simultaneously opening spaces of resistance (in other words, precisely because interpellation sometimes *fails*), agency is made possible and efficacious within these frames. "And if there is *agency*," Butler writes, "it is to be found, paradoxically, in the possibilities opened up in and by that constrained appropriation of the regulatory law, by the materialization of that law, the compulsory appropriation and identification with those normative demands. . . . Moreover, this act is not primarily theatrical" (*Bodies*, 12). The subject, in other words, is itself a product of interpellating codes, and therefore it cannot simply enforce a critical distance between itself and these codes. If there is to be any kind of effective subversion or reinscription of normative identities, it must be subversion from within, a reinscription rather than a supposed remaking ex nihilo.

"Failure," then, is one name for the potentially productive qualities of performativity; the performative always fails to become or remain a constative, and one could argue that this resistance is precisely its ethical quality. De Man remarks concerning the "deconstruction" of the performative/constative distinction, "The difference between performative and constative language . . . is undecidable; the deconstruction leading from the one model to the other is irreversible but it always remains suspended, regardless of how often it is repeated" (*Allegories*, 130). Or, as Žižek writes in another context, "it is not difficult to notice how the paradoxical logic" of something like performativity "repeats the deadlock of reflection: this feature is *stricto sensu* superfluous (added to the reflective totality of self-mediation), yet simultaneously a foreign body which undermines its consistency" (*Enjoy*, 88–89). In other words, just as totalization always fails because it is inherently hindered or "deadlock[ed]," so does totalized identity. Subjectivity is groundless, not a "constative" category, and thereby it must always and everywhere be performed. Something must inexorably be added to the subject; but that very necessity of addition consistently undermines the subject's supposed privilege precisely because, in the end, the performative subject is nothing other than this supposed "addition," nothing other than the failure to be complete.

So identity's necessarily performative character is at the same time the "positive" condition of identity *and* what Žižek calls the "hindrance which prevents the absolute self-transparency of the pure performative" (*Enjoy*, 88); it seems to follow that the performative subject can act ethically "*by affirming this void as such, in its priority to any positive entity that strives to fill it out*" (*Tarrying*, 39). In such a system, it is not the Bakhtinian or Levinasian plenitude of humanness that grounds ethics, but the "inhuman" void of subjective interruption and debt: the chiasmus.[7] The ethical subject affirms its lack, and it learns, perhaps, to enjoy its chiasmus.

Lack . . . of What?

As compelling as it may be, any negative discourse of performative hindrance or failure begs a very simple question: hindrance or failure *of what?* Both Žižek and de Man seem to insist that all identity is founded on a prior lack; but, one might naïvely ask, *lack of what?* The answer, it would seem, is lack of "totalization." In fact, as we have seen, this is the *specifically ethical* answer for negative critique: the inability to totalize the field keeps it inexorably open to other possibilities.

Of course, this answer only begs a somewhat different question. I, along with many others, thought we "postmoderns" didn't have stock in totalization anymore. As either de Man or Žižek (or both) make clear in their critiques of Derrida, two hundred years ago (or more) either Rousseau or Hegel (or both) made it obvious that totalization is impossible.[8] If that's too contentious a claim, we'd at least have to admit with de Man, Žižek, and a host of others that Lacan or Derrida (or Heidegger or Adorno or . . .) definitively closed the door to totalization more than three decades ago. So, one might profitably ask, why do we continue to deploy the categories of totalization through their sibling categories of lack? If *totalization* doesn't make any sense in a postmodern context, then *lack* doesn't make any sense either, insofar as *lack* is inexorably *lack of totalization: void* is *lack of plenitude, hindrance* is *lack of completion*, and so on.

In terms of the performative, it would seem that both de Man and Žižek ask us to thematize performative identity as an *ethical lack of constative identity:* lack of a sure or complete subject. But of course we know from J. L. Austin, the father of speech-act theory, that any supposed constative is really nothing other than a special case of the performative; as we saw in chapter 1, constatives are produced precisely by forgetting their performative grounding. That being the case, however, what would allow or tempt us to allegorize this process of performative founding as a *failure?* As Derrida asks concerning the supposed "slippage" of meaning in the "unhappy performative," if something happens always and everywhere, what allows us to thematize it as a contingency?[9] And, concomitantly, if ethics is fueled by an inability to appropriate, doesn't that (however surreptitiously) reinscribe the normativity of a horizon of appropriation, plenitude, and wholeness? Each time we "fail," in other words, don't we reify the impossible goal of success?

Of course, this is the brilliance of tarrying with the negative: failure *is* success! Žižek writes, "even the most crude judgements succeed *by means of their very failure*" (*For They Know Not*, 139 n): we need to recall again that it is the *inevitability* of failure that transforms the negative into a kind of truth. As de Man writes about Nietzsche, the allegory of reading's impossibility or failure "reaches truth by a negative road" (*Allegories*, 92). However, this "truth," which is supposed to *recommend* the work of the negative, seems to me nothing other than the best reason to be infinitely suspicious of it.

This expropriating work of the negative is supposed to be both revelatory and dangerous to the smugly humanist subject, who is exposed to the hazards of alterity by its recognition of the absences within itself. We may, however, need to hesitate here and ask a question much like Steven Shaviro's question to Lacanian film theory: "But is it really *lack*," he asks, that the subject finds "so dangerous and disturbing?" (16). Is it really *lack* that opens or keeps open ethical relations? Isn't it more likely that the inevitability of *lack* leads to an inevitable *resentment*, the reification of the imaginary desiring link to what is (supposedly) lacking? As Shaviro points out, discourses of lack—lack of totalization, lack of identity, lack of completeness—inexorably protect the "conservative, conformist assumption . . . that our desires are primarily ones for possession, plenitude, stability, and reassurance" (53). It seems, as Shaviro writes, that "even at its ostensibly most critical," tarrying with the negative "does nothing but reinscribe a universal history of lack and oppression" (66); in the process it protects the horizon of wholeness, if only as that which we can never attain.

Following Foucault and Deleuze, I would argue that the work of the negative is inadequate for describing or enacting the ethical in a postmodern society, where totalization or representation has given way to the proliferating intensity of production. As Shaviro reminds us, "power in postmodern society works as a process of production, rather than as a drama of representation—an affirmative play of affects and effects, and not a series of splits and absences unfolding according to a logic of negativity" (22). As I argued in chapter 1, the ethical force of performativity rests in the *emergence of* and *response to* the other, not in an inexorable allegory of subjectivity's failure to comprehend or assimilate otherness. Certainly, the subject-as-lack produces a "play of affects and effects," but preeminent among them seem to be resentment and reification rather than some kind of ethical opening to alterity.

Performing Lack: Butler Redux

Where, the reader might ask, does this leave us in terms of this book's opening question, posed by Judith Butler, concerning identity's "embarrassed 'etc.'"? Doesn't Butler's performativity, upon which I've been staking much of my discussion, likewise depend on a notion of identity's *failure* as an ethical or quasi-ethical opening of identity politics to its others? This is precisely the topic around which we need to pose a number of questions to Butler's discourse.

Although collective identifications under common-cause signifiers ("woman," "queer," "African American") are perhaps indispensable for the project of recognition within a conflicted democracy, Butler argues that "it may be precisely through practices which underscore disidentification with those regulatory norms by which sexual difference is materialized that both feminist and queer politics are mobilized. Such collective *disidentifications* can facilitate a reconceptualization of which bodies matter, and which bodies are yet to emerge as critical matters of concern" (*Bodies*, 4; my italics). Butler here emphasizes the importance of a kind of double movement: the necessity of identification, coupled with the necessity that this identificatory movement be open to reinscription. As she insists throughout *Bodies That Matter*, there is no stable site of "femininity" or "queerness," and, in fact, ensuring the multiplicity of such identificatory sites is critical to feminist and queer body politics.

I take the provocation of Butler's work to be that feminism, like any other identity-based movement, cannot protect its identificatory sites from being inhabited by drag queens, Phyllis Schlafly, James Joyce, or whomever. In fact, to turn a Foucauldian phrase, Butler asks us to consider what it costs us to protect such seemingly stable sites of contestation from contestation itself. In other words, what normativizing practices are reified and extended in protecting a site of stable identificatory femininity? This is perhaps Butler's most poignant question to identity politics; she writes, "It seems important, then, to question whether a political insistence on coherent identities can ever be the basis on which a crossing over into political alliance with other subordinated groups can take place, especially when such a conception of alliance fails to understand that the very subject-positions in question are themselves a kind of 'crossing,' are themselves the lived scene of coalition's difficulty" (*Bodies*, 115). However, and just as important, Butler's discourse is not merely an empty celebratory gesture toward a contentless "postmodern" multiplicity, where the other would never be determined or would be indetermination itself.[10] She writes, "one might be tempted to say that identity categories are insufficient because every subject position is the site of converging relations of power that are not univocal. But such a formulation underestimates the radical challenge to the subject that such converging relations imply" (229–30). But how is it, we might ask in response, that simply *recognizing* the insufficiency or lack of stable identity categories— and the concomitant recognition of the multiplicity of possible identificatory sites—"underestimates the radical challenge to the subject" that Butler wants to pose?

To answer this question, we need to (re)turn to Butler's continuing engagement with Lacan. Butler takes very seriously Lacan's Freudian vocabulary of "foreclosure" as the suturing constitution of the subject. Such foreclosure, of course, creates both the subject and the exclusions that she calls us to attend to. For example, Butler points out that within the constraints of Lacan's compulsory heterosexuality, the "feminized fag and the phallicized dyke" become the uninhabitable positions that are foreclosed in the taking up of compulsory heterosexuality, "a move that excludes and abjects gay and lesbian possibilities" (*Bodies*, 96). But what happens, Butler asks, when those abjected sites, by and through their very exclusion or foreclosure, become sites of subversive desire and identification? What happens, in other words, "if the taboo becomes eroticized precisely for the transgressive sites that it produces" (97)? Certainly, Lacan would have taught us that this is precisely how desire works, but what happens when we subject the Lacanian analysis of sexual difference to a kind of symptomatic Lacanian reading?

What happens (on Butler's reading) is that the monologizing Lacanian Oedipal law of signification—expropriation from the real into the symbolic under the threat of castration—seemingly loses its absolute privilege; castration, we might say, becomes *historicized* or *materialized*. Certainly, as Butler notes, Lacan's philosophical version of resistance to interpellating norms—desire necessarily cathecting onto forbidden objects, the power of the imaginary to resist the law of the symbolic—has proven productive for his feminist readers. In fact, the imaginary has proven to be the productive hinge by which to read Lacan against Lacan's own foreclosure of other economies. Butler writes:

> This version of resistance has constituted the promise of psychoanalysis to contest strictly opposed and hierarchical sexual positions for some feminist readers of Lacan. But does this view of resistance fail to consider the status of the symbolic as immutable law? And would the mutation of that law call into question not only the compulsory heterosexuality attributed to the symbolic, but also the stability and discreteness of the distinction between symbolic and imaginary registers within the Lacanian scheme? It seems crucial to question whether resistance to an immutable law is *sufficient* as a political contestation of compulsory heterosexuality, where this resistance is safely restricted

to the imaginary and thereby restrained from entering into the structure of the symbolic itself. (*Bodies*, 106)

Butler argues that we must pay attention to the material specificity of the subject's foreclosures and the concrete responding resistances that they enable; in other words, resistance to the law of the father or the law of lack is to be found in inhabiting and reinscribing *specific, material* abjected subjectivities rather than simply lamenting the necessity of such foreclosures or concentrating on the imaginary spaces of freedom that such foreclosures seem to allow. Finally, Butler suggests that this resistance of and to foreclosure breaks down the wall between the Lacanian symbolic and imaginary: "if the figures of homosexualized abjection *must* be repudiated for sexed positions to be assumed, then the return of those figures as sites of erotic cathexis will refigure the domain of contested positionalities within the symbolic" (109).

The key concept that Butler wants to rescue from Lacan is an explanation of the resistance to foreclosure through desire. Although Foucault and Derrida are helpful in the project of enabling resistance (showing how it is possible if not inevitable), it seems that for Butler, Lacan allows us to demonstrate how resistance happens, how it is engendered and made material through foreclosure and response. Butler departs from Lacan, however, by questioning his reduction of all such response or subversion to the very terms of the originary *loss* of the real; in other words, Butler questions the monologizing reduction in Lacan of all laws to the "immutable" law of failure, lack, and expropriation from the real. For Butler, as for Lacan, foreclosure or interpellation is the founding of the subject, the seemingly superfluous "addition" that in fact founds the subject in the first place. However, when Lacan reduces all resistance to a symptom of Oedipal expropriation, he thereby reduces the complexity of material, historical, and cultural power relations that pave the way for normativity by foreclosing specific identities at specific times.

In the end, it seems that the consistent failures or misrecognitions of the Lacanian subject all point to the same monologizing drama of Oedipal, phantasmatic expropriation from the real. Butler writes specifically about Žižek's rendering of Lacan that such a "rendition of the real presupposes that there is an invariant law that operates uniformly in all discursive regimes to produce through prohibition this 'lack' that is the trauma induced by the threat of castration" (*Bodies*, 205).[11] And, Butler suggests, such a fetishizing of lack protects the normativity of wholeness; for example, such "diagnoses presume that lesbianism is acquired by virtue of some failure in the heterosexual machinery, thereby continuing to install heterosexuality as the 'cause' of lesbian desire" (127).

For Butler, however, both subjective misrecognition and the production of desires call to be read otherwise, not as symptoms of the Law of the Father but as the condition of its subversion—not as a founding interpellative inscription of phantasmatic lack, but as a productive performative interpellation conditioned by a radically specific historical or political slippage or lack of wholeness. She writes, "The resignification of norms is . . . a function of their inefficacy, and so the question of subversion, of working the weakness in the norm, becomes a matter of inhabiting the practices of its rearticulation" (*Bodies*, 237; italics removed). There certainly is more than a trace of Lacanian "lack" running through Butler's work, but she will insist that this Lacanian "failure" is not in simple opposition to success, but rather a responding productivity or intensity that enables and calls for another reading, another response, another movement. As she writes, "it may be that the affirmation of that slippage, that failure of identification is itself the point of departure for a more democratizing affirmation of internal difference" (219). Interpellative disidentification or misrecognition is, it seems, the moment or movement of critique in Butler's work—the *exposure* of the weakness or "slippage" of the negative or normative. But finally it is this movement of *response*— "*affirmation of that slippage*," working that specific weakness by reinscribing it—that brings together the theoretical moment of alterity and the cultural moment of politics, opening onto a production of identities in the gaps or slippages of normativity's laws.

This is the point at which my analysis of performativity takes its departure from Butler, or at least poses a series of questions about the legacy of lack in her discourse. As nuanced as it is, Butler's moment of *response* remains inexorably tied to the primacy of a performative *failure*. As in de Man and Žižek, *failure* (and with it the horizon of normative wholeness) comes *first* in Butler; it remains the privileged moment, offering to the subject "the occasion for an allegory . . . that concedes the unrealizability of [a cultural] imperative from the start, and which, finally, cannot overcome the unreality that is its condition and its lure" ("Burning," 22–23). In "Burning Acts," Butler analyzes Nietzsche's famous performative dictum "there is no 'being' behind doing, effecting, becoming; 'the doer' is merely a fiction added to the deed—the deed is everything" (*Genealogy*, essay 1, sect. 13), emphasizing particularly the juridical notions buried within Nietzsche's theory of performative subjection. Butler explains, "In a sense, for Nietzsche, the subject comes to be only within the requirements of a moral discourse of accountability. The requirements of blame figure the subject as the 'cause' of an act" (200; see *Genealogy*, essay 2, sect. 3). Nietzsche shows that the constative notion of identity is made possible not only through a forgetting of performativity, but also through a discourse of accountability or blame: the subject's "causing" an action works *both* as an ontological category and a moral one; for the subject to imagine that it is free, it must ignore both the performative action and the prior moral discourse to which it is beholden. Butler goes on, then, to pose a question to Nietzsche's discourse: "If there is an institution of punishment within which the subject is formed, is there not also a figure of the law who performatively sentences the subject into being? Is this not, in some sense, the conjecturing by Nietzsche of a prior and more powerful subject?" (200).

Indeed, it is in and around this prior performative "law" of interpellation that Butler will locate both the subjection of the subject and its opportunities for response. To be sure, she argues, the law constitutes the subject as accountability; but it is precisely in the *failure* of the law to suture or enforce accountability—the failure fully to configure the subject in accordance with a representation of juridical norms—that subjective *response* and *subversion* of the law is made possible. In fact, she argues, there is no subject at all without this failure. As she explains in *The Psychic Life of Power*:

> Considered along Nietzschean and Hegelian lines, the subject engages in its own self-thwarting, accomplishes its own subjection, desires and crafts its own shackles, and so turns against a desire that it knows to be—or knew to be—its own. For a loss to predate the subject, to make it possible (and impossible), we must consider the part that loss plays in subject formation. Is there a loss that cannot be thought, cannot be owned or grieved, which forms the condition of possibility for the subject? (24)

As Butler shows, Nietzsche's reading of performative identity keeps our attention focused on a "subjection, without which no proper subject emerges" (66); Nietzsche shows time and again how the constative doer is backloaded from the performative deed as the action's supposed "cause." But what's not so clear in Nietzsche is how you get from this notion of inevitable subjection to the notion that subjection is the inevitable installation of "loss." As I perhaps naïvely ask above, loss of what? If, as Butler argues, there is no subject in Nietzsche but for the recoil of a performative act, where would this "predate[d]" loss come from?

As Butler claims in *Excitable Speech*, "The address that inaugurates the possibility of agency, in a single stroke, forecloses the possibility of radical autonomy" (26); again, there is always subjection where there is subjectivity. But how do we know the subject wants "radical autonomy," and wants it enough to recognize each time autonomy's failure? Where does that desire for wholeness come from? Butler insists that "Nietzsche offers us a political insight into the formation of the psyche and the problem of subjection, understood paradoxically not merely as the subordination of a subject to a norm, but as the constitution of a subject through precisely such a subordination" (*Psychic*, 66). This insight seems irreducible, but that simultaneity of subject and subjection being the case, subjective loss or lack can't exist always and everywhere. It seems contentious, in other words, to argue that the inscription of the social is synonymous with the inscription of lack.

Butler's discourse of performative identity goes a long way toward providing an alternative to the resentful discourses of identity politics, but the centerpiece of Butler's discourse—*failure of recognition or misrecognition*—in the end protects the very horizon of totalized identity that it seems she wants to question. In Butler's performative discourse, we remain symptoms; ye shall know us by our lack. And whether that lack of totalization is thematized as historically contingent or metaphysically primary, the problem remains the same: in its attempts to suture the founding gap or lack, the subject continues to protect the normativity of a wholeness that supposedly was lost. This sense of unattainable wholeness continues to rule over Butler's discourse as a phantasmatic normativity—made all the more powerful by its unattainable status, its inevitable yet irresistible "failure." In the end, normative or constative wholeness (and its impossibility) remains the necessary horizon and engine of Butler's discourse, just as it does in de Man's and Žižek's.

Just as lack presupposes totalization, a performative discourse of failure presupposes the privilege of totalized phantasmatic identity, and the concomitant thematization of the other as being finally *like* the self: lacking in wholeness. But for an alterity politics of response, there may be good theoretical and political reasons *not* to know who "the other" or "the self" is—not to get caught up in the chiasmic reversals of recognition, which is always recognition of a subject's lack. It is the insistence on *response* that I find so crucial in Butler's discourse; but if that response is always conditioned by a prior lack, it then seems destined to reinscribe the very problems that performativity seems so helpful in circumventing or deploying otherwise: resentment and the separation of the performative subject from what it can do or what it can become. If it is to be an affirmation of otherness, response can never be primarily response to a lack, as I will argue at some length in chapter 7. Indeed, as I have argued throughout and will continue to argue in the ensuing chapters, the seeming inability to know who the other is—or should be—constitutes *not* a failure or lack of response in the subject, but rather the positive necessity of the unforeseen, and therefore urgent: the positivity of a hesitating yet concrete response to alterity.

5 · *Is It the Shoes? Otherness and Exemplarity in Jameson, Heidegger, and Derrida*

We will begin with one of the canonical works of high modernism in visual art, Van Gogh's well-known painting of the peasant shoes, an example which, as you can imagine, has not been innocently or randomly chosen.
—Fredric Jameson, *Postmodernism*

How shall we discover what a piece of equipment truly is? The procedure necessary at present must plainly avoid any attempts that again immediately entail the encroachments of the usual interpretations. We are most easily insured against this if we simply describe some equipment without any philosophical theory. We choose as example a common sort of equipment— a pair of peasant shoes.—Martin Heidegger, "The Origin of the Work of Art"

I'll begin. What of shoes? What, shoes? Whose are the shoes? What are they made of? And even, who are they? Here they are, the questions, that's all.
—Jacques Derrida, "Restitutions of the Truth in *Pointure*"

I also begin this chapter with the question of shoes: the status of shoes caught between figure and discourse, between image and word, between exemplarity and singularity, among Jameson, Heidegger, and Derrida. In Fredric Jameson's hugely influential essay "Postmodernism, or The Cultural Logic of Late Capitalism," his distinction between modern and postmodern cultural production turns decisively on two paintings of shoes: Vincent Van Gogh's so-called "Peasant Shoes" (Figure 1) and Andy Warhol's *Diamond Dust Shoes* (Figure 2). Jameson begins his discussion with this, his first and most decisive, example of the "differences between the high-modernist and the postmodernist moment, between the shoes of Van Gogh and the shoes of Andy Warhol" (9).

For Jameson, Van Gogh's modernist presentation of the peasant shoes conjures up a sense of hermeneutic and historical depth, "stark rural poverty, and the whole rudimentary human world of backbreaking peasant toil" (7). As a reply to the fragmented and alienated world called forth within it, Van Gogh's painting stands as "a Utopian gesture, an act of compensation" (7) that tries to re-create or reimagine an authentic relation to the earth. The painting is an "act of the will" (9) that refuses to take as givens the anomie and alienation of modern life; in turn it calls the viewer likewise to reinvigorate this inauthentic world through his or her own interpretative act of will.

In contrast, Jameson reads Warhol's shoes as a celebration—or at least a passive acceptance—of the fragmentation or loss of the authentic, an almost gleeful presentation of "superficiality in the most literal sense" (9). Warhol offers the glittery commoditized postmodern shoes as objects removed from any useful human context and transformed into endless simulacra, fetishized orphan objects that can never be unified through any act of will or interpretation. Jameson writes, "There is therefore in Warhol no way to complete the hermeneutic gesture and restore to these oddments that whole larger lived context of the dance hall or the ball, the world of jetset fashion or glamour magazines" (8–9). In the now familiar narrative, postmodernism attests to the failure of modernism's critical and utopian dreams, and to the triumph of late capitalism; the critical challenge posed to the viewer by Van Gogh's orphan work shoes gives way to the neocelebratory "waning of affect" (10) traced in Warhol's commodity fetish.

It is from the secure base of this initial example that Jameson can go on further to discuss myriad examples of modernism's demise and the triumph of postmodernism's schizophrenic, surface-obsessed subjectivity. Insofar as they constitute Jameson's base examples, Van Gogh's peasant shoes and Warhol's *Diamond Dust Shoes* do a suspiciously large amount of work in setting up the terms of his essay. At

Figure 1
Van Gogh, *A Pair of Shoes*
(1886). (Van Gogh Museum,
Vincent Van Gogh Founda-
tion, Amsterdam)

Figure 2
Warhol, *Diamond Dust
Shoes* (1980). (© Andy
Warhol Foundation for the
Visual Arts/ARS, New York)

the same time, it does seem that the shoes fit: Jameson's examples work. It *is* the shoes that offer us an exemplary thread to unravel this thorny distinction between modern and postmodern.

This is not to ignore the fact that Jameson's essay has come in for its share of criticism; his definition of postmodernism as a spatial and synchronic phenomenon over against a diachronic modernist tempo- rality, as well as his Kantian notion of cognitive mapping and his per- haps all-too-modernist nostalgic stance have all been called into ques- tion over the years since the essay was written. In addition, several of his examples of a depthless, schizophrenic, "bad" postmodernism— among them, postmodern architecture and language poetry—have caused commentators to bristle, and to argue that Jameson has over- looked a critical edge or critical potential within these works.[1] And I suppose that one could follow such a line of reasoning here in several ways: arguing, for example, that Warhol's work *does* produce a certain critical displacement; or perhaps reading Heidegger against Jameson's somewhat odd presentation of "The Origin of the Work of Art," and in the process showing a postmodern moment already at play in the high modernism of Van Gogh and Heidegger.

Although I will follow such a reading of Heidegger's "Origin" against Jameson's reading and also try to read Warhol differently, such a rereading or critique is not finally what interests me in and around Jameson's text. Rather, I am interested in the performative logic of the example in "Postmodernism"—or, for that matter, in postmodernism: if, as Jameson argues, there is a flattening of discourse in a postmodern epoch, if critical distance cannot be secured—rendering "the luxury of the old-fashioned ideological critique . . . unavailable" (46)—then what is it that would allow Jameson to bring Van Gogh's and Warhol's figurations onto the scene as discursive examples of this or that overarching principle? In fact, even while rereading Heidegger in an attempt to complicate Jameson's presentation of him, we will still be left with Heidegger's all too abrupt exemplifying of Van Gogh's shoes, which are brought on the scene in "The Origin of the Work of Art" rather cavalierly as an "example [of] a common sort of equipment—a pair of peasant shoes" (32).

In this chapter, I'd like to take up the specificities of performative response by suggesting that important questions about ethics congeal around the example. More specifically, I will argue that the question of exemplarity is inseparable from the crucial postmodern question of alterity, insofar as exemplarity in its traditional form is the seeking out of difference and the concomitant reduction of difference to sameness, the corralling of radical specificity under the controlling rubric of the concept. As Levinas concisely writes about the exemplary relation, "In evidence the violence of the encounter with the non-I is deadened" ("Philosophy," 49).[2] Exemplary "evidence," in other words, does a certain violence to the non-I; it reduces the other to the categories of the same. And, perhaps more sinister, exemplarity simultaneously deadens or covers over that appropriating violence by sublating it within the supposedly transcendental movement of revelation. The example, like the performative, too quickly becomes subsumed under the rubrics of constative knowledge.

I will argue that an other or postmodern reading of exemplarity is necessary—and not merely to keep things philosophically tidy after the withdrawal of a transcendental ground. The project here, in other words, is not merely to account for or construct a nontranscendental notion of exemplarity.[3] Rather, it seems to me that such an exemplary rereading has much to add to this book's project of rethinking ethical

responsibility and setting into motion an alterity politics of acting or
responding otherwise in the postmodern world. Irene Harvey points
toward some of these general consequences when she writes about
exemplarity and alterity in Derrida's work: "Far from simply illus-
trating an argument or theory, the examples themselves re-orient
the text around them. . . . [T]hey entail the possibility of being read
otherwise such that they do not simply support or clarify the stated
argument, but rather exhibit another level and, hence, [another] law
operating within the text" (197). In a hypotactic economy of exemplarity, the example effaces itself before the conclusion: difference
effaces itself, sacrificing itself to the constative privilege of sameness. However, even in its seeming effacement before the conclusion
that it serves, the example simultaneously inscribes the possibility
of performatively responding otherwise, of paratactically leading to
other conclusions. The example lives on after its seeming sublation
because, as Rodolphe Gasché writes, the example "is a condition of
possibility that inscribes the possibility of *not* being *valid*, of its ex-
ception" ("God," 58). The example always inscribes or attests to an
other at the heart of the same, always points to the "one more" that
can be grafted onto any seemingly static chain.

There is, then, an odd ethical paradox at the site of the example. In
postmodern ethical discourse, we certainly cannot do without a fairly
traditional understanding of the example; we cannot attend or respond
to the other if this chimeric other cannot even be located, specified,
or singularized from within a larger network of possible responses.
Because pious generalizations about alterity, respect, and difference
will not stand in for concrete response to specific others, concepts—
for example, justice—must always be singularized or performed in
particular cases. And attending to such specificity calls for some
notion of exemplarity in order to identify the persons or contexts to
which one could or must render ethical response. But at the same
time, one cannot simply import transcendental ethical standards into
specific conflicted and complex situations, rendering automatic judg-
ments that, due to the very fact of their rote character, would be
no ethical responses at all.[4] In short, exemplarity is both necessary
and impossible for any performative ethics of response to the other:
one must identify or exemplify those to whom or that to which one
would respond ethically; but at the same time, "the persistence of
*dis*identification is equally crucial to the rearticulation of democratic
contestation," as Judith Butler writes in *Bodies That Matter* (4).

In thematizing and enacting such a radically democratic rearticulation of ethics, as Chantal Mouffe suggests, perhaps "what is needed is a new kind of articulation between the universal and the particular" (36), between the concept and the example. I will try to sketch out such a rearticulation in this chapter by attending to three specific texts: Jameson's "Postmodernism," Heidegger's "The Origin of the Work of Art," and Derrida's "Restitutions of the Truth in *Pointure*." These texts are, like any examples, not randomly chosen, but at the same time they have no essential necessity. Here, they are all brought together under the rubric of exemplarity itself, because each of them turns crucially on a painting of shoes. These paintings become, like all examples and all performatives, translated into something other in each of these discourses; it is precisely this becoming-other that I want to track in Jameson, Heidegger, and Derrida.

Jameson's Heidegger

Jameson reads Heidegger as an example of a modernist thinker nostalgic for the values of nature, values cathected in Heidegger's exemplification of Van Gogh's peasant shoes. For Jameson's Heidegger, "the mediation of the work of art . . . draws the whole absent world and earth into revelation around itself, along with the heavy tread of the peasant woman, the loneliness of the field path, the hut in the clearing, the worn and broken instruments of labor in the furrows and at the hearth" (8). Jameson argues that Heidegger's reading of Van Gogh's shoes "may be described as *hermeneutical*, in the sense in which the work in its inert, objectal form is taken as a clue or a symptom for some vaster reality which replaces it as its ultimate truth" (8). According to Jameson, this "ultimate truth" is the lost reality of the shoes in their original context, and Jameson suggests that both Van Gogh and Heidegger, in exemplary modernist fashion, valorize artistic revelation as a (perhaps pale) substitute for the lost revelation of authentic, immediate experience. In the absence of tangible ultimate truths, Van Gogh's painting offers hermeneutics, and Jameson argues that the question of (the shoes') truth for the modernist Heidegger likewise turns on reconstituting the artistic evocation of "the whole missing object world which was once their lived context" (8).

Certainly, this is all too quick. If Heidegger's "Origin" has any relation at all to what is traditionally called hermeneutics (and this is by

no means clear), it would seem that it is first and foremost an attempt
to think beyond the circles of hermeneutical inquiry, where "the artist
is the origin of the work. The work is the origin of the artist" ("Origin,"
17). For Heidegger, the question of "Origin" is elsewhere: "In themselves and in their interrelations artist and work *are* each of them
by virtue of a third thing which is prior to both, namely that which
also gives artist and work of art their names—art" (17). The tautological exemplifications of hermeneutics—where the "ultimate truth" of
the painting could be said to correspond to this or that propositional
example—are in fact the stakes of "Origin"; something like correspondence is made possible in and through this third term, with which
there can be no simple corresponding. Prior to the opposition between
art and artist, there is *aletheia*, an unconcealment that conceals.

   Why, the weary reader might profitably ask, do we need to take
up Heidegger here at all? What relevance does his incredibly esoteric
work on "Being" have for contemporary debates about performative
subjectivity, ethics, or agency? Well, one might answer, quite a bit
of relevance. Indeed, it remains somewhat baffling to me that, given
the flood of recent work on cultural identity and the possibilities of
agency, there has been relatively little work done on the so-called
existentialists, for whom these were *the* questions. At the risk of trying the reader's patience, I'd like to linger awhile with Heidegger and
try to track his sense of (un)concealed possibility and subjective response—not merely to recuperate or reify his analyses, but to try to
open up a space to think past them. I fear that if we avoid analyzing
Heidegger, we too easily fall back into or onto a Heideggerian sense of
the agent's solitary confrontation with possibility, and in the process
we lose the crucial ethical question of the other.

   To trace the path of *aletheia*'s (un)concealment, Heidegger spends
a good deal of time in "Origin" revisiting the distinction between the
being of the artistic work and the being of more mundane work with
equipment. Both can initially be understood in terms of usefulness
or "reliability" within the context of a specific end-oriented action. A
piece of equipment, for example, is the specific matter through which
a possible form can be realized. A tool is a tool only in use, in its
reliable employment toward a specific end: "Because it is determined
by usefulness and serviceability, equipment takes into its service that
of which it consists: the matter. . . . The material is all the better
and more suitable the less it resists perishing in the equipmental
being of the equipment" (46). For Heidegger, equipmental being is the

being that disappears into the activity of pursuing an end. The appropriateness of the tool is, in other words, given by the job to be accomplished; the more appropriate the tool, the "less it resists perishing in the equipmental being of the equipment." The tool, then, is best understood in terms of the myriad ends or jobs that it might assist in accomplishing; like the example, the tool is revealed as itself only when it is deployed toward a specific end, within a specific economy where form (ends) subsumes matter (means).

The material artwork, however, is not so easily subsumed within an equipmental or exemplary relation to an end or form. In fact, the artwork gestures toward something behind or before any particular use (or form/matter distinction), toward the very thing that makes any specific exemplary relation possible: the openness of being. Heidegger writes, "in setting up a world, [the artwork] does not cause the material to disappear, but rather causes it to come forth for the very first time and to come into the Open of the work's world" (46). The material work of art is not merely the flowering of some particular form or use, but is rather the opening of the space where any relation, equipmental or otherwise, could take place. Unlike the equipmental tool, the material artwork never merely disappears into a formal interpretation; it is not merely an example of a principle. In the artwork, we confront the multiple possibility of being's gift, that which rests— or, rather, buzzes with life—prior to matter's disappearance into a static form. Here, matter stubbornly remains in or as the open, attesting to still other possibilities, other interpretations, other uses, other examples: "The work holds open the Open of the world" (45).

But this openness of the world is not to be confused with the simple availability that characterizes equipment; the artwork reveals an openness that simultaneously shelters a kind of closedness or unavailability. The artwork holds something back even as it discloses multiple possibility. According to Heidegger, possibility as such "disappears in usefulness. The more handy a piece of equipment is, the more inconspicuous it remains" (65).[5] Because of this fact, matter must be drawn out of a merely useful relation if that relation is to (un)conceal what makes it possible, if we are to confront the open as the multiple availability that grounds any particular use. As Heidegger writes, the artwork is a privileged thread in tracing this relation: "Color shines and wants only to shine. When we analyze it in rational terms by measuring its wavelengths, it is gone. It shows itself only when it remains undisclosed and unexplained. . . . The earth appears

openly cleared as itself only when it is perceived and preserved as
that which is by nature undisclosable, that which shrinks from every
disclosure and constantly keeps itself closed up" (47). The work, in its
truth as (un)concealment, brings about a certain absence of work—in
unconcealment, it conceals. The useful work of interpretation is, in
other words, disrupted before the work of art, and rendered use-less.
Heidegger writes, "Every [interpretive] decision, however, bases itself
on something not mastered, something concealed, confusing; else it
would never be a decision" (55). Paradoxically, it is precisely this "concealed," "confusing" use-less character that allows us to confront the
essence of being as multiple availability—allows us to see that any
particular decision or action is both *based upon* and *conceals* myriad
others that could have been made.

In the language of exemplarity, the difference between the tool
and the artwork is precisely this difference between the "ontic" example (the tool that effaces itself before a particular conclusion) and
"ontological" exemplarity itself (the artwork as the very ground of
availability that allows and preserves the possibility of multiple em-
ployments toward many ends). All presence, according to Heidegger,
is derived from a state of multiple availability, and this radical multiplicity—the possibility of proceeding otherwise—remains concealed
within any constitution of presence. The essence of *techné*, in other
words, is *poesis*.[6]

It is in the service of preserving the artwork's radically plural
essence that Heidegger writes, "The work, therefore, is not the reproduction of some particular entity that happens to be present at any
given time; it is, on the contrary, the reproduction of the thing's general essence" (37). This "general essence" seems to be the untruth that
conceals itself at the heart of truth, the ontological multiplicity that
grounds any ontic specificity; likewise, it seems that this is the truth
that (un)conceals itself in the artwork: "Truth happens in Van Gogh's
painting. This does not mean that something is correctly portrayed,
but rather that in the revelation of the equipmental being of the shoes,
that which is as a whole—world and earth in their counterplay—
attains to unconcealedness" (56). In Heidegger's somewhat rarified vocabulary, Van Gogh's painting of the peasant shoes reveals the world
(as possibility, clearing, the *da*) held open by the earth (as concealment,
sheltering, *Sein*): earth and world work together, then, but not as a
dialectical form/matter distinction where the monologizing "form" of
the earth would absorb the heterogeneous "matter" of the world. Hei-

degger writes, "Clearing of openness [world] and establishment in the Open [earth] belong together. They are the same single nature of the happening of truth" (61). Like the relation between being and *Dasein*— where the *da* and *Sein* work together to create a thrown or projected whole, a space for the continual playing out and sheltering of being as possibility—the relation between being and the artwork is never merely an exemplary or form/matter distinction; rather, the artwork creates a clearing that can reveal the state of possibility or availability that rests prior to and remains concealed within any such distinction.

To return to Jameson, then, we see much that is perceptive in his brief reading of Heidegger in "Postmodernism." Certainly Heidegger does take the artwork to have an ontological and hermeneutical significance, though this significance is portrayed a bit histrionically by Jameson's phrasing: "the work in its inert, objectal form is taken as a clue or a symptom for some vaster reality which replaces it as its ultimate truth" (8). Certainly the play between ontic and ontological is crucial to Heidegger, for whom the "objectal form" of the ontic work clearly opens onto an ontological investigation of the conditions of possibility for any inquiry.

I would hesitate, however, before Jameson's phrases "vaster reality" and "ultimate truth." Such terminology is troubling not merely because it is overstatement, but because it is misleading: it thematizes Heidegger's text as a very traditional kind of metaphoric or transcendentalist thinking. In other words, it seems obfuscatory to argue that Heidegger's move to the ontological is an attempt to reify Van Gogh's painting, to get back behind the painting in order to capture its "hermeneutical" "vaster reality" once and for all. Recall that for Heidegger the "ultimate truth" of the shoes is untruth, and his move to the ontological level is an attempt to protect the artwork from disappearing under the simple exemplary substitutions of a metaphysical ontology, where the artwork would be subsumed into the work of interpretation. In fact, Heidegger thematizes such an exemplifying movement as a kind of "violence" that "makes an assault upon" the work ("Origin," 25).[7]

Ironically, then, on another reading Heidegger's seemingly "modernist" presentation of Van Gogh is actually very close to Jameson's thematization of Warhol's "postmodern" celebratory fragmentation. If Heidegger's appeal to the ontological "ultimate truth" reifies anything, it would seem to be precisely the "postmodern" sense of irreducible multiplicity that Jameson wants to use him to combat.

Figure 3
Warhol, *Two Hundred
Campbell's Soup Cans*
(1962). (© Andy Warhol
Foundation for the Visual
Arts/ARS, New York)

Certainly there is much (seemingly "modernist") talk of levels and depth in Heidegger's essay, but to explore these Heideggerian depths is to confront not stasis and reification but expropriation and fragmentation: "Truth is un-truth, insofar as there belongs to it the reservoir of the not-yet-uncovered, the un-uncovered, in the sense of concealment. In unconcealedness, as truth, there occurs also the other 'un-' of a double restraint or refusal" (60). Ironically, Heidegger's move to the ontological level refuses rather than appeals to the possibility of a static "ultimate truth," and places Van Gogh at a very "postmodern" moment indeed: the revelation of depth ("unconcealedness") in Van Gogh is simultaneously the revelation of surface ("the other 'un-' of a double restraint or refusal"); the uncovering of truth in the artwork leads to a denial of any static truth through the confrontation with multiplicity. In Heidegger's "Origin," hermeneutic depth turns out to be subject to or derived from a flat or depthless horizon of multiple reinscription or possibility. Behind Van Gogh's shoes one can almost hear the anonymous murmur of Warhol (Figure 3): Campbell's Campbell's Campbell's Campbell's Campbell's . . .[8]

The Example, for Example

Even if we accept this reading of Heidegger contra Jameson, we are nevertheless left with any number of similarities in their texts, not the least of which is the incredible amount of theoretical and rhetorical work done in both essays by a crucial example: Van Gogh's peasant shoes. For Jameson the shoes reveal the workings of modernism, and for Heidegger they reveal the (un)concealment of truth as untruth. Certainly, other examples in both texts can and do lead us to similar places, but finally it is the singular logic or economy surrounding this example that interests me here. Even when we reread Heidegger against Jameson's presentation of him as a nostalgic modernist, we are still left with the odd fact that both of these thinkers—each committed to accounting for a certain fragmented present that comes about in the absence of a transcendental, after modernism or after metaphysics— end up resorting to a very traditional hypotactic logic of the example.

For both Jameson and Heidegger, Van Gogh's painting "speaks" to the viewer, not coincidentally telling him or her the main points of either Jameson's or Heidegger's analysis: Heidegger writes of Van Gogh's shoes, "This painting spoke" ("Origin," 35), and it told us that "usefulness itself rests in the abundance of an essential being of the equipment" (34). Jameson takes the *via negativa* to the speech of the painting, writing that "Warhol's *Diamond Dust Shoes* evidently no longer speaks to us with any of the immediacy of Van Gogh's foot-gear; indeed, I am tempted to say that it does not really speak to us at all" (8). For Jameson, it seems that Van Gogh's shoes, unlike Warhol's, speak to us immediately—telling us of their lost horizons.

There remains, however, something very strange about all this. As Heideggerian postmetaphysicians or Jamesonian postmoderns, we should be somewhat suspicious when examples "speak" in this way. As Derrida writes of Van Gogh's shoes in another context, one should be surprised by "propositions of the type 'this is that' in which the copula ties a 'real' predicate to a 'painted' object. One is surprised that an expert should use all this dogmatic and precritical language. It all looks as though the hammering of the notions of self-evidence, clarity, and property was meant to resound very loudly to prevent us from hearing that nothing here is clear, or self-evident, or proper to anyone or anything whatsoever" (*Truth*, 313). This is a caveat well heeded: too often, clear and convincing examples cover over an essential ambiguity that demands attention. Of course, neither Jameson nor Heidegger merely reduces his examples to ham-fisted "propositions of the type 'this is that,'" but there is a sense in which both thinkers' gestures toward multiplicity and ambiguity remain tied to an oddly monologizing understanding of exemplarity.

In Heidegger, as I argue above, if Van Gogh's work is an example of anything, it is of the "ontological" character of exemplarity itself: Van Gogh's shoes trace availability in its pure form, possibility not subsumed under an equipmental or exemplary relation to a specific end. One is left, however, with a very odd notion of availability in Heidegger's text: for availability to be understood properly, it must be

Figure 4
Van Gogh, *Three Pairs of
Shoes, One Shoe Upside
Down* (1887). (Fogg Art
Museum, Harvard
University)

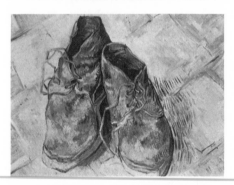

Figure 5
Van Gogh, *A Pair of Shoes*
(1887). (Van Gogh Museum,
Vincent Van Gogh Founda-
tion, Amsterdam)

Figure 6
Van Gogh, *A Pair of Old
Shoes* (1888). (Metropolitan
Museum, New York)

Figure 7
Van Gogh, *A Pair of Shoes,
One Shoe Upside Down*
(1887). (The Baltimore
Museum of Art: The Cone
Collection, formed by Dr.
Claribel Cone and Miss Etta
Cone of Baltimore, Maryland
BMA 1950.302)

shoes" over the course of his career (Figures 1, 4–7).[12] The last of this series, painting 1236 in the Hulsker catalogue raisonné (Figure 7), is reproduced in the text of Jameson's *Postmodernism.*

Given the multiplicity of Van Gogh's versions, one has to wonder how or why Jameson chooses to reproduce this particular portrait of the peasant shoes. Most obviously, it could be explained by the fact that this particular pair of peasant shoes presently finds itself housed in the United States, a " 'fact' " that nicely inflects Perloff's discussion of the "U.S.-centrism of his position" (128). However, a little legwork on Perloff's or Jameson's part—or a closer reading of "Restitutions," the essay where, as Jameson puts it, "Derrida remarks, somewhere . . . that the Van Gogh footgear are a heterosexual pair" (*Postmodernism,* 8; see Derrida's *Truth,* 332)—would have turned up the fact that Heidegger, Jameson's ostensible interlocutor, does not seem to be referring to Figure 7 in "Origin." Rather, to the best of Heidegger's recollection, he refers to Figure 1 (Hulsker 1124), which he saw in Amsterdam in 1930.[13] And the two paintings are, in " 'fact,' " not interchangeable.

Likewise, there is no singular or unproblematic "work called *Diamond Dust Shoes.*" Warhol in fact produced between twenty and twenty-five distinct *Diamond Dust Shoes* in or around 1980 (see, for example, Figures 2, 8–11).[14] Jameson sets the tone here by referring to the *Diamond Dust Shoes* series as if they were a singular painting, although, oddly enough, there are two very different versions of *Diamond Dust Shoes* reproduced in his *Postmodernism:* the brightly multicolored Figure 2 is reproduced in part on the cover of the book (Figure 12), but there is also a version of the painting in the text immediately following the reproduction of Van Gogh. In fact, it is to this second, flat black *Diamond Dust Shoes* (Figure 13)—after the style of Warhol's 1980 *Diamond Dust Joseph Beuys* (Figure 14)—that it seems Jameson refers in the "Postmodernism" essay, when he speaks of Warhol's use of "the photographic negative," "which confers its deathly quality to the Warhol image, whose glacéd X-ray elegance mortifies the reified eye of the viewer in a way that would seem to have nothing to do with death or the death obsession" (9).

Finally, however, what interests or concerns me here is not Perloff's emphasis on supposed " 'facts,' " but rather the economy of exemplarity in this series of texts. In taking one of Warhol's *Diamond Dust Shoes* or one of Van Gogh's "Peasant Shoes" to be exemplary of a concept or idea—modernism, postmodernism, openness to being, brutal marginality, shameless self-promotion—there is of course a narrowing

Figures 8–11
Warhol, *Diamond Dust Shoes*
(1980). (© Andy Warhol
Foundation for the Visual
Arts/ARS, New York)

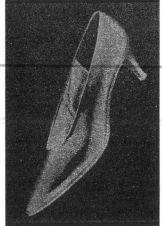

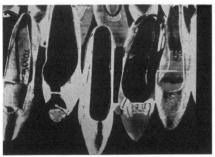

Figure 14
Warhol, *Diamond Dust
Joseph Beuys* (1980). (©
Andy Warhol Foundation
for the Visual Arts/ARS,
New York)

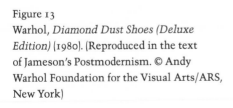

Figure 12
Cover of Jameson's *Postmodernism* (1991).
(Duke University Press)

Figure 13
Warhol, *Diamond Dust Shoes (Deluxe
Edition)* (1980). (Reproduced in the text
of Jameson's Postmodernism. © Andy
Warhol Foundation for the Visual Arts/ARS,
New York)

Figure 15
Warhol, *210 Coca-Cola Bottles* (1962).
(© Andy Warhol Foundation for the Visual
Arts/ARS, New York)

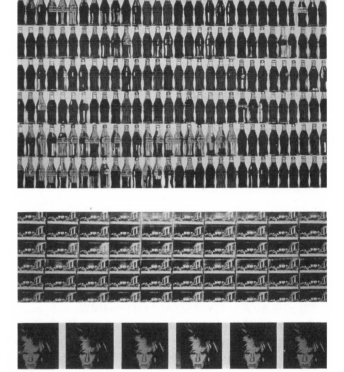

Figure 16
Warhol, *Sixty Last Suppers* (1986).
(© Andy Warhol Foundation for the Visual
Arts/ARS, New York)

Figure 17
Warhol, *Six Self-Portraits* (1986).
(© Andy Warhol Foundation for the Visual
Arts/ARS, New York)

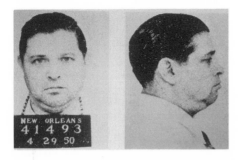

Figure 18
Warhol, *Most Wanted Men
No. 7, Salvatore V.* (1964).
(© Andy Warhol Foundation
for the Visual Arts/ARS,
New York)

Figure 19
Warhol, *Marilyn* (1964).
(© Andy Warhol Foundation
for the Visual Arts/ARS,
New York)

Figure 20
Warhol, *Elvis I and II*
(1964). (© Andy Warhol
Foundation for the Visual
Arts/ARS, New York)

there is at the same time no space offered in or by Warhol to recover any originary, untainted, or uninterpellated Norma Jean, Salvatore, or Elvis. The movement of Warhol's serial iteration seems to be a one-way movement outward, and none of us has any choice about whether or not to participate in it. Viewers' identities, Warhol suggests, are formed in the very same way as Salvatore's, Elvis's, or Marilyn's: through an iteration that functions to found identity as a performative effect without any simply recoverable cause or ground. Identity, for both commodity and human, is an effect rather than a cause of serial iteration. As Warhol writes about his own serial identity, "If you want to know all about Andy Warhol, just look at the surface—of my paintings and films and me—and there I am. There's nothing behind it" (in McShine, 457).

Of course, it is precisely his serial murder of the real that makes Warhol both available and efficacious as Jameson's primary example of postmodern "pastiche" (celebratory iteration without an original) over against modernism's more biting "parody" (which presupposes a distance from the real or original by which the example can be judged and found wanting). As Jameson writes, Warhol's iterations offer us no "feeling or emotion," but rather the "decorative exhilaration" of "gratuitous frivolity" (10). But is there, we might ask, another way to read Warhol's disruptions of the real? Are his serial iterations solely celebrations of depthless commodity fetishism, a giddy postmodernism that offers no space for intervention or analysis? Can Warhol's questioning of performative exemplarity be read other-wise? Can it in fact be read as an *ethical* movement?

In attempting to answer this question, I'd like to return to Derrida, another figure obsessed by serial exemplarity. Harvey writes, "one could argue that Derrida's work has from its inception never been concerned with anything *other* than exemplarity" (193).[16] Likewise, it is worth noting that much of Derrida's most explicit work on the question of exemplarity is done within his work on the visual arts, in *The Truth in Painting* and *Memoirs of the Blind*.[17] And this makes a certain amount of sense, insofar as the experience of viewing or organizing an art exhibit lends itself to questions about the serial example. In an organized or topical art show, how does one move from one painting or sculpture to another, protecting the integrity of each work but gesturing at the same time toward the overarching "theme" of the show? Obviously, to begin to answer these questions, one must confront a specific work of art. As Derrida writes, "In each case the

Figure 21
Warhol, *Cow* (1966). (© Andy
Warhol Foundation for the
Visual Arts/ARS, New York)

structure of exemplarity (unique or multiple) is original and therefore
prescribes a different affect. And in each case there remains to be
found out what importance one gives to the case" (*Truth*, 49).

So, we begin again—with a radically singular example: a cow, or,
more specifically, Warhol's silkscreen cow series, and his wallpaper-
design iterations of this same image of the cow (Figure 21). I had
always vaguely associated the cow in Warhol's iterations with Elsie,
the (now out-to-pasture) trademark Borden cow, but on a recent trip to
the Warhol museum in Pittsburgh, I found the "original" from which
Warhol cropped his "master cow" for the cow series. The portrait is
extracted from a book about judging dairy cows. Next to the picture
that Warhol cropped for the original in his series is this description of
the cow head in question:

> The Jersey is the smallest of the dairy breeds and naturally the
> head is in proportion to body size. In addition to being smaller
> and finer, the Jersey head is also characterized by a more pro-
> nounced dish in the face and a more prominent eye. Most of the

other points of consideration, however, are not essentially different [from other cows]. The face is well illustrated by a comparison
of the official score card with any of the other breed score cards.
The various breed score cards place about the same emphasis
upon feminine refinement, width of muzzle, openness of nos-
tril, fullness of eye, or strength of jaw. *The Jersey head featured
in [this] figure . . . possesses quality and refinement as well as
displaying evidence of strength. At the same time it is a typical
Jersey head and therefore shows breed character.* (Italics added)

Warhol's "original" Jersey head has an odd status indeed. It is, as a
representation of a prize-winning cow, compelling in its uniqueness,
possessing a "quality and refinement as well as displaying evidence
of strength"; the book's "figure" is, in other words, a rare and original
mix of stereotypically feminine ("quality and refinement") and masculine ("strength") traits. But, "at the same time, it is a typical Jersey
head." In other words, it's unique, but at the same time it is infinitely
repeatable. In fact, it is unique *because of* its iterability: the unique
features of this Jersey are locatable precisely insofar as they reinscribe
a general "breed character."
    Here, then, it is suggested that Jersey cows, like human identities or
commodities, do not exist as "originals"; they come into being as they
are named (and renamed). Jerseyhood, like personhood, is a hypostasis—the irruption of a substantive, constative, or noun within what is
already an ongoing performative process of interpellative elaboration.
And this insistence on the seriality of the process seems to entail that
the hypostatic substantive in question—"Jersey cow"—is made possible in the first place by the process of iteration itself: the irruption
of this figure as the new ideal mix of feminine and masculine Jersey
heads is brought about by and through the reinscription of preexisting juridical norms. We are, in other words, kept constantly in contact
with specificity through a certain repetition—the performative repetition that makes specificity possible or articulable (a repetition that
will be the major focus of chapter 6).
    Such a radically empirical Warholian working from and with spe-
cifics is what Derrida, in another context, refers to as "the authority
of this reflective hinge" (*Truth*, 52), the performative hinge of thinking that is the example. And the exemplary hinge, Derrida argues,
can swing either way: to open a discourse to further examples, or to
close a discourse by sublating or hypostatizing it within a transcen-

dental stopping point outside the conflicted surface of analysis. As he writes, the example is "neither simply outside nor simply inside" (54) the logics of thinking, but is in fact the condition of emergence for discourse with and about the other. Ironically, however, these hazardous dialogic or paratactic encounters often turn into transcendental arguments that consistently try to reduce or exclude the very open or serial nature of their conditions: "philosophical discourse will always have been *against* the *parergon*" (54)—not against the grain, but against the frame, against the very exemplary conditions that allow dialogic inscriptions to be made and remade.

In a traditional philosophical discourse, the example—as Warhol's series—seems to be a superfluous parasite that feeds on the plenitude of the thing itself; but as we saw above with Warhol, such an exemplary frame in fact may be the condition of possibility for there to be any supposed state of plenitude. Derrida thematizes this moment or movement of the example as "the instant when the singularity of the trait divides in order to link itself to the play, the chance, and the economy of a language" (*Truth*, 4). At the *moment* of the example, then, the *movement* of seriality is brought into play. And in exposing the economy of thematization to its condition, one enacts a law of serial alterity that "is written in the singular but the law of its agreements may require the plural" (13). The future necessarily haunts the responses of the present.

In other words, attending to the example teaches us not only that the radically singular or idiomatic always resists sublation; Hegel could have taught us that, and Heidegger certainly insists upon it when he recalls that something remains concealed within any unconcealment. Rather, focusing on the example in this way also calls us to map out the singular, productive resistance of *this* example to sublation. One responds, in other words, to the specific remainder in each case: one can't predict that/if there will even be such a remainder (and in many cases there may not be), and one certainly can't predict or offer a response before the fact. But there is, due to the exemplary condition of serial response, always the necessity for a (re)reading, for another response or inscription.

Though this may seem merely a metaphysical game of analysis and its impossibility, I would argue that the force of such a rereading—for example, of Warhol—would *not* primarily go to show that, because his conclusions can be reinscribed other-wise, Jameson's reading of Heidegger or Warhol or Van Gogh is somehow wrong or simply "un-

decidable." Rather, the point of such a rereading might be to show
that specific other responses are, in fact, necessitated by the intervention or inscription at hand. The question or project of deconstruction,
however broadly defined, would not then consist in showing the
monotonous remainder-producing undecidability of texts and other
cultural products, but rather in asking how we can and must enact
other, future reinscriptions of their sense. This would seem also to
offer another way to respond to Slavoj Žižek's critique of deconstruction—that it breaks down an open door. Recall, as I outlined in
chapter 4, Žižek's argument that "Hegel knows perfectly well that
reflection always fails" (For They Know Not, 89), so we don't need deconstruction to point this out through a laborious analysis. However,
deconstruction, as I'm trying to deploy it here, is not really concerned
with the demonstration of failure, lack, or insufficiency. Rather, it
is necessitated by response, inscription, production, performativity—
concerning itself primarily with the (re)inscription of the future, not
merely the monotonous interruption of an originary lack. As Derrida
insists in a recent interview, "any coherent deconstruction is about
singularity, about events, and about what is ultimately irreducible
in them" ("Deconstruction," 29). And one of the things that is "ultimately irreducible" in this sense is the serial reinscription that is the
future, the unavoidable necessity of response and negotiation—which
Derrida will elsewhere call "justice" (see "Force of Law").

The question of exemplarity is, in this way, a privileged thread by
which one could return to the question of performative ethics, insofar
as exemplarity (an economy of alterior reinscription or response) constitutes the necessary condition of thematization or sameness, as well
as the future reinscription that haunts any such presence. This materiality of performative exemplary reinscription is, then, that which
is to be accounted for in any such "deconstructive" discourse—and accounted for as the *necessity*, not so much the *possibility*—of alterity
within any supposed constitution of sameness. As Derrida writes,
perhaps "everything must be so calculated that calculation should not
have the last word over everything" ("At This Very Moment," 25); in
other words, perhaps examples must be consistently (re)deployed in
a serial performativity, so that a supposed transparentism of the example does not offer us "the last word over everything."

Like Derrida, it seems that Warhol would, in an exemplary fashion,
call us to attend to such material, serial reinscriptions somewhat differently, as other than mere examples of a larger theoretical or cultural

thematization. But maybe this refusal of the theme, the concept, and the same has a name we already know. As Gasché suggests, maybe the "name for thought's inclination to the Other, for the renunciation of the concept, the apriori and transcendental horizons of language in front of God, is *empiricism*" ("God," 63).[18] But this is an empiricism radically reconsidered as performative, serial reinscription. Perhaps it is this sort of empiricism that Butler tries to open up in her work on the performative. She writes, "If essentialism is an effort to preclude the possibility of a future for the signifier, then the task is surely to make the signifier into a site for a set of rearticulations that cannot be predicted or controlled, and to provide for a future in which constituencies will form that have not yet had a site for such an articulation or which 'are' not prior to the siting of such a site" (*Bodies*, 219). Such an iterative siting (or, perhaps, a *citing*) calls for a radical rereading of the example, an attempt to open up a reinscribed future of response rather than merely settling for or on a representative past. Such an ethical site may actually be one of myriad names for the elusive postmodern condition, that site where things "'are' not prior to the siting of such a site": a site where performative ethics, openness to the other, precedes ontology, where verbs precede nouns, and where each *other* would have to be attended to in its serial specificity. One by one, for example.

6 · Becoming-Black: Repetition and Difference in Baraka's Blues People *and Reed's* Mumbo Jumbo

Everything is itself and something else at the same time, i.e., what it is becoming.—Amiri Baraka, "The 'Blues Aesthetic' and the 'Black Aesthetic'"

One reterritorializes, or allows oneself to be reterritorialized, on a minority as a state; but in a becoming, one is deterritorialized. Even blacks, as the Black Panthers said, must become-black.—Gilles Deleuze and Félix Guattari, *A Thousand Plateaus*

Repetition and difference—those poststructuralist buzzwords—are certainly no strangers to African American cultural and political traditions. From the slave narrative to the postmodernism of Toni Morrison and Clarence Major; from *The Souls of Black Folk* to *The Signifying Monkey;* from what Amiri Baraka calls the "willfully harsh, *anti-assimilationist* sound of bebop" (*Blues,* 181–82) to rap; from Prince Hall to Malcolm X, African American traditions have deployed *repetition with a difference* as a key concept in maintaining a vibrant culture. Certainly there is a kind of repetition of standard Western forms in, for example, Harriet Jacobs's *Incidents in the Life of a Slave*

Girl or in the scholarly anthropological prose of W. E. B. Du Bois, but it is precisely the *difference*—the displacement, the question posed from within—that renders a singularity or irreducibility to African American traditions.[1]

Such repetitions cannot simply be conflated with received notions of imitation or representation. As Gilles Deleuze notes in *Difference and Repetition*, there are perhaps two kinds of repetition: the static, "reterritorializing" of repetition-as-representation; and the dynamic, "deterritorializing" of *repetition with a difference*. Deleuze writes, "The first repetition is repetition of the Same, explained by the identity of the concept or representation; the second includes difference, and includes itself in the alterity of the Idea, in the heterogeneity of an 'a-presentation'" (*Difference*, 24). When Charlie Parker covers "White Christmas," for example, what you get is not so much a representation of Irving Berlin's vacuous classic, but what Deleuze calls an "a-presentation": a presentation that marks and "includes difference" rather than effacing it. This "second" repetition—*repetition with a difference*—inhabits a traditional form in order to further open the "Idea" to "alterity" and "heterogeneity."[2] In Deleuze and Guattari's words, such a repetition inhabits an accepted form "in order to transform it from within, deterritorialize it" (*Thousand*, 349).

However, just as African American culture cannot simply be thought of as the "opposite" of a Euro-American tradition, for Deleuze and Guattari such a "deterritorializing" *repetition with a difference* does not exist in binary opposition to a "territorializing" representation or imitation. In fact, according to Deleuze, reducing the productive potential of repetition to a binary skeleton has gone a long way toward "confusing the concept of difference with a merely conceptual difference, in remaining content to inscribe difference in the concept in general" (*Difference*, 27). In other words, when difference is thematized as a "concept in general," it loses its "deterritorializing" power of becoming. When difference becomes a theme—merely to be found, pointed out, located—it loses its critical force to change or disrupt, to become-other.[3]

Likewise, when we take difference and repetition to be concepts, we mirror the mistake that Baraka argues critics have consistently made in the face of African American culture. In *Blues People*, which Bruce Tucker has called "the founding document of contemporary cultural studies in America" (v), Baraka argues that "assimilation" has demanded the imposition onto black culture of a narrowing, reterritorialized "parochialism" (*Blues*, 185). In mainline culture's appropriation of the blues tradition, a verb is made into a noun (212). As Nathaniel Mackey elaborates, Baraka's "'From verb to noun' means the erasure of black inventiveness. . . . On the aesthetic level, a less dynamic, less improvisatory, less blues-inflected music and, on the political level, a containment of black mobility, a containment of the economic and social advances that might accrue to black artistic innovation. The domain of action and the ability to act suggested by *verb* is closed off by the hypostasis, paralysis, and arrest suggested by *noun*" (266). To imbricate Mackey's Barakan vocabulary with Deleuze's, perhaps we could say that the deterritorializing, performative quality of African American culture is consistently reterritorialized (nouned, as it were), and that this movement from verb to noun is precisely a strategy of cultural and political "containment." So it's not just that a verb is mistaken for a noun by a culture that doesn't know any better; rather, the movement from verb to noun names the strategic closing down of escape routes — Deleuzian "lines of flight" — from what Baraka calls the "vapidity of mainline American culture" (*Blues*, 182). Benny Goodman is not crowned the King of Swing by mistake; his coronation is precisely one of the many complex, site-specific bulwarks against the becoming-black of America.

Insofar as it traces just such a series of "from verb to noun" containments, Ishmael Reed's *Mumbo Jumbo* comprises a kind of companion piece to Baraka's analysis in *Blues People*. Leaving aside for the moment Reed and Baraka's well-known aesthetic and political differences,[4] they can at least provisionally be brought together through a consideration of "Jes Grew," Reed's name for the performative, deterritorializing quality of African American *repetition with a difference*. From the beginning of *Mumbo Jumbo*, the stakes of Jes Grew's containment within American culture are clear. As the Mayor of New Orleans puts it, "Don't you understand, if this Jes Grew becomes pandemic it will mean the end of Civilization As We Know It?" (4). The Mayor goes on to warn that "if Jes Grew is immune to the old remedies, the saving Virus in the blood of Europe, mankind is lost" (18). Reinscribing the Mayor's vocabulary of "pandemic" sickness and contagion (repeating it with a difference), Reed thematizes Jes Grew in terms of an anti-virus or "anti-plague" (see 6, 25, 33), one carried specifically by Africans and African Americans. He writes, "Jes Grew carriers came to America because of cotton" (16); once Jes Grew enters a host culture, "It is self-propagating and you can never tell when it will hit" (5). Jes Grew—like Baraka's blues tradition—is never a constative, a noun, or a concept; as a performative "anti-plague," it exists and is efficacious only in action, by an embodied, active *responding* to the "Virus" of American culture.

Just as, for example, the Dionysian names the effects of minoritarian becoming-other in a European tradition, Jes Grew names the singular deterritorializations carried out in and by African cultural traditions. However, although Jes Grew does name the specificity of the African tradition, at the same time it cannot serve as the hypostatic, transcendental soul or mystical oneness of black folks precisely because of what James Weldon Johnson called this performative, verbal, "indefinable quality" (*Mumbo Jumbo*, 211). As Henry Louis Gates argues, "Reed criticizes the Afro-American idealism of a transcendent black subject, integral and whole, self-sufficient, and plentiful" (218).

In fact, in a painful paradox, it is precisely the specific material history of African Americans' marginalization, rather than some naturally contestatory African American spirit, that makes possible the active responses and myriad sites of black culture. As Baraka contends, the African American's "conditional separation from the mainstream spared him" (*Blues*, 181); in fact, Baraka sees it as the project of bebop "to make that separation meaningful" (186), to "restore jazz, in some sense, to its original separateness" (181). The unique contribution of the beboppers was the fact that they "reinforced the social and historical alienation of the Negro in America, but in the Negro's terms" (219). Such an "alienation" or "separateness" is, then, a *repetition* of mainstream segregation, but with an important *difference:* this is a repetition that reinscribes the forced segregation of blacks to create a deterritorialization, a line of flight for African American culture.[5] As Mackey writes, "This confinement to a predetermined status (predetermined stasis), the keeping of black people 'in their place,' gives rise to the countering, contestatory tendencies" (266) that make up the history of black culture in America. It is, in other words, precisely these nominative or normative containment strategies that offer the specific conditions for their performative *repetition with a difference,* what Mackey calls the responding "movement from noun to verb" (266). So perhaps we could say that if this "movement from *noun to verb*"—if this Jes Grew or this anti-plague—"is" anything at all, it "is" what we might call a *becoming*-black (rather than a hypostatized *being*-black). As Baraka insists in "The Legacy of Malcolm X," even "the Black Man must aspire to Blackness" (167): even prized nouns or identity categories must become-verb: whites must become-white, Asians must become-Asian, Latinas become-Latina.

In other words, there is no "ontology" of difference—no guarantee of otherness or subversion, no easily identifiable sites of hegemonic or antihegemonic culture. Deleuze maintains that the hypostatizing attempt to guarantee otherness by making it into a noun has in fact been "disastrous for the entire philosophy of difference: assigning a distinctive concept of difference is confused with the inscription of difference within concepts in general—the determination of the concept of difference is confused with the inscription of difference" (*Difference*, 32). If we take bebop or Jes Grew for transhistorical nouns rather than active site-specific verbs of African American deterritorialization, we perform both a historical and an artistic *mis*take: historically, a radically context-bound process is mistaken for a transhistorical end; artistically, the deterritorialization of becoming ("the *inscription* of difference") is mistaken for the reterritorialization of being (the "*concept* of difference"). And, Mackey insists, this mistake has wide-ranging consequences for theorizing African American identity and agency: "The inequities the recent attention to cultural diversity is meant to redress are in part the outcome of confounding the social with the genetic, so we need to make it clear that when we speak of otherness we are not positing static, intrinsic attributes or characteristics" (265). Being-black is finally no guarantee of being outside the mainstream, posing a question to dominant racist codes, just as being-white or -Asian is certainly no guarantee of antiblack racism;[6] it is, rather, in *becoming* that deterritorialized lines of flight might appear.

And though it seems clear that in both Reed and Baraka the vibrancy of African American culture exists through this inscription of otherness rather than resting in bland concepts (in the performative *enactment* of *repetition with a difference* rather than some intrinsic definition of authentic blackness), there does remain in each writer a seemingly odd mandarinism concerning African American authenticity. Recall, for example, Reed's obsession with bokors and houngans,[7] or Baraka's tirades on the inauthenticity of cool jazz and hard bop, where he pits the college-boy musician against the authentic, blues-tradition bebopper.[8] Of course, just because one holds that distinctions obtain only in specific inscriptive contexts, it certainly doesn't follow that distinctions are impossible to draw: to say that difference is not a static concept doesn't mean that one can't tell a bokor from a houngan, or Dave Brubeck from John Coltrane. It does, however, mean that such "authenticity" claims have to be made on different grounds—or, more precisely, they must be made on the shifting nonground of difference. Authenticity will need to be measured, it seems, not by prescriptive *grounds* of being, but rather by inscriptive *forces* of becoming.

But insofar as our dominant conceptual codes are not well set up to handle such a (non)concept, this is easier said than done. All too often, in a zeal to make claims about the contestatory nature of African American culture, we leave behind some of the complexities of the issues at hand. This has been especially noticeable, for example, in the so-called gangsta rap debate, where everyone from academic critics to talk-radio hosts has been quick to take sides: either gangsta rap is an authentic expression and extension of African American cultural traditions, or it's a commercial ploy that reinforces for white suburbanites all the most vicious stereotypes surrounding black culture. This debate poses an all too familiar either/or, and postmodernism has, if nothing else, made critics suspicious of the either/or: why either/or and not both/and, as they say?

Well, from the point of view of Baraka or Reed, the supposed postmodernist both/and solution to the either/or dilemma is actually more dangerous than the dilemma itself. All too often, this both/and names a moment of complete assimilation, the erasure of African American otherness altogether. If gangsta rap is *both* an authentic expression of contemporary black experience *and* a race-baiting sales ploy, this conveniently closes down a complex web of debate by totalizing and smoothing over all the categories involved: the both/and solution presupposes that we know enough about the categories under consideration—gangsta rap, African American experience, the music industry, white suburban youth—merely to conflate them or create a singular relation among them. But it seems that if, following Baraka and Reed along a Deleuzian line of flight, we are to take account of a culture of becoming-black, we cannot merely go from the dialectical separation of the either/or to the dialectical assimilation of the both/and; rather, we need a critical vocabulary to open the movement of becoming, to enact the *specificity* of the *difference* in *repetition with a difference.* To describe this open-ended movement of transformation, then, we need a force that goes not from either/or to both/and, but, as Deleuze and Guattari put it, from either/or to either or or or or or or or or or . . . ; not from difference to assimilation, but from difference to difference to difference.[9]

Becoming-Bird

Charlie "Bird" Parker has remained a towering figure in African American cultural history, and not surprisingly he continues to play a singular role in both Baraka and Reed: especially when the game turns to "authenticity," it seems that Bird always holds a trump card. For example, in *Mumbo Jumbo* "Charlie Parker, the houngan" (16), holds one of the privileged places in the Jes Grew pantheon: "Jes Grew, the Something or Other that led Charlie Parker to scale the Everests of the Chord. Riff fly skid dip soar and gave his Alto Godspeed" (211). And critics commenting on *Mumbo Jumbo* have likewise made much of Bird's influence on Reed's form and content. As Henry Louis Gates writes, for example, the best "formal metaphor for Reed's mode of writing is perhaps the bebop mode of jazz, as exemplified in that great reedist, Charlie Parker" (233). Joe Weixlmann concurs, offering Bird as one of Reed's most powerful metonyms: "Ultimately Jes Grew is the music of Charlie Parker, the 'second line' in a New Orleans funeral procession, the African American literary tradition—African American culture itself" (62).

Likewise, in *Blues People*'s celebration of '40s bebop as the authentic continuation of a polyrhythmic blues tradition, it is Bird—his "endless changing of direction, stops and starts" (194)—that Baraka hears most clearly. He asserts, "the 'harshness' and 'asymmetry' of bebop was much closer to the traditional Afro-American concept of music than most of its detractors ever stopped to realize" (210-19). And with surprisingly few exceptions (most notably, of course, Coltrane), Baraka reads the cool, progressive and hard-bop jazz of the mid- to late '50s as a blockage and containment of that deterritorializing bebopping moment—just as, for example, both he and Reed trace swing's assimilation as a blockage of the blues tradition's forces of becoming.[10]

In following these "from verb to noun" appropriations of the blues tradition in both the '30s and the '50s, Baraka's *Blues People* constructs a kind of genealogy of assimilation or containment. In both periods, he argues, jazz was directed away from the improvisatory anarchy of small groups by the standardizing of arrangement, a territorializing molded and made concrete by bourgeois control over performance venues, radio, and recording companies; and both the big white-led swing bands of the '30s and the interracial hard boppers and cool cats of the '50s are representative of this movement toward overarranged, notational jazz. He writes, for example, that hard bop is merely "*a style*, behind which there is no serious commitment to expression or emotional profundity" (*Blues*, 218). And such a hollow cathection onto "style," devoid of Bird's bebopping improvisatory force, further opens the door for the market-friendly platitudes of "cool" or "progressive" jazz: repetitions, Baraka might say, *without* a difference. The bebop of the 1940s remains jazz's most important moment, and "Parker was the soul and fire of the bebop era" (*Black Music*, 38).

However, the crucial importance of Bird within Baraka's cultural history doesn't come completely into focus until Baraka takes up the rejuvenation of jazz happening around him as he finishes *Blues People* in 1963. In the final pages, Baraka argues that musicians like Ornette Coleman and Cecil Taylor are helping to "restore to jazz its valid separation from, and anarchic disregard of, Western popular forms. They have used the music of the forties with its jagged, exciting rhythms as an initial reference and have restored the hegemony of blues as the most important basic form in Afro-American music. *They have also restored improvisation to its traditional role of invaluable significance, again removing jazz from the hands of the less than gifted arranger and the fashionable diluter*" (225; my italics). Here, I think, it becomes clear how Bird functions to help Baraka articulate a kind of paradoxical African American authenticity: it is the "invaluable significance" of *performative improvisation*—the enactment of a becoming-difference—that makes the blues tradition unique. As Baraka argues in *Black Music*, when Ornette Coleman "reestablishes the absolute hegemony of improvisation in jazz" (105), he thereby reinvigorates the link to bebop and the blues tradition. Improvisation, it seems, is the *difference* in *repetition with a difference*; and Bird, along with Louis Armstrong, was jazz's greatest improvisor.[11]

In the blues tradition, of course, *repetition with a difference* is linked to the structure of call and response,[12] and it is precisely in this urgency of performative *response* that one could, following Baraka, locate Bird as *the* exemplary figure within an "authentic" African American tradition of site-specific deterritorialization. Bird's improvisational performative reinscriptions stand in sharp contrast to the universalizing pretensions of the "less than gifted arranger and the fashionable diluter." As Henry Louis Gates notes, "Repetition of a form and then inversion of the same through a process of variation is central to jazz" (104), and it is through an informed weighing of or responding to the specific improvisatory "variation"—the difference—that Baraka suggests one could begin to broach a discourse of nonessentializing

African American "authenticity." When, for example, Baraka insists
that Coleman's "extemporaneous statements cannot be reproduced
by any notation" (Blues, 225), he invokes Bird's legendary improvisatory skills and the deterritorializing challenge they pose to the canons
of American music.[13] As Miles Davis recalls, summing up Parker's
singular place in the African American canon, "Bird was a great improvisor . . . His concept was 'fuck what's written down' . . . just the
opposite of the Western concept of notated music" (in Johnson, 2).

Perhaps, though, we need to hesitate here, insofar as we seem
to have arrived—or to be back—at a potentially pernicious binary
either/or: Bird's improvisations are "just the opposite of the Western
concept of notated music." As noted above, if an African American tradition is to have a specificity and verb-al quality, it cannot
be thematized as "just the opposite" of so-called mainstream American culture. If Bird's improvisations are read as "just the opposite"
of notational music, a potentially dangerous discourse about black
primitivity is surreptitiously reopened, a discourse that would thematize Bird's supposed musical illiteracy as the source and condition of
his (and, by synecdoche, African American culture's) unmediated in-
spirational genius.[14] In addition, both Reed and Baraka seem to agree
that African American cultural production cannot merely be read
as a parodic inversion. In fact, as Hegel (certainly no friend to an
African tradition)[15] demonstrates, it is precisely through dialectical
inversion that transgression is assimilated: verbs are translated into
nouns; forceful performative interventions are translated into ironic
hypostatized contemplations.[16]

The majority of critical literature on jazz continues to treat improvisation as ironic or parodic doubling. For example, Ingrid Monson's
essay, "Doubleness and Jazz Improvisation: Irony, Parody, and Ethnomusicology," argues that the great jazz improvisors "employ musical
reference in one form or another to communicate the ironic play of
difference" (303). There is a "doubleness, irony conveyed in jazz improvisation" (310), and Monson offers "John Coltrane's transformation
of Rodgers and Hammerstein's 'My Favorite Things'" as "the first example of irony" (292) to be discussed in her essay. She goes on to argue
that "jazz listeners generally view the transformations of [such] Broad-
way tunes as considerably 'superior' to the original material" because,
in their improvisational jazz incarnations, "these tunes are made to
swing by the addition of jazz grooves" (293).

To illustrate the problem with reading jazz improvisation as subjective irony, one need only compare Monson's rather contemplative vision of hipsters consuming Coltrane's improvisatory "grooves" to Baraka's decidedly un-ironic reading of Coltrane's interventions: "Coltrane seeks with each new onslaught to completely destroy the popular song" (*Black Music*, 105). As William J. Harris notes, this non-ironic reading of Coltrane is crucial for understanding Baraka's own multiple, nonformulaic writing practices: "Baraka's transformations are not always neatly expressed in terms of symmetrical inversions or formal assassinations; rather (once again like jazz) his creative destructions take many forms: rejection, extremism/completion, violence, dismemberment, creative anger, and revolution" (18). And, at the risk of autobiography, it seems to me that the experience of listening to the improvisations of Bird or Coltrane (or the experience of responding to Baraka's poetry) doesn't lend itself very well to a binary vocabulary of ironic reversal: the technical virtuosity and wide-ranging specificity of their improvisations isn't "just the opposite" or just a parody of anything. Bird's and Coltrane's interventions may be inhabiting certain forms of Western notational music, but their music neither merely reproduces nor merely opposes some chimeric Western tradition; as Harris insists, such improvisations go well beyond an inverted binarism to "take many forms: rejection, extremism/completion, violence, dismemberment, creative anger, and revolution."

This, perhaps, is where one could pose a question to Henry Louis Gates, whose theory of African American "signifyin(g)" seems to depend on a repetition that *reverses* a prior binary opposition. As he explains, the Signifying Monkey "is our trope for repetition and revision, indeed our trope of chiasmus, repeating and reversing simultaneously" (52). He later clarifies, "the Monkey's process of Signifyin(g) turns upon *repetition and difference, or repetition and reversal*" (63; my italics). It seems to me that this ironic sense of chiasmic reversal in the end protects the harmonious binary oppositions that it wishes to break down. To put it in Deleuzian terms, a repetition as "reversal" is not necessarily a repetition that introduces "difference." Deleuze's vocabulary of deterritorializing is precisely an attempt to chart a line of flight from the binary oppositions that have been bequeathed to us by a very suspicious tradition. That being the case, however, how do we understand performative improvisatory interventions and their singular place in the African American cultural canon? If they're not ironic or chiasmic reversals, then what exactly are they?

To try to get a handle on a vocabulary for describing or enact-

ing such improvisations, I'd like to return to Deleuze and Guattari's
deterritorialization. As I argue above, reterritorialization and deterritorialization do not exist in some sort of binary or dialectical struggle,
each playing ironically off the other. Rather, as Deleuze and Guattari
insist, "each code is in a perpetual state of transcoding or transduc-
tion" (*Thousand*, 313). The "white" mainstream, in other words, is
no more a *singular* entity than the "black" counterculture. Similarly,
given this mutual deterritorialization, there can be no simple "representation" or "imitation" because those concepts presuppose the
self-evidence of the so-called original and the concomitant fallen,
secondary status of the copy.[17] For Deleuze and Guattari, when we
understand artistic endeavor in terms of representation or imitation
(even if we understand it in terms of ironic reversal), we've once again
traded mere concepts for the forces of becoming that are traced so
well in art. They write: "Suppose a painter 'represents' a bird; *this is
in fact a becoming-bird that can occur only to the extent that the bird
itself is in the process of becoming something else*, a pure line and
pure color. Thus imitation self-destructs, since the imitator unknow-
ingly enters into a becoming that conjugates with the unknowing
becoming of that which he or she imitates. . . . Becoming is never
[simply] imitating. . . . One does not imitate; one constitutes a block of
becoming" (305; my italics). Here we again confront the circuits of becoming that Baraka and Reed ask us to consider—the forces that they
in fact perform in their own works. When Baraka and Reed "imitate"
or "represent" Bird as an exemplary figure in African American culture, they enact and thematize what Deleuze and Guattari call here a
"becoming-bird." For Deleuze and Guattari's artist, painting a bird is
actually a confrontation with the processes of becoming to which the
artist and bird are both subject: the painter comprises a "becoming-
bird," but the bird also moves along a line of flight, becoming "pure
line and pure color." There is, in other words, a simultaneous series of
deterritorializations: each term (representer, represented, conditions
of representation, etc.) becomes-other in the artistic inscription.

Likewise, what we might call the "becoming-*Bird*" in Reed's or
Baraka's discourse is precisely *not* an attempt to capture, imitate, or
ironize some quality in the man Charlie Parker (and in turn, Bird is
not merely attempting to imitate or ironize Western forms in his performative improvisations). Rather, what one iterates in becoming-bird
(or in becoming-Bird) is becoming itself: an active response, joining
"a block of becoming." Baraka calls this the "'going out' quality of

African-American culture" ("Blues Aesthetic" 104), where the "highest thought is a doing, a being, not an abstraction" (107).

And this brings us back to Deleuze and Guattari's odd claim that even blacks must become-black. As they go on to clarify, "if blacks must become-black, it is because only a minority is capable of serving as the active medium of becoming, but under such conditions that it ceases to be a definable aggregate in relation to the majority" (*Thousand*, 291). If indeed we all must become-other, this becoming-other presupposes remaining in a minority status—in a state other than "whole." Becoming-minority is, in other words, a status that "ceases to be a definable aggregate in relation to the majority" because the majority is itself deterritorialized by the minority's *repetition with a difference*.[18] As Baraka writes about the specificity of African American cultures, "Without the dissent, the struggle, the *outside of the inside*, the aesthetic is neither *genuinely* Black nor Blue" ("Blues Aesthetic," 109; my italics). The deterritorialization performed by the "Black" aesthetic or the "Blue[s]" tradition deploys directional, conflicted vectors of becoming—the forceful interruptive movement of "the outside of the inside," the minority's alteration of the majority. Both blackness *and* whiteness are inexorably transformed by the performative movements of becoming-black.

All that having been said, however, we still seem to find ourselves within a familiarly binary vocabulary: even if it is not exactly the opposite of majority reterritorialization, minority deterritorialization seems clearly to be the privileged, good term of active becoming, with the static weight of some chimeric "mainstream" having been left in the dust. So-called whites, it might seem, must simply abandon their whiteness and become-black. But, if this is indeed the case, what get iterated in deterritorialization are the stale platitudes of the twentieth-century white avant-garde, sentiments increasingly translatable into late capital's orientalizing lingo of advertising: calling for site-specific improvisation—deterritorializing lines of flight—seems merely a call to "make it new."

If, for example, we use the distinction between harmonious sound and dissonant noise to outline a definition of music, and go on to celebrate a "new" or "noisy" music as unproblematically deterritorializing, we've again made the mistake of supposing that we know what all those terms mean—that they are binary terms of being rather than dynamic terms of becoming. As Deleuze and Guattari insist, the "difference between noise and sound is definitely not a basis for a definition of music. . . . Rather, it is the *labor of the refrain:* Does it remain territorial and territorializing, or is it carried away in a moving block that draws a transversal across all coordinates. . . . Music is precisely the adventure of the refrain" (*Thousand,* 302).[19] For Deleuze and Guattari, newness or noise or irony or antiassimilationism (or whatever) is not in itself deterritorializing within the field of music. The territorializing or deterritorializing qualities within a piece of music would each time have to be located in terms of the *effects* of a specific, hazardous musical event, in what they call "the adventure of the refrain." The senses of "noise" and "music," as well as the senses of "deterritorializing" and "reterritorializing," are specific to any particular "refrain"— to any performance or repetition—and are not actually available to be celebrated or anticipated before the event of their inscription. Variously transgressive and reappropriative elements necessarily exist side by side in any cultural production; as Deleuze and Guattari contend, "in each case we must simultaneously consider factors of territoriality, deterritorialization, and reterritorialization" (303).

It is crucial to recall within such a consideration that deterritorializing in Deleuze and Guattari does not name a liberation or teleological forward-moving progress. They write in *What Is Philosophy?*, for example, that "A stick is . . . a deterritorialized branch" (67). Of course, a stick is no more or less "free," no "better" or "worse," than a branch; it's simply different from a branch, no longer intimately tied to arboretic systems of becoming that are branchlike. There may be compelling ways of talking about a stick as more or less "liberated" than a branch, but this finally is not the interesting or operative question for Deleuze and Guattari, just as an avant-garde notion of progressive subjective freedom is not at stake in their notion of deterritorialization. Rather, the singular weighing of becoming-different in the event is paramount.[20]

Of course, this would seem to create any number of problems for harnessing Deleuze and Guattari's deterritorialization in an analysis of black culture, where the question of freedom is central. Baraka argues, for example, that there "cannot be an authentic reflection of the main thrust of the African-American aesthetic without dealing with the Question of Freedom" ("Blues Aesthetic," 109). Note, however, that for Baraka the crucial marker of an "authentic" "African-American aesthetic" is the performative "*Question* of Freedom," not the nominative *answer* of freedom. As Cecil Taylor notes, perhaps in both music and politics, "it is not a question of 'freedom' as opposed to 'nonfreedom,' but rather of recognizing different ideas and expressions of order" (in Hartman, 70).

In other words, although there certainly is a kind of liberatory dialectic operative in Baraka's work, it is not a Eurocentric Hegelian dialectic of subjective freedom's progress.[21] Rather, Baraka repeats dialectic with a difference. For example, when he writes of "the change from one quality or element to another. The dialectic of life itself" ("Blues Aesthetic," 106), Baraka goes on clearly to tie his dialectic to Lenin's reading of Marx. But Baraka here argues for a *different* dialectic; he argues in fact for what we might call the "Black Panther dialectic" of becoming that Deleuze and Guattari allude to in our epigraph. Compare, for example, Baraka's critique of dialectics in his preface to *The LeRoi Jones/Amiri Baraka Reader:* "We go from step 1 to step 2 and the crushed breath away from the 'given' remains unknown swallowed by its profile as what makes distance. But there is real life between 1 and 2. There is the life of the speed, the time it takes, the life there in, in the middle of, the revelation, like perception, rationale and use. To go from any where to any there" (xi). Here, the important moment of dialectics for Baraka is the moment or movement of transformation: what's important is not the "distance" from the "'given'" seemingly made possible by the hypostatizing movement "from step 1 to step 2," but rather the "speed," the "middle," the "life" that is necessary "To go from any where to any there." It's actually *movement* (becoming) that makes *stasis* (being) possible, not the other way around: "As Fred [Hampton] said, 'No progress without struggle'" ("Blues Aesthetic," 106), and that "struggle"—the "Question of Freedom"—is an ongoing, necessarily open-ended and transformative one, not merely the work of the negative which shows freedom always to be lacking. Rather, this work of freedom is the specificity of African American culture's *repetition with a difference*, what Baraka calls in a 1966 essay "The Changing Same."

Although I'm not arguing that deterritorialization in Deleuze and Guattari is somehow equivalent to Baraka's ongoing "Question of Freedom" or Reed's Jes Grew, considered together they do create certain productive relations, especially insofar as Deleuze and Guattari are willing, perhaps more than other poststructuralists, to hazard a positive use of the word or concept "freedom."[22] They write, for example, "free the line, free the diagonal: every musician or painter has this intention" (*Thousand*, 295). But how are we to understand such a deterritorialized freedom? Isn't it, despite their protestations, just a

disguised Hegelian dialectic or a progressing avant-garde? To antici-
pate an answer, Deleuze and Guattari will argue that "freedom" can't
be thematized through the labor of the individual subject, or the labor
of the Hegelian negative; rather, they argue that it is the odd "labor of
the refrain" that parses out deterritorialization, the "movement from
noun to verb."

Refraining

In *A Thousand Plateaus*, Deleuze and Guattari thematize the labors
of the refrain through their narrative of a small boy returning home
from a walk by himself. The refrain—a phrase or verse repeated
at intervals throughout a song—is deployed differently in the three
movements they examine: on the boy's way home, at his home, and
on the next trip out. On the way home, the refrain comes into play as
a stable point of familiarity: the boy humming to himself to ward off
feelings of impending danger. Deleuze and Guattari expand: "lost, he
takes shelter, or orients himself with his little song as best he can. . . .
[The refrain] jumps from chaos to the beginnings of order in chaos and
is in danger of breaking apart at any moment" (311). When the boy arrives safely at home, the repetition of the refrain performs a different
kind of work: "Now we are at home. . . . But now the components are
used for organizing a space, not for the momentary determination of a
center. The forces of chaos are kept outside as much as possible. . . . A
mistake in speed, rhythm, or harmony would be catastrophic because
it would bring back the forces of chaos" (311). Unlike the refrain's
work on the trip home, at home its labor is no longer "the momentary determination of a center." Rather, at home the refrain works to
effect the ambient rhythm of a stable holistic environment, a rhythm
that nonetheless remains threatened by the inherent instability of the
refrain's effect; the refrain remains haunted, in other words, by the necessity of its repetition: it must be repeated to produce its stabilizing
effects, but in the repetition there is always the specter or possibility
of producing a different effect. Because it is necessary to repeat the
refrain to create interiorizing effects, the refrain necessarily remains
threatened by the interruption of the outside or difference that makes
the inside possible.

But then there is an other moment. From within the stable pace of
the home refrain's closed circle of repetitions, an other event intrudes:

the boy wishes to venture out again. "Finally, one opens the circle a crack, opens it all the way, lets someone in, calls someone, or else goes out oneself. . . . *One launches forth, hazards an improvisation. But to improvise is to join with the World, or meld with it.* One ventures from home on the thread of a tune" (*Thousand*, 311; my italics). Finally, perhaps, the vocabularies of Deleuze and Guattari and Baraka and Reed come together here, where deterritorialization meets improvisation at the labor of the refrain. The refrain deploys repetition, the seemingly secure baseline (or bass line) of song. However, the refrain's repetitions function not according to stable con*cepts*, but in active response to unstable con*texts*: on the trip home, at home, and venturing from home. In each of these moments or movements the refrain does different work: sometimes momentarily reterritorializing a hostile landscape, sometimes mapping out a stable territory, sometimes marking a movement of deterritorialization toward the outside.

So, the point is not that there are inherently deterritorializing refrains or genres; in keeping with the performative emphasis of the refrain, it would be futile to say, for example, that all jazz is or isn't deterritorializing. Deterritorializing doesn't come in universalizing nouns; it is only available, so to speak, in site-specific verbs. Due to the necessity of repetition and response highlighted in the moments of the refrain, it wouldn't even make much sense to say that all movements in any particular tune are deterritorializing. For example, Bird has to lay down a particular set of riffs to set up the potentially deterritorializing movements of improvisation: the refrain first becomes a reterritorialization, a kind of home from which the improvisor repeats with a difference. As Deleuze and Guattari maintain, "a musician requires a *first type* of refrain, a territorial or assemblage refrain, in order to transform it from within, deterritorialize it, producing a refrain of the *second type* as the final end of music: the cosmic refrain of a sound machine" (*Thousand*, 349).

(Re)Territorializing, then, is not in itself a "bad" or negative thing; nor is it merely a regrettably necessary moment in the inexorable evolution of deterritorializing. The movements Deleuze and Guattari examine

> are not three successive movements in an evolution. They are three aspects of a single thing, the Refrain. . . . Sometimes chaos is an immense black hole in which one endeavors to fix a fragile point as a center. Sometimes one organizes around that point a

calm and stable "pace" (rather than a form): the black hole has be-come a home. Sometimes one grafts onto that pace a breakaway from the black hole. . . . And all three at once. Forces of chaos, terrestrial forces, cosmic forces: all of these confront each other and converge in the territorial refrain. (*Thousand*, 312)

So, in the conflicted, multiple "territorial refrain" that is, say, Bird's "Ornithology," there are necessarily many moments: there are frag-ile centers, calm paces, and breakaways; but this does not mean that "Ornithology" is three tunes, or that because it begins and ends on a point of relative stability, "Ornithology" isn't deterritorializing— though those points of relative stability don't necessarily mean that it's merely reterritorializing either. "Ornithology" itself constitutes a block of becoming, with us becoming Bird as we listen, and Bird becoming sound, and sound becoming flight, and flight becoming . . .

There is no simple stability or simple instability in the refrain: there are forces of becoming. And jazz improvisation seems a privileged site to explore those becomings, to venture out on the wings of a tune, to meld with the movements that are the world.[23] As Baraka writes in *Black Music*, "the content of The New Music, or The New Black Music, is toward change. It is change. It wants to change forms. From physical to physical (social to social) or from physical to mental, or from physical-mental to spiritual" (199). For Baraka, there are *changes* to and from all sorts of forms; there are becomings-other.[24]

In other words, what I've been calling becoming-black names a singularity of deterritorializing sites and movements, the transforma-tive African American tradition that Baraka and Reed both rightly insist upon and extend. As Reed wrote on the original book jacket for *Mumbo Jumbo*, "The big lie concerning Afro-American culture is that it lacks a tradition."[25] But this tradition itself is not simply or wholly privileged over other becoming-sites and -movements in American culture. It is, after all, precisely this responsive, metonymic linking of sites and territories—an openness to the other and the future—that effects the dynamism of becoming-black, and one can't simply appre-hend or arrest the molecular improvisatory flows that are becoming. Rather, one ventures from home on the thread of a tune.

On the surface, perhaps this deterritorializing movement of becoming-black seems like a hopelessly aestheticized project, an effete appreciation or formalization of otherness rather than a kind of revolutionary alterity politics. In fact, it is precisely around the question of the politics of transformation that the *disputes* between

Reed and Baraka—rather than the similarities—need to be taken into account. For Baraka, Reed is a bourgeois apologist, too concerned with aesthetic formalism and political individualism, with content-less transformation in the abstract. Reed insists that he's "not into black-confrontation politics" (*Shrovetide*, 220), but for Baraka this is already a confrontational politics: "I think Ishmael Reed is very political," Baraka says in a 1980 interview, "but it's just a reactionary politics" ("Interview," 178). Specifically, Baraka takes Reed to task for a certain kind of ethereal formalism that he associates with the re-actionary stances of the new critics: "The emphasis, necessarily, was on technique, on *how* something was said, not *what* was being said. The bourgeoisie must always emphasize formalism, form over con-tent, because if people check out what's being said they will not give too much of a shit how; or they will at least reject what and try to learn from how. . . . [O]ur works [must] be aesthetically powerful and politically revolutionary. . . . We cannot be one-sided, though it must be obvious that *content is principal!* What you are *saying*" ("Afro-American," 6, 12). According to Baraka, overemphasis on aesthetic transformation misses or neglects social specificities. Celebrating the formal individualist power of mere saying—*how* something is said—runs the risk of slighting the importance of *what* you are saying (and, he might add, *where* you are saying it from). Exclusive emphasis on form blurs the importance of content. For Reed, on the other hand, Baraka's kind of political scripting is precisely the problem with those "sullen, humorless critics of the Black Aesthetic movement" who have "forgotten that the mainstream aspiration of Afro-America is for more freedom, and not slavery—including freedom of artistic expression" (*Shrovetide*, 257). According to Reed, an animated, desiring "artistic expression" cannot simply be reduced to a reified, political "content" or message: *how* cannot simply be reduced or subordinated to *what*. In fact, when critics like Baraka present a call for such a reification, for Reed they simply conjure a new "slavery" of the politically correct.

Reed, then, might be said to turn the dialectical tables on Baraka: Reed accuses Marxian critics of fetishizing content over form. How-ever, I suggest that Baraka doesn't so much simply privilege content over form ("We cannot be one-sided," he insists), but rather questions what I'd call a fetishizing of defetishization, a territorializing of de-territorialization. In other words, it is tempting to fetishize artistic creation—the "saying"—as itself transgressive or transformative, but in the process this position runs the risk of ignoring "*What* you are *saying*": sure, one could admit, misogyny and racism are self-defeating or self-overcoming, but is that finally an adequate response to them? Do certain cultural texts need to be attended to differently because of *what* they say?

Hardly a simple *declaration* of approved content, I take Baraka to be posing a question to any poetics where the principal force is deployed as a merely contentless process of becoming, speaking, or performance. Such a "formal" emphasis will, in Baraka's view, inexorably romanticize the resistance of the individual's saying, and de-emphasize the concrete response that is called for by what is said. As I argue above, this risk haunts any deployment of the notion of deterritorializing. There is no liberatory deterritorializing—no freedom or transformation—per se; there are only specific, more or less forceful imbrications of form and content that can respond to—disrupt and reinscribe—existing norms. Deterritorialization, if it happens, always happens in a specific context, in response to a specific content. That having been said, however, it seems to me that *Mumbo Jumbo*'s insistence on the social force of African American traditions—and the politics of containment directed at these traditions—makes it difficult to reduce Reed's text to a simple formalistic affirmation of the individual artist's transformative power.[26] As Reed points out in *Mumbo Jumbo*, both Jung and Freud saw and were horrified by the collective effects of becoming-black in American culture: "Europeans living in America have undergone a transformation. Jung calls this process 'going Black'" (209). Compared to the effects of this becoming-black, white avant-garde interventions into American culture—think of the nostalgic modernism that led to the expatriation of Pound or Eliot—pale in their social impact, in terms of what their productions ask or have forced American culture to *do* or *become*. When NPR informs us today that jazz is "America's classical music" and white high school kids in Indiana get beat up by their peers for "dressing black" while young black men are being incarcerated in record numbers, another round of complex calls and responses are set in motion. And it is perhaps best to understand *Mumbo Jumbo*'s extensive bibliography as a kind of tool kit for enabling such response, as a kind of Hoodoo instruction manual to cash out the social content of Reed's artistic form.

Indeed, despite their differences, both Baraka's and Reed's texts reveal that African American life and cultural politics become imbricated precisely around these questions of *specific* performative or improvisatory reinscriptions. Neither Jes Grew nor the blues tradition is *simply* concerned with formalist aesthetics or philosophy; rather, both are committed to the *necessity* of change and alterity in American political life. Recall Baraka's subtitle to "The 'Blues Aesthetic' and the 'Black Aesthetic' ": "Aesthetics as the Continuing Political History of a Culture." As he insists in this essay, talk of aesthetics "is useful only if it is not depoliticization of reference," if we remain careful not to "disconnect the historical continuum of the Blues from its national and international source" (101) in African and African American cultures. Recall in the same vein, pace Baraka, that Jes Grew's finding its text in *Mumbo Jumbo* is important precisely so that African American traditions *aren't* mistaken for mere aesthetic trifling: "Jes Grew needed its words to tell its carriers what it was up to. Jes Grew was an influence which sought its text. . . . If it could not find its Text then it would be mistaken for entertainment" (211). Reed's *Mumbo Jumbo*, in some sense, is that interventionary text, insofar as it calls not for more textuality, but gestures beyond reading or appreciation to the necessity of interventionary *response*. It all boils down to the interventionary force of specific transformations: in becoming-black, an ironic or aesthetic textuality gives way to interventionary *production*, to the production of concrete *effects*. As Baraka writes in "Black Art":

> Poems are bullshit unless they are
> teeth or trees or lemons piled
> on a step. Or black ladies dying
> of men leaving nickel hearts
> beating them down. Fuck poems (*Reader*, 219)

In the end, the vectors of becoming-other that we call the blues tradition or Jes Grew are two of the most productive sites of irreversible social transformation that we have in and against the American grain. Thought together as *both* an aesthetics and a politics, perhaps one could say that the becoming-black of American culture—through Jes Grew or the blues tradition—enacts a kind of dual *jamming* of the machinery: becoming-black jams this machinery by *disrupting* it, and likewise jams this machinery by *riffing on* it, reinscribing the language elsewhere, opening it to its others. Both of these moments are irreducibly "aesthetic" *and* "political," the aesthetic become-political through the performative deterritorialization that is African American culture's *repetition with a difference*: "And so struggle, chance, struggle, unity, change, movement and more of, the movement, the motion" (Baraka, "Preface," xii).

7 · *White Male Anger: Failure, Resentment, and*
Performative Political Theory

> Those who link desire to lack, the long column of crooners of castration,
> clearly indicate a long resentment, like an interminable bad conscience.
> Is this to misunderstand the misery of those who really do
> lack something? —Gilles Deleuze, "Psychoanalysis and Desire"

As I noted in the introduction and in chapter 4, the ethical claims
made by a performative politics of identity are usually claims concerning the subjective agencies opened up by the *failure* of interpellating
social norms. Insofar as identity is always constructed or performed,
social norms both provide a script for "proper" subjectivity and simultaneously offer points of resistance: one is compelled to act in accord
with the norm's imperatives; but because one must always repeat the
performance of one's subjectivity, the possibility of proceeding otherwise always haunts so-called normative subjectivity.

Within a performative theory of subjectivity, the norms of interpellative subjectivity *produce* certain subjects and thereby *exclude*
others; the reproduction of compulsory heterosexuality, for example,

necessarily abjects gay, lesbian, and bisexual possibilities. However, social norms don't found subjects in lockstep ways. Due to this double movement of producing/excluding, norms work *both* to uphold normative subject positions *and* to offer possibilities for subverting the very categories of normativity itself. The subject is never completely sutured to normative imperatives, and in this way the terrors of the social norm—its demands for totalization—are simultaneously the tools of its undoing: the normativity that is the heterosexual family, for example, both excludes "deviant" subjectivities and serves as an engine for producing them.

Concomitantly, proponents have argued that the politics of performative identity is necessarily open-ended and ethical because "I" am nothing other than this failed cultural structure, and hence I must constantly identify (myself) with and through a series of alterities and shifting cultural subject positions. I must perform my identity, and, as Ernesto Laclau writes, thereby "I am *condemned* to be free, not because I have no structural identity as the existentialists assert, but [rather] because I have a *failed* structural identity. This means that the subject is partially self-determined. However, as this self-determination is not the expression of what the subject *already* is but the result of its lack of being instead, self-determination can only proceed through processes of *identification*" (*New*, 44). Because my identity is structurally "failed," I must constantly renegotiate it in and through social engagement with others. In a theorized identity politics of lack like Laclau's, then, my freedom or agency exists *not* as the product of a transcendental absence that I must bravely or resolutely fill with my authentic actions, but rather through a hesitating negotiation among necessarily incomplete hegemonic subjective identity positions, *performative* subject positions of identification or disidentification among founding (but incomplete) cultural norms. Within such a performative identity politics, as Judith Butler contends, "loss [both] inaugurates the subject and threatens it with dissolution" (*Psychic*, 23).[1]

Certainly, this thematization of subject construction—production/exclusion, failure, and performative reinscription—does a tremendous amount of work in theorizing a politics of identity; it focuses our attention on the alterity or "etc." that, as Butler points out, inevitably keeps open the list of subaltern identity positions: race, class, gender, sexual orientation, etc. The inability to suture or close the gap between the subaltern and the norm—the "etc." or failed

totalization that both founds the subject and keeps the subject open—
entices us finally to read this *failure* of totalization as the specifically
ethical upshot of a performative theory of subjection or identity.

Among the latest groups to add its name to the "etc." of subaltern
performative identity positions is the white heterosexual male. White
men are *angry* these days, and this chapter will try to mobilize and
focus some of the interventions that I've been performing throughout this book in a diagnosis of a particular performative political
subject, the North American "white angry male" (hereafter, WAM).
More specifically, I'm interested in doing a performative reading that
is *not* driven primarily by a notion of ethical performativity revolv-
ing around *lack* or *failure*. My interest in doing so is compelled not
so much by a perverse desire to extend the critique of lack that I've
been making throughout in this book; rather, as Robin D. G. Kelley
points out, it seems that we need to revisit an identity politics of lack
or performative failure precisely because "it has also become a noose
around the necks of oppressed people, as in the case of white racism or
certain variants of black nationalism" (85). At this point in its history,
identity politics offers solace to virtually any subject position, as long
as it claims to be a minority oppressed by the weighty and influential
norm, as long as the norm has *failed* a given subject position. For example, Tom Metzger, leader of the White Aryan Resistance and former
Grand Dragon of the California Knights of the KKK, has argued that he
and his WAM buddies are the real political victims of recent years: "we
see ourselves, if you'll pardon the expression, as the new niggers" (Savran 127). Metzger's predecessor at the California Knights of the KKK,
failed Louisiana gubernatorial candidate David Duke, left the Klan to
form the National Association for the Advancement of White People
(NAAWP), a "white civil rights organization" (in Ross, 179) dedicated to
redressing the wrongs perpetrated on white people everywhere.

And it's not merely the lunatic fringe of white American society
making such claims of victimage or exclusion from the norm. In the
name of reverse racism, the "mainstream" WAMs of California and
Texas have effectively repealed affirmative action in higher educa-
tion. At Penn State, the student government has recently recognized
the group STRAIGHT, an identity-based lobby for "underrepresented"
heterosexual interests in the queer utopia that is rural Pennsylvania.
The U.S. State Department, full to the gills with white men, recently
commissioned the "Report on U.S. Policies to Eliminate Christian
Persecution," a study on the worldwide suppression of Christianity as
a "minority" religion.[2] Indeed, from the Promise Keepers to the Men's

Movement, from the Wise Use Anti-Environmentalism movement to the recent academic craze for "whiteness studies," various WAMS have found a series of big-time ways to cash in on an identity politics of failure, ushering in what Cindy Patton describes as a "discursive convergence of left and right, or at least, their arrival on the same turf" (234).

At first, this may seem a bit strange, insofar as identity politics has been first and foremost a movement dedicated to a critical interrogation of the (white, straight, male) norm—its exclusion of alterity—and a concomitant affirmation of minority experience. However, as George Yúdice points out, claims of victimage by the WAM and his kin are inevitable because under a politics driven by identity, "the ultimate legitimizing move is the claim to oppression. . . . Even a white male identity politics makes a claim upon it" (281). It may have taken the WAM a while to figure out how to cash in on what David Gates calls "the moral clout that comes with victimhood" (49), but tune in any right-wing radio talk show, and you'll get an earful concerning the "oppressed" or "endangered" status of the WAM. "The white male," complains one Rush Limbaugh listener interviewed by *Newsweek*, "is the most persecuted person in the United States" (in D. Gates, 51).

Oddly enough, along with this victim discourse from the WAM comes a seemingly contradictory insistence on *anger* or *force*. In fact, the frontline performers of this white male anger—Pat Buchanan, G. Gordon Liddy, and Limbaugh—take themselves to be a certain type of popularized Nietzschean:[3] unwilling to hear anything about "victims" (other than themselves), they perform their rhetoric of self-overcoming in front of a growing audience of angry followers.

Of course, on further examination, this WAM discourse shows its pedigree not in Nietzsche, but precisely in that which Nietzsche set out to analyze in *On the Genealogy of Morals* and so much of his other work: resentment. Because white men are now overtly marked as a group, they find themselves besieged by the double consciousness that other groups have long had to manage within American culture, and they're deeply resentful about this.[4] The white male has been marked with its own difference, and the performers of resentment take this as their own special brand of victimization. Though the WAMS understand themselves to be Nietzschean "great birds of prey," in the end they show themselves to be closer cousins to his "little lambs," bleating the refrain "you are evil; therefore, I am good" (see *Genealogy*, essay 7, sect. 13).

Gilles Deleuze writes in *Nietzsche and Philosophy* that such a resentful subject "makes the object responsible for [the subject's] own

powerlessness. . . . It is venomous and depreciative because it blames
the object in order to compensate for its own inability. . . . This is why
ressentiment's revenge, even when it is realized, remains 'spiritual,'
imaginary, and symbolic in principle" (116). From Pat Buchanan's
new *Kulturkampf*, to Rush Limbaugh's demonization of the welfare mother; from the various "independent republics" set up in the
western United States, to Timothy McVeigh's symbolic reasons for
bombing the federal building in Oklahoma City, the purveyors of WAM
are first and foremost resentful purveyors of anger-as-revenge, artists
of resentment who constantly construct a symbolic metaphorization
out of what they take to be a wounding or expropriating act.

As became clear at his trial, for example, McVeigh was convinced
that the order to attack the Branch Davidian compound in Waco was
given from the federal building in Oklahoma City (which, it turns out,
is not the case). In an act fraught with symbolism, exactly two years
later on April 19, 1995, McVeigh blew up the building as revenge.
Kathy Marks points out that April 19 is a highly symbolic date for
the WAM: in addition to the Waco raid on April 19, 1993 (which, in
a nice metaphorical touch, McVeigh used as the date of issue for his
forged South Dakota driver's license), April 19 is also the anniversary
of the 1775 Battle of Lexington ("the shot heard 'round the world" that
began the American Revolutionary War), and the execution of Richard
Wayne Snell (a member of the right-wing Covenant, Sword and the
Arm of the Lord) for the murder of a Jewish businessman and a black
police officer (see Marks, 101). April 20, we should note, is Hitler's
birthday, a date that remains highly overdetermined for many in the
WAM movement.

Of course, to argue that the resentful type has this tendency toward
"symbolic" revenge is *not* to say that the economy of resentment is
somehow unreal, or that killing federal workers is *merely* a symbolic
act. It is, rather, to insist that WAM resentment creates effects on
the sociopolitical level through a pernicious symbolic economy of
othering, creating enemies solely to bolster the WAM's own sense of
inherent goodness. As Nietzsche writes, "picture 'the enemy' as the
man of *ressentiment* conceives him—and here precisely is his deed,
his creation: he has conceived 'the evil enemy,' '*the Evil One*,' and
this in fact is his basic concept, from which [the man of *ressentiment*]
then evolves, as an afterthought and pendant, a 'good one'—himself"
(*Genealogy*, essay 1, sect. 10). The resentful WAM has an identity only
insofar as he is angry at someone else, an "Evil One."

So why even bother to reopen a discourse about *anger?* Why not just cede the field to the rancorous chorus of whiners and moaners, and try to perform another mode of comportment toward the other: communicative rationality, the ethical face-to-face, the openness to alterity stressed in leftist political, feminist and postcolonial discourses? Indeed, can there really be any kind of ethically or politically productive anger, insofar as anger seems intimately associated with the renunciation of alterity? Isn't "anger" as a category of political analysis irrevocably tainted by a kind of reprehensible xenophobia?

To take up these questions, we first need to make a distinction between resentment and anger. As Nietzsche shows in the *Genealogy*, resentment is the first and last safe harbor for the stable subject, who "from the outset says No to what is 'outside,' what is 'different,' what is 'not itself'" (essay 1, sect. 10). Such subjective resentment is different from anger because resentment never properly sets out from itself: the rancorous subject's "No" to alterity is assured "from the outset" (or, really, from *before* the outset). Rancor admits of no alterity and gives rise to nothing other than self-assured smugness; resentment preeminently produces more reified, effective, and pernicious versions of resentment. It cannot, in Nietzschean parlance, create *affirmative* values.

Anger, on the other hand, can be deterritorializing at certain sites; it can produce something other, a line of flight. Anger does not accrue quite so easily to an assured movement of subjective appropriation and control. It is in this sense that Jean-Luc Nancy writes, "Anger is the political sentiment par excellence. It brings out the qualities of the inadmissible, the intolerable. It is a refusal and a resistance that with one step goes beyond all that can be accomplished reasonably— in order to open possible paths for a new negotiation of the reasonable but also paths of uncompromising vigilance. Without anger, politics is accommodation and trade in influence; writing without anger [merely] traffics in . . . seductions" ("Compearance," 375). Perhaps one could say that resentment is being angry at-the-other, for the sake of the self. Nancy's anger as a "political sentiment," however, is precisely anger for-the-other: political anger does not merely say no to difference, but precisely "brings out the qualities of the inadmissible, the intolerable." In short, anger can produce a response that is more than a repetition of the same: anger is perhaps another of the myriad names for a movement outside the self that does not merely return to the self.

To put it slightly differently, resentment necessarily presupposes and reifies existing categories of recognition; it judges injury by the failure to attain a phantasmatic ideal. Resentment, then, is always a metaphoric or *representational* type of anger, which protects an interior space from interrogation and contamination. For Nietzsche, resentment brings about the reinterpretation of bodily suffering as an *"orgy of feeling"* (*Genealogy*, essay 3, sect. 19). Deleuze expands on this claim: "the word *ressentiment* gives a definite clue: *reaction ceases to be acted in order to become something felt (senti)"* (*Nietzsche*, 111). *Ressentiment*, then, is the (non)reaction that characterizes the victimized bourgeois subject, the one who consistently translates exterior provocations—opportunities to respond—into interior states or representational "feelings," slights to be felt and remembered, each new trauma a metaphor for all the others that have robbed me of my autonomy and happiness.

In contradistinction, what we might call the political anger of transformation introduces a metonymic movement that calls for(th) an attention and response to alterity. The metaphorical speech act "Feel my pain" is in this way at considerable odds with the more angry speech act "Do something about pain." Anger produces or gestures toward new categories, rather than pleading in the name of existing ones; and a political anger would thereby open a space for us to respond to subjective or communal expropriation in other than resentful ways.

To paraphrase Deleuze and Guattari, I'm trying to suggest that anger can be a factory (a site of *production*) for subjectivities rather than primarily a theater (a site of *representation* or *recognition*) for the staging of an already reified drama of failed subjectivity. Indeed, I argue throughout this book that the ethics of performative subjectivity rests primarily not in the recognition or representation of expropriation or failure, but in the *production* of subjectivities: ethics is mobilized in performative *responses* to subjection, but these responses are not territorializable before the fact by the constative categories which are their outcomes. Certainly, normative exclusion can be an *outcome* of subjection; but, under a logic of performativity (which asks after the effects of a process), normativity and/or its lack can hardly function as the birth of all subjectivity.

To further sharpen the distinction between anger and resentment, I would argue that resentment is always based on or in some notion of *failure, absence,* or *lack:* I resent the other because the other has something that I do not; or, in more properly Hegelian or Lacanian language, this inevitable lack is tied to the fact that I always desire or derive recognition from the other. I both desire and lack completeness, and I resent the social fact that I must submit to the other in order to attain a measure of this completeness. However, as Tania Modleski writes, the project of ethical or political resistance to the expropriating phallic law of the father "is doomed to failure . . . unless the father is frankly confronted and the entire dialectic of abjection and the law worked through; otherwise, as Deleuze's analysis confirms, the father will always remain in force as the major, if hidden, point of reference" (70). As Modleski suggests in the context of another argument,[5] as long as "lack" is the engine of an analysis, you can be sure that the other side of lack's coin—the plenitude of "the father"—lurks somewhere nearby, "the major, if hidden, point of reference." The bolstering of the norm—its inevitable power and desirability—is the free glass you get with a fill-up of lack.

This paradoxical insistence on normativity is the resentment buried deep in identity politics: the resentful subject takes an effect (exclusion or expropriation from the sociopolitical norm) for a cause, thereby reifying and bolstering its own inherent sense of goodness: it's your fault that I'm not recognized, and that makes me angry. As Wendy Brown maintains in *States of Injury*, "In its emergence as a protest against marginalization or subordination, politicized identity thus becomes attached to its own exclusion both because it is premised on this exclusion for its very existence as identity and because the formation of identity at the site of exclusion . . . augments or 'alters the direction of the suffering' entailed in subordination or marginalization by finding a site of blame for it" (73–74). To redeploy Brown's Nietzschean insight slightly differently, in a normative reading of identity politics and its lacks, recognition becomes a zero-sum game: because somebody (else) has recognition, I don't; somebody wins, so everybody else loses. Of course, as any Lacanian knows, it's more complicated than this because finally nobody wins; nobody "has" this normativity. All recognition is misrecognition, but that fact doesn't rob the norm of its phantasmatic power to attract. And round and round we go. As Slavoj Žižek writes about Laclau, for example, "as soon as we constitute ourselves as ideological subjects, as soon as we respond to the interpellation and assume a certain subject-position, we are a priori, *per definitionem* deluded; we are overlooking the radical dimension of the social antagonism, that is to say, the traumatic kernel the symbolization of which always fails" ("Beyond," 251). Under a psychoanalytic regime of performative failure, recognition remains a kind of phantasmatic Lotto: somebody's got to win, but you know when you buy your ticket that it's (almost) certainly not going to be you. And that should make you angry, but you keep buying the tickets, "*per definitionem* deluded" by an impossible plenitude.

And this double whammy of normativity's plenitude—its necessity and impossibility—is especially evident in the overdetermined performative identity position of the WAM: somewhat like the structural position of "woman" in Lacan, the WAM both "is" the phantasmatic norm and simultaneously embodies the yearning "lack" of access to the norm. Yúdice asserts, "Precisely because straight white men are perceived by progressives within identity politics and multiculturalism as the center of the dominant culture, they are not permitted to claim their own difference. There is an irony here, for the very objective of progressive politics today—to dismantle privilege—ends up keeping in place in our imaginary an even greater monolith of power" (280). The iteration of normativity's exclusionary function—the critical project of dismantling privilege by showing its lacks—ironically ends up reinstituting the very phantasmatic power of the monolithic normativity that we are trying so desperately to deconstruct: the claim of exclusion from the norm legitimizes the victimized group, but it simultaneously trumps that legitimation insofar as it bases itself on the even greater legitimacy or desirability of the norm from which the victim has been expropriated. And this is especially clear in the predicament of the WAM, his structural identity consisting primarily of a desiring link to an impossible norm, and heaps of resentment.

Let's Be Reasonable: Performative Being and Doing

Deleuze shows us throughout his reading of Nietzsche's *Genealogy* that resentment and its lack-inspired kin are poisonous because they always separate the subject from what it can *do*; resentment always downplays the affirmative *acts* of subjective performativity and subordinates them to the constative, conceptual language of recognition. As Patton puts it, "if . . . identity is performative or a performance, then identity is necessarily always in context or in practice" (227). In a kind of shorthand, then, one might say that resentment is the denial of active performativity, the territorialization of all response on reactive force. Nietzsche writes, "The slave revolt in morality begins when *ressentiment* itself becomes creative and gives birth to values: the *res-*

sentiment of natures that are denied the true reaction, that of deeds, and compensate themselves with an imaginary revenge" (*Genealogy*, essay 1, sect. 10). The resentful subject who is the WAM ignores the angry affirmation of the sociopolitical dice throw, and opts instead for an "imaginary revenge," convincing himself that someone else has rigged the table before the game even started. Immigrants, Affirmative Action recipients, feminazis, liberal media moguls, the UN: they supposedly rule the field, and refuse recognition of the WAM's expropriation. For example, William Pierce, founder of the National Alliance and Cosmotheist Church (after he splintered from the National Socialist White People's Party in 1970) and author of the infamous *Turner Diaries*,[6] asserts that there are several ways to get "free money" in America: "be an 80-IQ welfare mom having illegitimate children every nine months; be a homosexual 'performance artist'; a foreign dictator in the good graces of New World Order elitists; someone who burns their own neighborhood" (in Marks, 59). As Marks goes on to explain, Pierce holds "that this 'free money' is not available to working white Americans because their job is to provide this 'free money'" (59).

As any number of critics have pointed out, it's simply not reasonable to believe that welfare moms and homosexual performance artists have been the big winners in the upward redistribution of wealth carried out over the past twenty years in America. It's simply not reasonable to believe that lower-middle-class white men have more to fear from Andres Serrano or Holly Hughes than they do from Donald Trump or Bill Gates; and many diagnoses of the WAM phenomenon concern themselves with seeking ways to transform the WAM's resentment against women, immigrants, and minorities into a political anger aimed at the more likely causes of their expropriation: transnational corporations, the Republican upward redistribution of wealth carried out during the '80s and '90s, corporate welfare, union busting through so-called right-to-work legislation, and so on.[7]

Although this effort certainly makes sense, and one must always affirm such attempts at reasoning out a problem, I think we should also hesitate before such "reasonable" argumentative solutions, precisely because *reason* has very little to do with WAM discourse: no one could reasonably believe that the National Endowment for the Arts, which has a budget slightly less than the U.S. Marine Corps Band,[8] is the major instrument for the sinister redistribution of wealth and the legitimation of homosexuality in America; no one could reasonably believe that women on welfare have more children simply to tack a

few dollars a month onto their check; no one could reasonably believe that the L.A. uprisings following the Rodney King verdict were
masterminded by secretive African American groups in order to fleece
the American government out of urban renewal monies. Of course
these things make no "reasonable" sense; but the anger of resentment
doesn't work reasonably.

In fact, as Stanley Aronowitz has suggested, new social movements—both rightist movements like the WAM and leftist movements
like ACT-UP—really have had one thing in common: the rejection of
a certain kind of "reason" that would link political identity or liberation to universalizing categories. Aronowitz writes, "the appearance
of a postmodern politics may be ascribed to a multiplicity of devel-
opments that signify a major shift in the cultural and intellectual
presuppositions of political life. Chief among these is that the category of 'reason' proposed by modernity as an unimpeachable standard
against which politics and culture may be measured has become a
contested category" ("Against," 379). A certain critique of reason puts
the "new" in the "new social movements," right or left.[9] Likewise, the
gains of these movements are seldom accomplished through the sole
deployment of reasoned arguments: sure, most "reasonable" people
would agree that African Americans deserve the same rights as other
Americans and that discriminating on the basis of gender or sexual
orientation is absurd. But the most successful strategies of the civil
rights eras have been *performative* ones that highlight or stage discrimination and provoke an ethical response to it.

What new social movements like ACT-UP learned from the radical
wing of the civil rights movement was precisely this: when trying
to create action—effects to counter other effects—the performative
staging of political anger will usually prove more effective than arguments and counterarguments concerning the merits of social policy.
As Aronowitz points out, such a performative political strategy
passes up the traditional wisdom of electoral politics—build a broad-
based coalition, elect your candidates, work with them to introduce
procedural legislation, and so forth—and opts instead for direct micro-
intervention that "tacitly challenges the *ethical* legitimacy of the
majority" ("Against," 362). *Anger*, it seems, can be performatively
mobilized much more quickly and decisively than reason's constative categories; simply recalling George Bush's "Willie Horton" ads or
spending an afternoon listening to Rush Limbaugh will confirm that
the new right has learned this lesson just as well as, if not better than,
the new left.

Certainly, then, no single deployment of a knockdown reasoned argument will solve the WAM problem once and for all. The only thing that seems clear politically is that any productive intervention would first have to redirect or restage this WAM anger, make it productive of something other than blame and resentment. It is increasingly unclear, however, that reason or reasoned arguments about the "real" culprits of the WAM's expropriation are going to get us there, or that the WAM's problems can easily or simply be "cured" at all. As Deleuze writes, within an affirmative frame, "the possibilities of a cure will be subordinated to the transformation of types" (*Nietzsche,* 116). If it is to be *mobilized* otherwise, the anger of the WAM first needs to be *described* differently, to be offered a line of flight other than mere resentment.

For the purposes of the present argument, then, I am—following Nietzsche's metaphorics of sickness and health—most interested in a *diagnosis* of the WAM phenomenon. Specifically, I'm interested in exploring the theme of lack that runs through both the resentful, right-wing WAM discourse and the more radical, left-wing discourse that would attempt to redirect or redeploy the WAM's ire. Both right and left seem to agree that the system has *failed* these people, and WAMs need to respond to their expropriation by re-representing themselves to the public at large.

But this is where the birds of prey who are progressive or liberal political theorists meet up again with the newly born little lambs of angry white maledom—where the theorized identity discourse of the left meets the WAM: both share this notion that lack is the inevitable state of things in the political world. And this is also where performative social theory meets its own brand of resentment, its own fetishization of *failure.* William Connolly, for example, overtly thematizes his political theory as a performative end run around the debilitating political effects of resentment. "The Nietzsche/Foucault ideals of self as work of art," he writes, are an important component of the "drive to move the subject of desire away from *ressentiment*" (*Ethos,* 55); as he clarifies, such performative models of subjectivity "begin to subdue subterranean resentment of the *absence of wholeness* in what one is, treating the *absence as a source of possibility* for experimental engagement" (69; my italics). Here we see the Hegelian shell game of negativity (the very *engine* of resentment) oddly reintroduced by Connolly as its own cure: it's a matter of learning to live with "absence of wholeness," learning to tolerate difference, representing your own expropriation for the other to recognize in him-, her-, or

itself. Though Connolly thematizes his project as the "introduction
of a new possibility of being out of old injuries and differences" (xv),
it seems that on another reading his theory reproduces and reifies
the very lack-inspired economy that gives rise to resentment in the
first place: the recognition or reinscription of *absence* or *failure* again
reifies the privilege of presence or wholeness.[10]

Indeed, the inevitability of lack leads to an inevitability of resentment, an allegory of inexorable failure.[11] But the problem with
such an allegorical reading of performative failure is that it makes
or leaves only certain paths available for transformational *anger*,
especially something like white male anger. Certainly, one of the
greatest successes of the new social movements and their theorized politics of identity has been the mobilization of anger-as-lack:
women, minorities, and queers, for example, can mobilize around a
critique of the completely unjustified and unjustifiable privilege of
the straight-white-male norm in American society. For some, perhaps
for everyone, normativity inexorably fails; one is never fully sutured
to one's subaltern subject position, and the angry demand for recognition that comes from outside the norm—"We're here and we're
queer!"—will necessarily disrupt and reconfigure that norm through
the deployment of performative strategies that highlight the cultural
construction of subject positions. As Patton argues, the performative
"strategy of linking identity, minority, and civil rights was enor-
mously successful in creating a political mass and in achieving more
favorable status for at least some of the bodies in resistance" (239). The
norm fails to account for or recognize subaltern identities, and under
a performative topological reading of forces, which always asks after
the *effects* of an interpretation rather than some inherent meaning,
an anger based in normativity's lack and its reinscription certainly
can do productive work in many political contexts.

But what if one *is* the supposed norm—the straight white male—and
one is nevertheless stuck with a certain kind of inevitable "failure"?
How does one deploy or redeploy that performative anger, that failure, that normativity? At oneself? At other versions of one's subject
position? Are there not differing effects and differing deployments of
force? Can *all* force be understood as a reaction to failure? Is all anger
territorializable as anger over loss? Within a political discourse of normativity's lack, is there a subject position available to the WAM other
than xenophobia or self-flagellation, the twin towers of *ressentiment?*

White Angry Masochists?

In fact, several recent critics have argued that contemporary male subjectivity is nothing other than the combination of xenophobia *and* self-flagellation. David Savran argues, taking his cue from Kaja Silverman's *Male Subjectivity at the Margins*, that perhaps the WAM is nothing other than a "reflexive sadomasochist," "the man whose violent instincts are turned not only against others, but also against the self" (130). Savran in fact contends that "reflexive sadomasochism has become the primary libidinal logic of the white male as victim" (146). The WAM's role as victim, however, has led not so much to a humbling of WAM claims to masculine normativity, but to a compensatory imaginary deployment of hypermasculinity. Savran writes of the WAM, his "very occupational and emotional instability simultaneously inspires him—if only in his fantasies—to enact a hypermasculinized heroism, as if in compensation for his perpetually misplaced virility" (129).

In fleshing out this argument, Savran pays particular attention to the masculine body in Sylvester Stallone's *Rocky* and *Rambo* movies, with their portrayals of hypermasculinized victims responding to the lost economic and cultural normativity of white heterosexual masculinity. Since the mid-'70s, he maintains, the WAM has been ousted from the center of the American normative imaginary by a series of historical failures: the "failure" of the Vietnam War; the erosion of white male centrality brought about by the growth and influence of minoritarian identity movements; the loss of "good" (i.e., industrial) jobs in America due to the globalization of transnational capital; and the much-discussed "feminization of labor" in the new service economy.

As Savran persuasively holds, it is this genealogical confluence of historical factors—rather than some transcendental failure of subjectivity—that begins to explain the plight of the today's expropriated or failed WAM. Indeed, Savran makes it clear that he differs from many psychoanalytic critics through his insistence on the *material* status of subjective lack, failure, or expropriation. Like Butler, he argues that one needs to historicize failure, or it will inexorably remain a transcendental category, unable to do specific diagnostic or political work. As Savran writes about psychoanalytic theorists of masculine subjectivity like Silverman, it is the "insistent substitution by these theorists of psychoanalysis for history, which renders them incapable of analyzing the material forces that have foregrounded the masochistic white male subject at this particular historical moment" (145).

Although it's not entirely clear that Silverman is quite so naïve about the social nature of masculine subjectivity—as she insists, "masochism in all of its guises is as much a product of the existing symbolic order as a reaction against it" (*Male Subjectivity*, 213)— Savran does seem to have a point here: a psychoanalysis that does not historicize itself—does not make lack or expropriation *concrete*— seems destined to mystify social formations and their functions. However, as I argue throughout this book, it seems that making the functioning of lack "concrete" or "historical" doesn't get you off the transcendentalizing hook that Savran locates. In other words, once you've decided that subjectivity proceeds by expropriation from the norm—recall Butler: "loss inaugurates the subject and threatens it with dissolution"—it seems that you've already made a suspiciously transcendentalizing move. Subjectivity is then necessarily fueled by a phantasmatic resentment, and this conclusion seems destined to remain the same whether you fill in the details from a strictly theoretical discourse or from a sociopolitical one.

Of course, as Silverman maintains, psychoanalysis is from the start a discourse concerned with the social conditions of subjectivity; this is precisely why, for example, the family and its Oedipalization processes play such a large role. The theoretical rendering of the law of the father—expropriation from the real, desire, and gender coding—is inseparable from the functioning of the bourgeois family as a territorializing social norm of compulsory heterosexuality. Oedipalization, as Silverman insists, is always already a "material" discourse, drawn from the normative, dominant social codes of bourgeois life: those narratives in fact provide us with the scripts for our performative reinscriptions. Therefore, Silverman writes, "until our dominant fiction undergoes a radical metamorphosis, . . . subjectivity will always carry the imprint of the family. And even in the event of such a metamorphosis, the subject will still be defined by lack and alterity" (*Male Subjectivity*, 213). Silverman here seems to preempt Savran's objection by insisting that the distinctly social conditions of "lack and alterity" are already foregrounded by a theoretical psychoanalysis, insofar as the institutional and conceptual frameworks of the discourse are drawn from the "dominant fiction" that is the narrative of bourgeois family life.

This imbrication between the theoretical and the historical being the case, Silverman asserts in *The Subject of Semiotics* that one could reread the infamous psychoanalytic privilege of the phallus or notion of penis envy as socially descriptive claims: white heterosexual males have held social power and privilege and thereby functioned as a kind of normativity in recent bourgeois capitalist history. As she argues toward a critique and reinscription of Lacan, "the continuity of lack from one regime to another ultimately overrides everything else, and makes impossible any real critique of the present cultural order. However, once we deny this primordial lack, we are free to understand all ideal representations as culturally manufactured. . . . We are able to conceptualize . . . desire as belonging to a culturally and historically determinate Other—to a particular symbolic order, and not one which is universal or absolute" (192). In a kind of proleptic response to Savran, Silverman argues that psychoanalytic claims of "lack" are inexorably also historically descriptive claims, drawn from and responding to specific social formations in twentieth-century bourgeois life.

It seems, in other words, that social or materialist brands of psychoanalysis like Savran's can be reconciled with seemingly more "theoretical" or transcendentalizing deployments of the discourse of lack. However, the claim that both versions share is what interests me here, the claim nicely summed up in Silverman's statement about the present social status of the family and the potential for this "historically determinate Other" to change over time: "even in the event of such a metamorphosis, *the subject will still be defined by lack and alterity.*" This claim, rather strikingly "transcendental," runs through all identity politics of lack, materialist and theoretical: no matter what the historical formation of the past, present, or future, *lack defines and will define the subject.* This, it seems to me, is the claim that is finally impossible to defend in psychoanalytic readings of subjectivity, whether they emphasize supposedly material practices or supposedly transcendental categories.

That the subject is "always" defined by "alterity" seems a claim that can be both theoretically and historically defended—subjects do not simply get to choose the social contexts and the categories of social interaction that they are born into. It seems contentiously transcendentalizing, however, to link this sense of "alterity" with "lack": this is the moment where an inevitable resentment is smuggled into a politics of identity. If it is always figured as "lack," then "alterity" is necessarily translated to the subject as loss, theft, expropriation: the other is inexorably the marker of the subject's failure to be complete, and thereby the other remains my enemy, that which stands between me and an impossible return to wholeness. In fact, Butler herself voices a similar reservation about her own work in an exchange with Laclau: "But I do wonder whether failure, for both of us, does not become a kind of universal condition (and limit) of subject formation; a way in which we still seek to assert a common condition which assumes a transcendental status in relation to particular differences" ("Exchange," 10).

Just as queer theorists like Eve Kosofsky Sedgwick argue that conclusions from essentialism/constructionism debates in feminism cannot simply be imported into queer politics (where essentialism does substantially different work in responding to those who would thematize queerness merely as the perverted social construction of a "lifestyle"),[12] it is not at all clear that subjective lack or failure as a theoretical engine of political analysis and response can simply be imported into the discourse of any specific identity. "Alterity," in other words, is not always and everywhere synonymous with "lack." In the case of the WAM, for example, such a discourse of alterity-as-lack leaves no other than resentful possibilities for response. This is *not*, as I insist above, to say that this discourse doesn't do a *tremendous* amount of work in analyzing and redeploying political angers in other contexts. But the overarching reach of the theoretical frame itself—the fact, as Butler puts it, that "conscience doth make subjects of us all" through an allegory of loss—seems a bit suspicious, and not because it doesn't do *enough* work; rather, I'd suggest that perhaps this frame does *too much* work, because it seems to explain virtually everything on the political horizon in terms of representing and recognizing the subject's lacks and failures.

In an identity politics of lack or performative failure, the diagnostic topology of performative subjectivities—how much and what kind of force is manifest in a particular situation?—gets territorialized on one kind of force, and hence one kind of subjectivity: the one who lacks. Though performative theories of subjectivity make it clear that there is always subjection—the subject is never simply in control of its itinerary—and such subjections call forth responses, in the end not all response is territorializable as response to loss: all action is not necessarily resentful, and all consciousness is not necessarily bad conscience. Following the primary lesson of performativity (wherever one sees a *constative* noun, there has been a *performative* action), one would always need to do an analysis—a performative diagnosis or interpretation—to find out what forces were at work in a particular economy.

Although, strictly speaking, there is no such thing as purely active (i.e., unconstrained) performative force—all such force is deployed in response to subjection—this does *not* evacuate the diagnostic distinction between various varieties and deployments of active and reactive forces. For example, though they are both reactions to previous deployments of force, an ACT-UP disruption of a press conference and the bombing of the federal building in Oklahoma City are simply not of the same order. As we saw in chapter 6, repetitions respond to and carry force, but inherently those forces are neither territorializing nor deterritorializing, reactive nor active; it is, rather, the *effect* of the performative deployment in a social space that decides: reactive forces work to arrest a flow; active forces work to speed up a flow. This is most definitely *not* to argue that blowing up the federal building is "reactive" and "bad," whereas disrupting a Jesse Helms press conference is "active" and "good" (or vice versa); the discourse of morality is completely beside the point. Although all force creates effects—all force is in this way "active" force—there remains a diagnostic political decision to be made about the effects themselves—what states those effects produce—and whether those states and effects should or can be further accelerated or decelerated.

Of course, for psychoanalytically inflected thinkers, this notion of active or affirmative force is hopelessly naïve. Butler argues, for example, that such a neo-Deleuzian evaluation of lack is necessarily premised on an opposite and symmetrical phantasmatic investment in lack's dialectical other, the originary plenitude of active force. Butler maintains that Deleuze's "theory proceeds in two complementary ways: (1) as a critique of desire as negativity and (2) as the promotion of a normative ideal for desire as affirmation" (*Subjects*, 205). Insofar as Deleuze's assessment of the dialectic contains such a secret dialectic, Butler holds that Deleuze's critique of lack or reactive force is necessarily premised on a dialectical celebration of "a natural eros which has subsequently been denied by a restrictive culture" (214). The project of overcoming negativity, then, remains naïve insofar as "the appeal to a precultural eros ignores the Lacanian insight that all desire is linguistically and culturally constructed" (214).

According to Butler, such an affirmative critique of lack or failure is implicitly a denial of any social construction—an essentialist, apolitical, metaphysical dream of plenitude: "the postulation of a natural multiplicity appears, then, as the insupportable metaphysical speculation on the part of Deleuze. . . . The Deleuzian critique of the prohibitive law and the subsequent reification of desire as that which is always already repressed, requires a political strategy that explicitly takes account of the cultural construction of desire, that is, a political strategy that resists the appeal to a 'natural' desire as a normative ideal" (214). This is a common response to the Deleuzian critique of lack: because it wishes to activate a series of forces not tied essentially to repression and negativity, it fails to account for the social construction and canalization of desire. Indeed, it seems that what Butler calls the "normative ideal" of " 'natural' desire" may in fact be more politically dangerous than the work of the negative that it critiques; for example, it seems that this notion of active force opens the door for the most violent WAMs and other political extremists to justify their use of force through a mystifying appeal to the "natural" movements of deterritorializing desire.[13]

It seems to me, however, that such an assessment of Deleuze and Guattari misses the force of their intervention altogether. They have in fact been tireless in distinguishing their theory of desire from a theory of natural plenitude or pure active force that must be liberated from its social constraints. Deleuze writes:

> we run up against very exasperating objections. They say to us that we are returning to an old cult of pleasure, to a pleasure principle, or to a notion of the festival. . . . Above all, it is objected that by releasing desire from lack and law, the only thing we have left to refer to is a state of nature, a desire that would be natural and spontaneous reality. We say quite the opposite: *desire only exists when assembled or machined.* You cannot grasp or conceive of a desire outside a determinate assemblage, on a plane which is not preexistent but which must itself be constructed. ("What Is Desire?," 136)

Deleuze's analysis of lack gets off the ground precisely through the radicalization of a performative logic: there *quite literally* is no thing there until there is the deployment of a certain performative force. There is no natural plenitude of desire: objects and relations are performative effects; they do not preexist their articulation—their machinic assemblage—in a field.

In fact, far from being an *appeal* to a ubiquitous presence within desire, Deleuze and Guattari's critique of lack begins through the *questioning* of a ubiquitous presence in pyschoanalysis's theory of desire, lack's transcendental status with relation to particular differences and desires. As Guattari expands, "Our conception of desire was the opposite of an ode to spontaneity, of a praise of disorderly liberation. It was precisely to underscore the artificial 'constructivist' nature of desire that we defined it as 'machinic' " (*Soft*, 272). In other words, *it is precisely because desire is socially constructed and engineered that it cannot coherently be characterized as "lacking" in each and every instance.* Deleuze contends that the social cannot be characterized as either "lacking" or "full" before the fact because the social is under constant performative construction and reinscription: "the construction of the plane is a politics, it necessarily involves a 'collective,' collective assemblages, a set of social becoming" ("Psychoanalysis," 114).

Hardly a retreat from a social space of performativity to a place of natural plenitude, such conceptions of desire and active force are the further deployment—to what might be called the logical extreme—of a performative notion of identity. The subject is interpellated, to be sure; but precisely because there is no subject aside from interpellation, the subject cannot automatically be described in terms of loss or failure: there is literally *nothing to lose* because there is no subject but for the performance of a subjectivity; there is *nothing to fail* insofar as the machine that is the subject is under constant performative (re)construction. Deleuze insists, "Far from presupposing a subject, desire cannot be attained except at the point where someone is deprived of the power of saying 'I.' . . . But who has you believe that by losing the coordinates of object and subject you lack something?" ("Psychoanalysis," 113). Finally, Deleuze argues that if performative political and ethical theory is to live up to a theory of social construction, it *must* jettison the ontological or founding status of lack.

The ethical force of what I'm calling a political anger comes about in the *emergence of* and *response to* the other, not in an inexorable allegory of subjectivity's failure to comprehend or assimilate otherness or its failure to be recognized in and for its lacks. Certainly, the subject-as-lack also produces "a play of affects and effects," but preeminent among them seem to be resentment and reification rather than some kind of opening to alterity, and the WAM is par excellence this style of "failing" subject: the WAM *knows* that he has been expropriated, denied recognition; the WAM knows the norm has failed, and that he himself is nothing but this failure. And, at least in the case of the WAM, such an allegory of necessary failure leads to the inevitability of resentment: the WAM already lives within an understanding of subjectivity as failure to approximate the norm, and he responds with the symbolic violence that we've all come to know and fear. The WAM is the man of *ressentiment*, but it seems the only thing available to him under a system that would understand subjectivity as an allegory of failed normativity. Because he "is" this phantasmatic norm, the WAM's failed anger has no productive place to go. This is the predicament of the WAM, lacking a privilege that was never really there, consistently reconstituting and reifying his phantasmatic links to that (non)lost (non)privilege with each resentful phone call to G. Gordon Liddy: "Norm, are you there?"

To put it bluntly, the angry performative political subject is—or needs to be—angry over something more than its losses or failures. If failure is indeed the only engine of performative subjectivity, then the resentful anger of the WAM is both well-founded and here to stay, perhaps functioning as the paradigm of subjectivity itself. In the end, it seems that an ethics or politics of originary lack knows too well how to be angry; it too quickly thematizes the other as somehow like the self in its identity. The subject is angered when it is seemingly expropriated by the other or the others.

Finally, in taking into account the social interpellations of the subject, it seems that one would be obliged to account for an "unfree" subject as otherwise than a "lacking" or "failed" subject. As Nietzsche writes in the *Genealogy*, "*This* is precisely what the ascetic ideal means: that something was *lacking*, that man was surrounded by a fearful *void*—he did not know how to justify, to account for, to affirm himself; he *suffered* from the problem of his meaning" (essay 3, sect. 28). The primary concern for politics is not an ontological or epistemological question (What does it *mean?*), but rather a performative one (What does it *do?*). Following from the action—the reflexivity or recoil—that is the subjectivization of the subject, certainly there can be lacking or negative or failing *effects*, but an allegorical installation of those effects as a founding interpellative moment tends to territorialize all production of performative effects around the production of losses.

So What's a White Guy to *Do?*

As Henry Giroux points out, this is something of a tricky question for someone steeped in leftist academic theory, because the liberal identity politics of the '70s and '80s "has said practically nothing about how racial politics might address the construction of Whiteness as an oppositional racial category" ("Rewriting," 294). Insofar as identity politics construes the white straight male norm as an oppressive or hegemonic formation, the performative *disruption* of that normativity has occupied most theoreticians' attention. Recently, however, there has been a mini-explosion of "whiteness studies," which attempts to understand normativity itself as a performative category. As David Roediger writes, whiteness studies attempts to "pay attention to the most neglected aspects of race in America, the questions of why people think they are white and whether they might quit thinking so" (12).

Ironically, much of the discourse surrounding whiteness argues that the best way to deal with the phantasmatic and oppressive privileges of whiteness is by renouncing the category altogether. Perhaps, Roediger writes in *Towards the Abolition of Whiteness*, whiteness simply has to go:

> It is not merely that whiteness is oppressive and false; it is that whiteness is *nothing but* oppressive and false. We speak of African American culture and community, and rightly so. Indeed the making of disparate African ethnic groups into an African American people . . . is a genuine story of an American melting pot. . . . Whiteness describes, from Little Big Horn to Simi Valley, not a culture but precisely the absence of culture. It is the empty and therefore terrifying attempt to build an identity based on what one isn't and on whom one can hold back. Almost no left initiatives have challenged white workers to critique, much less to abandon, whiteness. (13)

There is much for so-called white folks to chew on here. At one level, Roediger argues for a move familiar in other versions of a performative identity politics: for example, Butler argues that feminism as a performative political project must give up the normative analytic category "woman," and many theorists of racial identity have argued that essentialized notions of race have hindered rather than helped in redressing racism's effects.

Roediger, however, goes another step, arguing for the thoroughgoing renunciation of the category "whiteness" in a way that feminists or theorists of race never would: certainly, for example, no feminist of any credibility would or could plausibly argue that the history of feminism "is *nothing but* oppressive and false." It seems that whiteness's special status as the proper name for normativity itself makes

~~it an irrevocably tainted category. Indeed, if whiteness is "empty" and~~
at the same time "oppressive and false," then there is simply no point
in trying to fill the category otherwise or perform it differently.

So what's a white guy to do, according to Roediger? He argues,
"Our opposition should focus on contrasting the bankruptcy of white
politics with the possibilities of nonwhiteness" (17). It seems that
Roediger here offers a kind of Deleuzian call to "become-black," to
focus on the nonmajoritarian lines of flight rather than the static,
territorialized categories of whiteness. Roediger writes, "If even MTV
realizes that there is a mass audience for the critique of whiteness,
we cannot fail to attempt to rally, and to learn from, a constituency
committed to its abolition" (17). Despite appearances, Roediger's here
is far from a Deleuzian intervention, insofar as Deleuze's notion of
becoming-black is most assuredly not a call for whites to swap subject
positions and thereby take advantage of the deterritorializing "possibilities of nonwhiteness" that alterity might offer.

The ethical problems surrounding such an enabling "renunciation"
of whiteness seem obvious: first, subjection teaches us that we don't
get to *choose* the categories we're interpellated into; second, and
perhaps more troubling, Roediger's notion of abandoning whiteness
allows for so-called white people simply to reconfigure themselves
around a series of new and improved, "other" authenticities of blackness or ethnicity: MTV, an example somewhat poorly chosen by
Roediger, very clearly promotes this kind of hipster white-negroism
in its presentations of rap and other contemporary "black" music to
its largely suburban "white" audience. Finally, Roediger's notion of
abandoning whiteness places us all in a hip MTV fantasy world where
we can choose our own subjectivity; and thereby we can leave behind
the "empty" husk of whiteness to be the burden borne by unreflective
Hee Haw–watching squares and rednecks.

This notion of "renouncing" whiteness is based on a very oddly
"constative" notion of identity. According to Roediger, whiteness "is"
oppressive, and therefore it "is" terrifying and false: it inherently lacks
any possibility or potential to be anything other than brutally territorial, so we should leave it behind. However, following the affirmative
performative emphasis I've been trying to work out in this book,
the question of whiteness would need to be posed somewhat differently: not around what whiteness supposedly *is*, but rather taking
up what whiteness *does*, and what it *can do*. Certainly, whiteness
has produced oppressive and terrifying results, as well as progressive

and deterritorializing effects; concomitantly it is those performative effects—rather than the constative category itself—that one might hope "white" people could be mobilized to abandon or join with.

In any case, the answer to resentment—the way to redeploy or redirect reactive force—is never more resentment, more lack, more denial, more renunciation. As Giroux suggests, the situation of whiteness is not so much an undecidable no-win decision between upholding or renouncing the history of whiteness (as if either were possible); rather, the provocation of whiteness is better configured within an injunction to "mediate critically the complex relations between Whiteness and racism," where white people might be encouraged to deal with this legacy "not by repudiating their Whiteness, but by grappling with its racist legacy and its potential to be rearticulated in oppositional and transformative terms" ("Rewriting," 301). What demands attention and response is not so much the *normativity* of whiteness—Is it "good" or "evil"? Do we work with it or abandon it?—but rather its *effects:* how can the forces of whiteness be deployed otherwise? What can the wam become, other than resentful? These, it seems, are the crucial questions for an analysis of whiteness or maleness or anger, and in the end they are not primarily questions about dealing with an originary normativity and its loss; any such discourse of lost privilege will continue the wam down an inexorable resentful road.

Of course, there certainly are ways in which arguments about the origins of the subject have real relevance concerning the effects that subjects create or can create. Depending on how one describes or diagnoses the wam phenomenon, for example, you could be looking at an expropriated group of victims, at a hegemonic wolf in sheep's clothing, a reflexive masochist, a sadist, a fetishist, a historical symptom of yet another mutation in capital, a familiar resentful story, a wholly new subject position, and so on. The terms of the debate or diagnosis can go quite a long way to recasting the debate around what a subject can do, how the anger in white male anger can find a productive way to play itself out. But to insist that a normative lack founds all subjects is, in Deleuze's words, "to misunderstand the misery of those who really do lack something. . . . Those whose lack is real have no possible plane of consistence which would allow them to desire" ("Psychoanalysis," 114). The critique of lack is at least partially undertaken in the name of shifting the terms of debate, which in turn joins the process of building a social plane upon which subjects can produce other effects. As Patton writes, "discursive agonistics do *more* than affect the terms of debate: insofar as some terms undergird the production of the spaces occupied by bodies, discursive intervention is itself material" (223).

After all this sound and fury, however, we're still left with the question What's a white guy to do? An affirmative performative emphasis—like the one I've been trying to articulate and argue for throughout this book—offers at least three concrete strategies for ethical or political engagement with and around the WAM, strategies that follow the lines of flight laid out by Foucault in his preface to Deleuze and Guattari's *Anti-Oedipus:*

1. "Free political action from all unitary and totalizing paranoia" (xiii). Discourses of normativity and lack mirror and feed the paranoia of the WAM, and also play into the nostalgic narrative of former WAM dominance (and subsequent WAM resentment of the present); giving up such a discourse allows a more fluid description of the WAM's complex relation to myriad social discourses—economic, race-based, political, ethical, religious, and so forth—that does not territorialize the WAM (or any other phantasmatic subject position, for that matter) as the impossible normativity, hated but yet striven for by all. One potential way to loosen the shackles of WAM resentment is to abandon a totalized picture of the social and its lacks, ruled over by monolithic norms that simultaneously oppress and attract.

2. "Develop action, thought, and desires by proliferation, juxtaposition, and disjunction, and not by subdivision and pyramidal hierarchization" (xiii). There are many WAM positions, just as there are myriad positions that make up the category woman or Asian American; and not all—not even most—of those who might be called WAMS are mobilized around a wholly reactionary agenda. The anger of the WAM can proliferate in other directions, and can mutate if it's given a plane on which to work, a plane other than resentment on which to produce its effects. For example, the style of WAM that Ross Perot represents, though dangerously nostalgic and leaning toward megalomania, has shown that some WAMS and their kin can be mobilized around concern for the future, around a certain kind of odd generosity that could be deployed to protect some form of the social institutions that other politically connected WAMS have been crusading to shut down. If specific intensities are delinked from an organizational or hierarchical pyramid of forces, they can potentially be shuffled into new combinations.

In fact, it is here—in strategies of intensification rather than sublimation or lack—that possibilities return for arguments concerning the WAM's historical genealogy. At some level, politicians, the FBI and transnational corporations deserve all the scorn that the WAM can heap on them; but it is not simply because transnational corporations have "taken something away" that one might mobilize anger against them. In concert with a series of other complex genealogical factors, such corporations have rather produced an economic plane of consistency on which strong unions and good industrial jobs are things that need to be struggled over in different ways.[14] However, the politics of nostalgia—hierarchized around a lost moment of plenitude—is not going to get the reorienting job done for the WAM.

3. "Do not think that one has to be sad in order to be militant, even though the thing one is fighting is abominable" (xiii). As any number of critics have asked, where's the leftist version of Rush Limbaugh, dishing out barbs at the far right? One major reason WAM anger has been easy for the right to orchestrate and territorialize is precisely because many on the left, like Roediger, have asked WAMs merely to abandon their guilty subject positions, rather than ask what effects they can produce with the resources that accrue to them. Without a doubt, guilty renunciation is *doing* something, but it is hardly an active deployment or line of flight for further action. As Giroux points out, the difficulty or impossibility of simply renouncing a subject position is seen most clearly in and around pedagogical issues: asking young WAMs in schools merely to abandon their whiteness, anger, or male identity is indeed a go-nowhere strategy, and leads only to more resentment and retrenchment on their part ("Rewriting," 296–300). Again, the question is not how to *abandon* such a WAM subject position, but how to *mobilize it otherwise*.

Certainly, all this is not to say that there is some simple or obvious cure for the WAM diagnosis; and of course, there are myriad other sites and cites around which white male anger could be mobilized otherwise. Indeed, as I've tried to outline it in this book, performative ethics is activated in articulating responses, not in offering templates or rules for social action.

One way or the other, it seems that we are destined to see more WAM deployment of what Nietzsche calls "the most dangerous of all explosives, *ressentiment*" (*Genealogy*, essay 3, sect. 15). But an affirmative performative diagnosis of the WAM phenomenon can at least direct our attention toward the anger in a different way, away from the question of what the WAM lacks, and toward the question of what the WAM can become. As Molly Ivins writes, "O.K., the U.N. and the black helicopters are not the problem. But don't underestimate the anger itself" (5).

Conclusion · Choosing Ethics, Affirming Alterity

I do not believe that today there is any question of *choosing*.
—Jacques Derrida, "Structure, Sign and Play"

Toward the end of Jacques Derrida's "Structure, Sign and Play," the essay well-known for ushering in a specifically *post*structuralist ethos, he lays out a distinction between two ways of thematizing play: the "saddened, *negative*, nostalgic, guilty . . . side of the thinking of play whose other side would be the Nietzschean *affirmation*, that is the joyous affirmation of the play of the world and of the innocence of becoming" (292). For Derrida, such a Nietzschean "*affirmation then determines the noncenter otherwise than as loss of the center*" (292). In other words, such an affirmation of alterity supersedes "the structuralist thematic of broken immediacy" (292): a *post*structuralism would concern itself first and foremost with a gesture other than mourning for an absence or lack. "There are," Derrida continues, "thus two interpretations of interpretation, of structure, of sign, of play": one remains "turned towards the lost or impossible presence of the absent origin," while "the other, which is no longer turned toward the origin, affirms play and tries to pass beyond man and humanism" (292).

I would venture to say these are among the most-quoted lines in the theory business, and for good reason. Though delivered in 1966, these words nicely stage the distinctly ethical component of a theoretical choice that seems *still* to lie before us today: Do we opt for nostalgia—recuperating the stable subject and/or mourning its lacks—or do we follow the line of flight that is the affirmation of difference, responsibility, and becoming-other? Do we continue to fear or mourn the other as the lack of the same, or do we choose to affirm alterity?

It is very tempting to stop reading Derrida's essay at this point, taking its upshot to be this choice between two interpretations of otherness. The existential feel of these passages has a nice pathos to it, and most any reader can feel confident that he or she has made the ethical choice: No nostalgia for me, thank you; I'll take some of that alterity, please.[1] And one assumes we make this affirmative choice with Derrida's wholehearted approval.

Of course, the essay does *not* end on this choice. Derrida continues: "For my part, although these two interpretations must acknowledge and accentuate their difference and define their irreducibility, I do not believe that today there is any question of *choosing*" (293). But what exactly might this mean—*no choosing*? There seems to be a clear choice laid out here between ethical response-ability to the other and unethical resentment of the other. And, as Zygmunt Bauman suggests in *Postmodern Ethics*, wouldn't a poststructuralist or postmodern ethics precisely be one in which "I assign the right to make me responsible" (86) in and through entering a dialogue with the other? Wouldn't *choosing* responsibility toward the other then be the founding moment of ethics?

Indeed, it would seem that this necessary turning over of "the right to make me responsible"—this *choice* of the ethical—is the founding act for any ethics of performative responsibility or answerability to the other. For there to be an ethical subject, I have to give up my dreams of mastery and recognize my cohabitation with the other, aspiring to become what William Connolly calls "a self that works on itself to develop critical responsiveness to that which it is not" (*Ethos*, 70).

And this perhaps reopens a distinctly ethical way to understand the paradoxical role of the self in performative subjectivity. As Bauman suggests in the context of his reading of Levinas, perhaps one could understand subjectivity precisely in terms of the self's ability to sacrifice, the refusal to project oneself into the space of the other. Bauman writes, "The readiness to sacrifice for the sake of the other burdens me with the responsibility which is *moral* precisely for my acceptance that the command to sacrifice applies to me and me only, that the sacrifice is not a matter of exchange or reciprocation of services" (51). Maybe, as Bauman suggests, there is a way to humble the self precisely in terms of its specific "acceptance" of the "command to sacrifice" that is the confrontation with alterity; whatever privilege the ethical self might harbor is gladly relinquished before the other.

As tempting as this may sound, from the performative point of view that I have been deploying throughout this book, such a generous relinquishing merely reconfirms the privilege of the founding subject, who cheerfully allows himself or herself to be drawn into the orbit of responding. In other words, such a conception of generous alterity and responsibility nevertheless protects the privilege of an originary freedom—protects the privilege of the self that can *choose* to be responsible or *choose not* to be responsible. But, as Derrida insists, it is not today a question of *choosing*.

Bauman tellingly writes that ethical subjects who *choose* to sacrifice "are *unique* people, people who do things other people shirk—being too afraid, too weak, or too selfish to do them . . . a standard only I can set for myself" (52). Here, the smugness of the purportedly ethical subject seems fairly clear, and the alterity under consideration seems one that exists merely to reinforce the altruistic good feelings of the self. As Bauman continues on the virtues of this "choosing" responsibility, its deep ethical problems become clearer: "No universal standards then. No looking over one's shoulders, to take a glimpse of what other people 'like me' do. No listening to what they say they do or ought to be doing—and then following their example, absolving myself for not doing anything else" (53). Here I think we begin more clearly to see the difficult question for an ethics of voluntary obligation, for an ethics of *choosing:* it seems to hold open the door for the worst kind of self-assurance. For Bauman, I am authentic and ethical precisely insofar as I live in *contempt* for the other(s)—"no listening to what they say they do or ought to be doing." Though I owe my allegiance to them, it seems more likely that other people distract me from my path of righteousness: "Only in that stout and proud refusal of 'having a reason,' of 'having a foundation,' responsibility sets me free" (77–78).

We seem to have come full circle to a subject that is in fact reassured and bolstered in its freedom by the ability to sacrifice, by its ability to *relinquish* or *refuse* totalization and bravely *choose* ethics.[2] As Bauman continues, he clearly reveals the convoluted logic of this ethic

of sacrifice: ~~"I am fully and truly *for* the Other, since it is I who give~~
her the right to command, make the weak strong, make the silence
speak, make the non-being into being through offering it the right to
command me. 'I am for the other' means I give myself to the Other
as hostage. . . . It is I who take the responsibility, and I may take that
responsibility or I may reject it" (73–74). The ethical hubris in this
passage is close to unbearable. However, it does show very nicely that
the supposed privilege of the other is a specious one in a system where
that privilege is fully and completely a function of my efforts, my deci-
sions, my *choice:* "it is I who give her the right to command, make the
weak strong, make the silence speak, make the non-being into being."
And by the way, I write the songs that make the whole world sing.

This kind of hubris remains inscribed in even the most seemingly
generous self-centered ethical discourses. In a passage that could be
taken as a gloss on Derrida's "I do not believe that today there is any
question of *choosing,*" Levinas writes that in his work "ethical consciousness itself is not invoked . . . as a 'particularly recommendable'
variety of consciousness, but as a concrete form of a movement
more fundamental than freedom, the idea of infinity" ("Philosophy,"
58). Levinas explains in *Otherwise than Being,* "The for-the-other
characteristic of the subject can be interpreted neither as a guilt
complex (which presupposes an *initial* freedom), nor as a natural be-
nevolence or divine 'instinct,' nor as some love or some tendency to
sacrifice. . . . Substitution frees the subject from ennui, that is, from
the enchainment to itself" (124). In Levinas, one does not give up one's
freedom and somehow allow oneself to be subjected. Rather, there is
a necessity to Levinas's performative discourse: I am nothing other
than a function of the infinity of the other; I am subjected rather than
doing the subjecting. To put it slightly differently, Levinas certainly
concurs with social constructionists that "The idea of infinity is the
social relationship" ("Philosophy," 54), but within that relationship
the I is not the locus of power and privilege: the I is nothing other
than performative response, that which says I after the others. There
is, in other words, no originary freedom to be given up or alienated
in Levinas. There is the movement of desire, the movement outward
that does not return to the self: "The idea of infinity . . . is experience
in the sole radical sense of the term: a relationship with the exterior,
with the other, without this exteriority being able to be integrated
into the same" (54). As Gilles Deleuze and Félix Guattari concisely
sum up the stake of this point, "immanence is not immanent 'to'
consciousness but the other way around" (*What Is Philosophy?,* 49).

So responsibility is not merely *choosing* to respond, at least if this responsibility is to be an *affirmation* of alterity. And this, as I have argued in various ways throughout this book, is precisely the ethical component of performative subjectivity. Perform*ative* subjectivity is not simply a perform*ing* subjectivity, which somehow decides what part it will play or what mask it will wear today. The ethics of performativity rest not, as Bauman writes, in the insight that "taking responsibility as if I was already responsible is an act of creation of the moral space" (75); the ethics of performativity rests *not* in choosing the role of "responsible one." Rather, the ethics of performative subjectivity is enacted precisely in and as a *response* to the always already exterior, to the other that is the ground of the same. The point is not that I need always to remember to act "*as if* I was already responsible"; rather, "I" *am* nothing but this responsibility. This notion of performative subjectivity could never, then, guarantee *an* ethics, but this is precisely its ethical component as a necessary yet halting *affirmation* of response to alterity.

Judith Butler's work on performative identity has helped me to articulate this crucial affirmative moment throughout the course of this book. As Butler insists, obligation and response are inseparable in or as performativity: "constraint calls to be rethought as the very condition of performativity. Performativity is neither free play nor theatrical self-presentation" (*Bodies*, 94–95), but rather response to the call of the other. She writes, the other's "call is formative, if not *per*formative" (121), for the response of the "self." Such a notion of performativity, as I have argued throughout, leaves the foundation of the subject always in question, always open to an other performative call or response. Indeed, as I have argued in various ways throughout this book, the primary difficulty with a politics of identity is that it remains unresponsive to the other because it judges otherness always in terms of sameness or a lack of sameness. So, as Butler suggests, "the subject" is not the sole or productive focus of performative inquiry — the subject is never the founding ethical, political, or social moment: "if power orchestrates the formation and sustenance of subjects, then it cannot be accounted for in terms of the 'subject' which is its effect" (9). Identity is always a question of response, of difference, of alterity.

As this text has progressed, Deleuze and Guattari's work has become increasingly central to its site-specific ethics of response, especially in articulating an alterity politics of response that does not begin by figuring otherness as "lack." As Deleuze insists, the diagnosis and deployment of subjectivities is not a dialectical ballet—

the either/or of the subjective essentialism/constructionism debate—
but a hesitating negotiation among the effects that performative
interventions produce: "What counts in desire is not the false alternative of law-spontaneity, nature-artifice; it is the respective play of
territorialities, reterritorializations, and movements of deterritorialization" ("What Is Desire?," 139). Here Deleuze names "what counts"
in performative ethics: examining the production of effects, not the
zero-sum game of deciding what an identity or movement really or
authentically "means." Call its origins socially constructed, call them
essential; either way, the stake of the subject and its ethical force
remains a question of effects: the crucial question is not primarily a
hermeneutic one, but rather a performative one—not What does it
mean? but rather What can it do, how can it respond (otherwise)?

It remains difficult, of course, to theorize or thematize this response, because if you begin by arguing that theoretical philosophy
cannot pretend to be first philosophy, you are then necessarily left
in a space *before* the categorization of *an* ethics—before right versus wrong, legitimate versus illegitimate, self versus other. You find
yourself in an ethical realm rather than inside *an* ethics: in the realm
of performativity rather than doing a performance, responding to
the specific emergence of alterity rather than examining otherness's
transhistorical conditions of possibility. However, I would argue that
this is not a shortcoming nor a cause for lament. Ethics, if it is to be of
any use at all in a postmodern context, has to be precisely an ethics of
response *both* to the concrete other *and* to the emergent other—the
unforeseen other, the wholly other. And just as one does not simply
choose to be a performative subject, one does not merely choose or
not choose an ethics of response: all constatives—all identities and
moralities—are always already performatives.

Perhaps this returns us again to Derrida's "Structure, Sign and Play."
After the seeming call to *choose* ethical affirmation is strangely with-
drawn or called into question, the essay gets even stranger. It ends
not with a *conclusion* about the inadequacy of mourning or a call to
choose poststructuralist alterity, but rather with a *question*. The end
of the essay reads as follows:

> Here there is a kind of question, let us still call it historical,
> whose *conception, formation, gestation,* and *labor* we are only
> catching a glimpse of today. I employ these words, I admit, with
> a glance toward the operations of childbearing—but also with a
> glance toward those who, in a society from which I do not exclude

myself, turn their eyes away when faced by the as yet unnamable
which is proclaiming itself and which can do so, as is necessary
whenever a birth is in the offing, only under the species of the
nonspecies, in the formless, mute, infant, and terrifying form of
monstrosity. (293)

An odd ending indeed. The ethical, Derrida suggests, rests not solely or
even primarily in choosing or refusing to be responsive to this or that
existing category of otherness. Those who turn or respond only to what
they know "turn their eyes away when faced by the as yet unnamable."
But it is toward this wholly other, this "monstrosity," that affirmation is deployed, and whether one "chooses" affirmation or denial,
the "decision" is inexorably based on an affirmation, an otherness, an
event that—like the decision that grows out of it—has future relays
far beyond the control of the subject. Both affirmation and denial are
acts that create effects, irreducibly affirmative acts, and something
other—something monstrous—is necessarily born(e) in affirmation.
Monstrosity is, I think, a word very deliberately chosen by Derrida to
name these incalculable effects of calculation. As Mary Shelley shows
us, even in the attempt to replicate existing categories, monsters
are nevertheless born. The wholly other is performatively conceived,
formed, gestated, and born within the categories of the same.[3]
   In a brief essay on Derrida, "Wholly Otherwise," Levinas references
this inexorably ethical production of alterity in a slightly different reg-
ister. Levinas recalls the exodus from Nazi-occupied France in 1940.
From "these in-between days," he recounts "a symbolic episode":
"somewhere in between Paris and Alençon, a half-drunk barber used
to invite soldiers who were passing on the road to come and have a free
shave in his shop; the 'lads' he used to call them in patriotic language
which soared above the waters or floated up from the chaos. With his
two companions he shaved them free of charge—and it was today"
(4). Of what, one might wonder, is this "episode" "symbolic," in the
"today" of 1940 and/or the "today" of today? Perhaps what we see here
is Levinas's affirmation of the Derridean "monstrous": a performative
affirmation of the "wholly otherwise," the as-yet-unseen, the yet-to-
emerge. The power of the ethical, its line of flight in any "today,"
is precisely the (un)anticipated, monstrous event or emergence of
the future: the impossible, implausible, or nonsensical gesture of the
shave on the retreat, in the midst of a war with no end in sight, when
everything looks its bleakest.
   Levinas suggests that it is precisely in such "in-between days,"

days perhaps all too familiar in recent history, that affirmation of the
wholly other takes on its greatest urgency. By enacting difference,
producing an other "today," the odd and seemingly marginal "episode"
that Levinas recounts here is not so much a symbol as it is a concrete deployment of the ethical as a performative act: the seemingly
impossible yet irreducibly affirmative gesture toward an other future,
an other act. Derrida writes about the ethics of such performativity,
"There would be no event, no history, unless a 'come hither' opened
out and addressed itself to someone, to someone else whom I cannot
and must not define in advance—not as subject, self, consciousness,
nor even as animal, God, person, man or woman, living or dead" ("Deconstruction," 32). To end, then, with this: a performative response
that produces "today" otherwise. Perhaps, in the end, the ethics of
performativity is nothing other—but nothing less—than such a specific, material affirmation of difference.

Introduction · Alterity Politics: Toward an Ethics without Lack

1   As Aronowitz argues, part of its strength lies in the fact that "identity politics narrows the purview of emancipation" ("Situation," 48) and sets out realistically accomplishable goals that are particular to groups of common interest. Therein, however, lies the problem. Aronowitz continues: "From human freedom, [identity politics] dedicates itself to 'our' freedom. This shift has had devastating consequences for any kind of solidarity politics whose presupposition is the underlying community of interest of all oppressed and marginalized groups" (48).

2   For a critique of liberal multiculturalism's identity politics, see Giroux's "Post-Colonial Ruptures," 13–18.

3   In "The Politics of Identity in Late Modern Society" Goldstein and Rayner write, "Identity-claims depend on others for their viability but this fact is rarely acknowledged by the claimants, for to do so would be to acknowledge dependency, *and this is precisely what the claimants want to deny.* This helps explain why the politics of identity fosters grievances that are so difficult to resolve" (371).

4   For a somewhat different analysis of founding performatives, see Derrida's "Declarations of Independence."

5   Deleuze and Guattari's *Anti-Oedipus*, though not cited here, has provided much of the inspiration for this critique of lack. See chapter 7 for a more sustained engagement with this argument.

6   See Grosz, *Volatile Bodies*, on the possibilities for feminism in Deleuze and Guattari's critique of psychoanalysis: "Lack only makes sense insofar as some other, woman, personifies and embodies it for man. Any model of desire that dispenses with the primacy of lack in conceiving desire seems to be a positive step forward, and for that reason alone, worthy of careful consideration" (165).

1 · Today; or, Between Emergence and Possibility: Foucault, Derrida, and Butler on Performative Identity

1   At the end of his 1991 essay on Foucault, Derrida writes: "I am still trying to imagine Foucault's response. I can't quite do it. I would need him to take it on himself" ("'To Do Justice,'" 266). Today, the debate with Foucault remains workless, "in this place where no one can answer for him, in the absolute silence where we nonetheless remain turned toward him" (266).

2   See *The Discourse on Language*, where Foucault posits chance, materiality, and exteriority as privileged sites of intervention within transcendentalizing discourses.

3   See chap. 3 of my *Double Reading*, "Exteriority and Appropriation: Foucault, Derrida and the Discipline of Literary Criticism," for another attempt to think them together.

4   "The reduction of performativity to performance," Butler writes in *Bodies*, "would be a mistake" (234).

5   Though note that Susan Bordo's (fairly representative) critique of Butler is precisely a critique of her "textual" Derrideanism. In *Unbearable Weight*, Bordo argues that Butler is "more the Derridean than the Foucauldian": "Butler's world is one in which language swallows everything, voraciously" (291).

6   Compare Butler's "Poststructuralism and Postmarxism," where she gestures toward a possible intervention between Derrida and Foucault: "At stake in such a comparison will be the production of logical possibility as an effect of power" (11). See also *Bodies*, 244–46.

7   Compare a more recent interview, where Derrida reiterates this commitment: "any coherent deconstruction is about singularity, about events, and about what is ultimately irreducible in them" ("Deconstruction of Actuality," 29). See chapter 5 for a more complete discussion of his point.

8   See *Archaeology*, 126–34.

9   This insistence on violence or force is in fact the substance of Derrida's disagreement with Levinas. See Derrida's "Violence and Metaphysics" and "At This Very Moment."

10 See Foucault's *Archaeology of Knowledge*: "Should we say . . . that a statement refers to nothing if the proposition, to which it lends existence, has no referent? Rather the reverse. We should say not that the absence of the referent brings with it the absence of a correlate for the statement, but that it is the correlative of the statement—that to which it refers, not only what is said, but also what it speaks of, its 'theme'—which makes it possible to say whether or not the proposition has a referent: it alone decides this in a definitive way" (89–90).

11 See Nietzsche's *Genealogy*, essay 3, sect. 16.

12 See, for example, Derrida on foreclosure: "The perpetual threat, that is, the shadow of haunting . . . does not challenge only one thing and another; it threatens the logic that distinguishes one thing from another, the very logic of exclusion or foreclosure" ("'To Do Justice,'" 242). Foucault, I think, would be suspicious of the wholesale nature of haunting's consequences here—the perhaps too quick movement from the singular to the universal, from a specific foreclosure to the conditions of its (im)possibility. Though as Derrida points out, the "quasi-transcendental law of seriality" necessitates "each time, in fact, that the transcendental condition of a series is also, paradoxically, a part of that series" (235).

2 · The Ethics of Dialogue: Bakhtin's Answerability and Levinas's Responsibility

1   See, for example, Nancy's collection *Who Comes after the Subject?*

2   On the imbrication of desire and mastery in Hegel, see Kojève, *Introduction to the Reading of Hegel*. On the deployments of Hegelian desire in contemporary French thought, see Butler's *Subjects of Desire*.

3   A few necessary caveats concerning my usage of Bakhtin's texts: first, it seems prudent to remain agnostic concerning the authorship of the disputed Voloshinov and Medvedev texts; hence I will concern myself exclusively with texts that are undisputably from Bakhtin's hand. For a concise summary of the controversy surrounding the disputed texts, see Morson and Emerson, *Rethinking*, 31–48. Of course, if one takes the controversial texts to be Bakhtin's, one reads a very different (more obviously Marxist) author. As Bialostosky writes, in the texts "published under the name Voloshinov and as Medvedev and Bakhtin, the emphasis shifts somewhat from the unity of person and idea to the context of persons ideologically invested in social and historical worlds occupied by such other persons" (796 n). As befits his polyvocal discourse, there are many

Bakhtins—Bialostosky's "rhetorical" Bakhtin, Carroll's "poststructuralist" Bakhtin, Emerson's "humanist" Bakhtin, Gardiner's "Marxist" Bakhtin (in *Dialogics*), and others—so I should make it clear that my primary concern here is with the "ethical" Bakhtin most closely associated with Holquist's work. Also, I should note that I do not read Russian, and am therefore wholly dependent upon—and beholden to—Bakhtin's translators.

4   See, for example, Emerson's "Russian Orthodoxy and the Early Bakhtin."

5   Certainly, links between Levinas and Bakhtin have been noted by other scholars; see especially Patterson, "Signification, Responsibility, Spirit," and Gardiner, "Alterity and Ethics."

6   Compare Bakhtin from *Problems:* "a living human being cannot be turned into some secondhand, finalizing cognitive process" (38). As he elaborates elsewhere, "beginning with any text—and sometimes passing through a lengthy series of mediating links—we always arrive, in the final analysis, at the human voice, which is to say we come up against the human being" (*Dialogic,* 253). It is perhaps here that one could launch a critique of the unquestioned anthropomorphism that runs deep in both Levinas and Bakhtin; see chap. 3 for the beginnings of such a critique of Levinas.

7   On the irreducibility of the face-to-face relation in Levinas, see *Totality and Infinity,* especially 79–81 and 194–216.

8   This Levinasian notion of the subject-as-hostage differs crucially from Bakhtin's "non-alibi in Being." Bakhtin's non-alibi concerns *my* uniqueness over against the other: "I occupy a place in once-occurrent Being that is unique and never repeatable, a place that cannot be taken by anyone else and is impenetrable for anyone else" (*Toward,* 40). In contrast, Levinas's "not-being-able-to-slip-away-from an assignation" thematizes my uniqueness as a function of the other's call, a function of the fact that my being is constantly penetrated by the others. For Levinas, my uniqueness arises from the fact that I am infinitely substitutable: *always*—rather than Bakhtin's *never*—repeatable.

9   See also Bakhtin's *Toward a Philosophy of the Act* on the authenticity of the self: "I, as once-occurrent, issue or come forth from within myself, whereas all others I find on hand, I come upon them: this constitutes a profound ontological difference in significance within the event of Being" (74). Compare Holquist's *Dialogism:* "The other is in the realm of completedness, whereas I experience time as open and always as yet *un*-completed. . . . [I]n a world filled with the determining energies of impersonal social force, it [i.e., my uncompletedness] is a potential source of freedom" (26).

10 Recall, pace Holquist, that Hegel's *Phenomenology* relentlessly criticizes a Romantic mystified privilege, the idea that subjective experience "is to be felt and intuited" (4). Hegel calls such mysticism a childish "immediacy of faith" that inexorably leads back to the "satisfaction and security of the certainty that consciousness then had" (4). In short, Hegel finds this

totalizing intuitive Romanticism "as prevalent as it is pretentious" (4), and critiques it for providing "edification rather than insight" (5).

11 Though note that the seeds of resentment loom in the margins of Holquist's *Dialogism:* "A dialogic world is one in which I can never have my own way completely, and therefore I find myself plunged into constant interaction with others—and with myself" (39).

12 Holquist goes out of his way to discount what he calls the American liberal misreading of Bakhtin, but when he pens sentences like "There is, then, in Bakhtin's aesthetic an emphasis on the primacy of lived experience in all its bewildering specificity" ("Architectonics," xliv), he holds open the door for a fairly familiar brand of optimistic liberal experience fetishization. Bakhtin doesn't help matters any with sentiments like "At [the novel's] core lay personal experience and free creative imagination" (*Dialogic,* 39). In "Getting Bakhtin, Right and Left," an extended review of Gardiner, Emerson argues (quite persuasively) for the liberal humanist Bakhtin: "To be sure, Bakhtin insists that the self arrives at its unique responsible position in the world through uninterrupted dialogic processes and not through solipsistic withdrawal or identification with transcendent forms. But there is nothing poststructuralist about this move at all. . . . [I]n fact, Bakhtin subscribes to almost *none* of this de-centering business" (294).

13 Compare Holquist, who argues that for Bakhtin, "the basic difference is between self-perception and other-perception. This division cannot be overcome; it can only be mediated. . . . Everything must be approached from the point of view of—point of view" ("Architectonics," xxviii).

14 See Butler's *Subjects,* 1–24, and Smith's *The Spirit and Its Letter,* 1–28, on the rhetorical and narrative complexities of Hegel's *Phenomenology.*

15 See Ziarek, "The Language of Praise," on Levinas's critique of intersubjectivity: "Dialogue is predicated upon a common frame of reference, that is subjectivity, which reduces the otherness of the other to another subject. The other becomes then like myself, an/other me. . . . Thus the other holds no mystery: (s)he, in fact, no longer is other. For Levinas, intersubjectivity then constitutes, under the guise of a mutually respectful dialogue with the other, the domination of the Same in Western philosophy" (95). See Carroll, "The Alterity of Discourse," 74, for a similar critique of intersubjectivity that specifically takes up Holquist's reading of Bakhtin.

16 See Bakhtin's *Art:* "The productiveness of the event of a life does not consist in the merging of all into one. On the contrary, it consists in the intensification of one's own *outsideness* with respect to others, one's own *distinctness* from others: it consists in fully exploiting the privilege of one's own unique place outside other human beings" (88).

17 Compare Bialostosky: "Dialogics as I have represented it has no a priori defense against powerful voices, however apparently distant their concerns or different their subject matters. The only dialogic defense, as some

of Dostoevsky's heroes make clear, is an active, articulate defensiveness that reveals embarrassment at not living up to other people's standards even as it tries to answer their claims and define its identity in terms other than theirs" ("Dialogics," 791).

18 Readers of Levinas will recognize my argument as a version of his critique of Heideggerian *Dasein*. Any number of critics have pointed out the relations between Bakhtin's discourse and Heidegger's; see, for example, Holquist, "Architectonics," xxxvi, and Roberts, "Poetics Hermeneutics Dialogics," 119–23.

19 Here, I perhaps am playing Bakhtinians against Bakhtin himself, who has little patience for a kind of social constructionism or relativism. Though he is clear about the privileges of practical reason—recall that "theoretical philosophy cannot pretend to being a first philosophy" (*Toward,* 19)—he is equally suspicious of any sort of social constructionism: "What follows from this least of all, of course, is any kind of relativism, which denies the autonomy of truth and attempts to turn truth into something relative and conditioned" (9).

3 · "Junk" and the Other: Burroughs and Levinas on Drugs

1 Addiction is from the Latin *addictus,* "given over," one awarded to another as a slave.

2 Although they share similar concerns, Levinas's conception of desire and alterity remains in sharp contradistinction to Lacan's, insofar as the Lacanian horizon of desire for the "great Other" is tied to a conception of lack. For both Lacan and Levinas, desire is animated by its object, but the Hegelian conception of desire as lack or insufficiency (failure to complete itself) remains characteristic of desire in Lacan: the upshot of the Oedipal drama is the lamentable expropriation of the self from the real into the symbolic. Though ostensibly the locus of ethics in Lacan, the Other in fact remains my enemy, the marker for that which constantly frustrates the animating ontological desire of returning to "essence," returning to myself. As Lacan writes in book 2 of the *Seminar,* desire is "a relation of being to lack. This lack is the lack of being properly speaking. It isn't the lack of this or that, but the lack of being whereby the being exists" (223). Compare Levinas, where desire is "an aspiration that is conditioned by no prior lack" ("Meaning," 94). As he writes, "Responsibility for another is not an accident that happens to a subject, but precedes essence. . . . I exist through the other and for the other, *but without this being alienation*" (*Otherwise,* 114; my italics). In Levinas, being for-the-other—which he will call "substitution"—exists *before* essence, before the real; hence, for Levinas there can be no alienation from and/or nostalgia for the re-

turn to self: "Substitution frees the subject from ennui, that is, from the enchainment to itself" (124). For Lacan, need (as loss of the real) subtends and traverses desire. For Levinas, the opposite is the case: any conception of loss or lack is subtended by the infinity of substitution, which exists before the distinction between lack and plenitude.

3 For his engagement with Sartre, see Levinas's "Reality and Its Shadow." Certainly more could be said on this topic, insofar as Sartre's *Nausea* likewise owes a tremendous debt to Heidegger's 1929 lecture on the nothing, "What Is Metaphysics?" Suffice it to say, Levinas is interested in something *other than* the distinction between being and nothingness. See *Otherwise:* "Not *to be otherwise,* but *otherwise than being.* And not to not-be. . . . Being and not-being illuminate one another, and unfold a speculative dialectic which is a determination of being. Or else the negativity which attempts to repel being is immediately submerged by being. . . . The statement of being's *other,* of the otherwise than being, claims to state a difference over and beyond that which separates being from nothingness—the very difference of the *beyond,* the difference of transcendence" (3).

4 The horror of the *il y a* is, in Levinas's concise words, "fear *of* being and not [Heideggerian] fear *for* being" (*Existence,* 62; my italics).

5 For more on this point, see Llewelyn's "The 'Possibility' of Heidegger's Death": "The distinction between a possibility which something *has* and a possibility which something *is* compels us to take notice that Heidegger writes not only of death as a possibility of being, a *Seinsmöglichkeit,* but also of death as a *Seinkönnen.* A *Können* is a capacity, power or potentiality. Ontic potentialities are qualities which things have and may develop, as a child may develop its potentiality to reason. But being towards death is an ontological potentiality, a potentiality of and for being. Dasein *is* its death itself" (137).

6 See Heidegger's *Being and Time:* "Dasein is authentically itself only to the extent that, *as* concernful Being-alongside and solicitous Being-with, it projects itself upon its ownmost potentiality-for-Being rather than upon the possibility of the they-self" (308). For more on this question, consult Manning, *Interpreting Otherwise than Heidegger,* 38–53.

7 Here Levinas seems to have much in common with Butler's work on performative identity in *Gender Trouble.* For Butler, like Levinas, to say that subjective agency is "performative" is *not* to say that agency doesn't exist or that all agency is merely an ironic performance; rather, it is to say that such agency is necessarily a matter of *response* to already given codes. Certainly, focusing on the question of gender would open up a considerable gulf between their projects, but there is at least some traffic between Butler and Levinas on the question of identity and performativity.

8 See *Otherwise:* "In its *being,* subjectivity undoes *essence* by substituting itself for another. Qua one-for-the-other, it is absorbed in signification, in saying or the verb form of the infinite. Signification precedes essence. . . .

Substitution is signification. Not a reference of one term to another, as it appears thematized in the said, but substitution as the very subjectivity of a subject, interruption of the irreversible identity of the essence" (13).

9 Levinas specifically points his reader to Blanchot's *Thomas the Obscure* for the experience of the *il y a* (*Existence*, 63 n). See also Levinas's *Sur Maurice Blanchot*, especially 9–26, and his interview on the *il y a* in *Ethics and Infinity*, 45–52. For more specifically on Blanchot, Levinas, and the *il y a*, see Critchley, "*Il y a*" especially 114–19; Libertson, *Proximity*, 201–11; Wyschogrod, "From the Disaster"; and Davies, "A Fine Risk."

10 Levinas writes in a similar context: "One watches on when there is nothing to watch and despite the absence of any reason for remaining watchful. The bare fact of presence is oppressive; one is held by being, held to be. One is detached from any object, any content, yet there is presence, . . . the universal fact of the *there is*" (*Existence*, 65).

11 See, for example, Habermas, *Philosophical Discourse*, 296–98.

12 Compare Levinas's *Totality and Infinity:* "The idea of infinity, the overflowing of finite thought by its content, effectuates the relation of thought with what exceeds its capacity. . . . This is the situation we call welcome of the face" (197).

13 See Nietzsche's *On the Genealogy of Morals*, essay 3, sect. 28.

14 See Levinas's "Reality and Its Shadow," 131.

15 Levinas wishes to rescue a notion of transcendence as phenomenological self-overcoming, but shorn of its ontological intentionality. Davies defines "transcendent" as follows: "that is to say, for Levinas, [the transcendent subject] can approach the other *as* other in its 'approach,' in 'proximity'" ("A Fine Risk," 201).

16 This may be more accurately, or at least philosophically, posed as a "good infinite, bad infinite" situation, which would bring us to a consideration of Hegel, for whom Levinas's alterity would be precisely a kind of bad (unrecuperable) infinite. It seems clear what Hegel protects in his exiling of the bad infinite: it keeps the dialectical system safe from infinite specular regression. Here, however, I would like to fold Levinas's skepticism concerning Hegel back onto Levinas's own text: Why the exiling of the *il y a* as a bad infinite, and what privilege is—however surreptitiously— protected by or in such a move? See Gasché's "Structural Infinity," in his *Inventions of Difference*, for more on the Hegelian bad infinite.

17 Compare Derrida's discussion of AIDS in "The Rhetoric of Drugs": "The virus (which belongs neither to life nor to death) may *always already* have broken into any 'intersubjective' space. . . . [A]t the heart of that which would preserve itself as a dual intersubjectivity it inscribes the mortal and indestructible trace of the third—not the third as the condition of the symbolic and the law, but the third as destructuring structuration of the social bond" (20).

18   This is Levinas's wording in the interview "The Paradox of Morality," 169.

19   This is contra Peperzak's *To the Other*, which casts Levinas as a metaphysician profoundly disdainful of the social or material world:

> The secret of all philosophy that considers society and history to be the supreme perspective is war and exploitation. . . . As based on the products of human activities, the judgment of history is an unjust outcome, and if the social totality is constituted by violence and corruption, there seems to be no hope for a just society unless justice can be brought into it from the outside. This is possible only if society and world history do not constitute the dimension of the ultimate. The power of nonviolence and justice lies in the dimension of speech and the face-to-face, the dimension of straightforward intersubjectivity and fundamental ethics, which opens the closed totality of anonymous productivity and historicity. (178–79)

20   For more on the question of animality in Levinas, see Llewelyn's *The Middle Voice of Ecological Conscience*, 49–67. See also Critchley's treatment of this topic in *The Ethics of Deconstruction*, 180–82.

21   Compare Heidegger's translation of this Aristotelian privilege in "The Origin of the Work of Art": "Language alone brings what is, as something that is, into the Open for the first time. Where there is no language, as in the being of stone, plant and animal, there is also no openness of what is. . . . The primitive . . . is always futureless" (73, 76).

22   For a critique of Levinas's thematization of the feminine, see Irigaray's "The Fecundity of the Caress" and her "Questions to Emmanuel Levinas: On the Divinity of Love." For an outline of the debate and something of a defense of Levinas, see Chanter, "Feminism and the Other."

23   The third epigraph to *Otherwise*, *Pensées* 112, reads: "'. . . That is my place in the sun.' That is how the usurpation of the whole world began."

4 · *Enjoy Your Chiasmus! Ethics, Failure, and the Performative in Žižek and de Man*

1   See Cohen, *Anti-Mimesis*, for an example of thinking de Man and Žižek together.

2   De Man tends to describe this legacy as Nietzschean (see the Nietzsche chapters in *Allegories*); however, Warminski, *Readings in Interpretation*, and Gearhardt, *The Interrupted Dialectic*, among others, demonstrate the essential links between Hegel's chiasmic work and a de Manian tradition of criticism.

3   It might be interesting to compare Derrida's own deployment of this popular trope against Searle throughout *Limited Inc.*

4   For a version of that argument, see my *Double Reading*, especially chap. 2.

5 As de Man argues, this figurality or rhetoricity names the "literary" qualities of Rousseau's text, "literary" here meaning "any text that implicitly
or explicitly signifies its own rhetorical mode and prefigures its own misunderstanding as the correlative of its rhetorical nature" (*Blindness*, 136).
And de Man contends that Derrida shares this literary rhetoricity with
Rousseau.

6 Compare Žižek's very similar critique of the "traditional 'deconstructionist' reproach to Hegel: true, Hegel acknowledges this radical withdrawal
of the subject into itself, this 'night of the world,' but only as a passing
moment which is quickly sublated (*aufgehoben*) in a new spiritual reality
of names" (*Enjoy*, 50). Again, Žižek argues that this Derridean critique
has gotten it wrong by trying to insert the theme of lack or failure as a
critique of Hegel, when in fact the Hegelian system *runs on lack*. As he
writes, Derrida "falls short of the crucial accent of Hegel: the experience
of 'abstract negativity,' the 'psychotic' withdrawal of the subject into self
(the 'night of the world'), is not a passing moment" (50).

7 Žižek writes, "What we forget, when we pursue our daily life, is that our
human universe is nothing but an embodiment of the radically inhuman
'abstract negativity,' of the abyss we experience when we face the 'night of
the world' " (*Enjoy*, 53).

8 Žižek writes in *Tarrying*, "in Hegel's philosophy, 'reconciliation' does not
designate the moment when 'substance becomes subject,' when absolute
subjectivity is elevated into the productive ground of all entities, but
rather the acknowledgment that the dimension of subjectivity is inscribed
into the very core of Substance in the guise of an *irreducible lack which
forever prevents it from achieving full self-identity*" (26; my italics). See
also 88–91 and *Enjoy*, 50–53.

9 See Derrida's "Signature."

10 Butler writes about this kind of postmodern pragmatist constructionism
in *Bodies That Matter*: "it is important to resist that theoretical gesture of pathos in which exclusions are simply affirmed as sad necessities
of signification" (53). Butler likewise remains suspicious of the "liberal"
multiculturalist position that would ask us to walk a mile in the other's
shoes: "sympathy involves a substitution of oneself for another that may
well be a colonization of the other's position *as* one's own" (118).

11 See, for example, Žižek on a Lacanian notion of history: "the only way to
save historicity from the fall into historicism, into the notion of the linear
succession of 'historical epochs,' is to conceive these epochs as a series of
ultimately failed attempts to deal with the same 'unhistorical' traumatic
kernel" (*Enjoy*, 81).

5 · Is It the Shoes? Otherness and Exemplarity in Jameson, Heidegger, and Derrida

1 See, for example, Bernstein, *A Poetics*, especially 90–101; Currie, "Andy Warhol"; and Leitch, "Postmodern Culture," especially 119–22.

2 Levinas continues: "To understand the non-I, access must be found through an entity, an abstract essence which is and is not. In it is dissolved the other's *alterity*. The foreign being, instead of maintaining itself in the inexpungable fortress of its singularity, instead of facing, becomes a theme and an object. It fits under a concept already. . . . It falls into the network of a priori ideas, which I bring to bear, so as to capture it" ("Philosophy," 50).

3 Though philosophical tidiness has its own sociopolitical import, as Derrida reminds us in the following remarks on Marx: "I persist in believing that there is no theoretical or political benefit to be derived from precipitating contracts or articulations, as long as their conditions have not been rigorously elucidated. Eventually, such precipitation will have the effect only of dogmatism, confusion or opportunism" (*Positions*, 62).

4 See, e.g., Derrida's afterword to *Limited Inc.*, 148–49.

5 Compare Heidegger's famous analysis of instrumentality and the hammer in sections 15–16 of *Being and Time*.

6 For more on *techné* and *poesis*, see Heidegger's 1953 "The Question Concerning Technology," especially 294–317.

7 I would argue that this attempt to protect the artwork from a certain scrutiny is the most keenly "modernist" component of Heidegger's project. See, however, Cumming's "The Odd Couple" for an attempt to use this Heideggerian autonomy of art as a bulwark against Derrida's reading of "Origin." Cumming writes that, in the end, "Heidegger might well view Derrida as conspiring with the 'assault' that super-imposes preconceptions deriving from the artefact" (520).

8 I steal these, Foucault's final words on Magritte, from *This Is Not a Pipe*, 54.

9 See, for example, Heidegger's (in)famous analysis of the inauthenticity of *das Man* (the "they") in *Being and Time*: "The self of everyday *Dasein* is the *they-self* [*das Man-selbst*], which we distinguish from the *authentic self*—that is, from the self which has been taken hold of in its own way. As they-self, the particular *Dasein* has been *dispersed* into the 'they,' and must first find itself" (167).

10 For more on Derrida's reading of Heidegger in "Restitutions," see Franklin, "A Differant Quest for Truth and Shoes," and Payne "Derrida, Heidegger, and Van Gogh's 'Old Shoes.'"

11 Another example: as Charles Bernstein argues concerning Jameson's reading of language poetry, it is somewhat specious for Jameson to conclude that any contemporary paratactic writing practice is merely symptomatic of late capital's pernicious influence:

juxtaposition of logically unconnected sentences or sentence frag-
ments can be used to theatricalize the limitations of conventional
narrative development, to suggest the impossibility of communication, to represent speech, or as part of a prosodic mosaic constituting
a newly emerging (or then again, traditional but neglected) meaning
formation. These uses need have nothing in common. . . . Nor is
the little-known painter who uses a Neo-Hellenic motif in her work
necessarily doing something comparable to the architect who incor-
porates Greek columns into a multimillion-dollar downtown office
tower. But it is just this type of mishmashing that is the negative horizon of those discussions of postmodernism that attempt to describe it
in unitary socioeconomic terms. (A Poetics, 91–92)

12   In "The Still Life as Personal Object," Schapiro argues that there are at
least eight paintings of shoes found in Van Gogh's collected works (205).
Undoubtedly, one could find many more or many less: aside from the foot-
gear featured in three other still lifes (Hulsker 920, 1233, and 1364), shoes
also figure prominently, for example, in many of the early figure studies
(Hulsker 201–283) and the "working peasant" paintings of summer 1885
(Hulsker 826–910).

I encountered difficulty in securing copyright permissions to reproduce
all of these images, but I trust the sampling of Van Gogh's shoe paintings offered here gives some indication of the complexity of his serial
composition practices.

13   If we take Heidegger at his word that he refers to a painting he saw in
Amsterdam in 1930 (see Schapiro, "Still Life," 205, citing a 6 May 1965
personal correspondence from Heidegger), we should note that, aside from
Figure 1, the only other version of "peasant shoes" displayed at this show
was Figure 4. Heidegger might, however, have had the opportunity to view
Figure 8 at a show in Basel in 1926, about the time he would have been fin-
ishing Being and Time in Marburg. One can only conjecture concerning
the identity of the mysterious "picture on the wall" in sect. 44 (260).

14   I thank Neil Printz, consulting editor for the ongoing Andy Warhol Catalogue Raisonné, for his help in coming to this ballpark number, which is
provisional and does not include Warhol's editioned multiples.

15   See, for example, Baudrillard's Simulations: "For the sign to be pure, it has
to duplicate itself: [but] it is the duplication of the sign which destroys its
meaning. This is what Andy Warhol demonstrates also: the multiple repli-
cas of Marilyn's face are there to show at the same time the death of the
original and the end of representation" (136).

16   For more on Derrida and exemplarity, see Gasché, "God"; Ulmer, Applied
Grammatology; and Warminski, Readings in Interpretation—all treated,
and found wanting, by Harvey. Also, see Naas's introduction to Derrida's
The Other Heading, which takes up exemplarity and/as the political in
Derrida.

17   Though it may seem that Derrida's interest in the visual arts is a recent
     or tangential development, we should recall one of his earliest published
     texts, *Speech and Phenomena*, especially the (in)famous finale of that Der-
     ridean analysis of Husserl: "There was never any perception" (103). This is
     a justifiably famous and oft-cited passage, but we should likewise keep in
     mind the passage cited by Derrida from Husserl's own text as an example
     of this point: " 'A name on being mentioned reminds us of the Dresden
     gallery. . . . We wander through the rooms. . . . A painting by Terniers . . .
     represents a gallery of paintings. . . . The paintings of this gallery would
     represent in their turn paintings, which on their part exhibited readable
     inscriptions and so forth' " (*Speech*, 104, citing Husserl's *Ideas I*).

18   Compare Derrida: "As always, empiricism has a vocation for heterology"
     (*Specters*, 123).

6 · Becoming-Black: Repetition and Difference in Baraka's Blues People *and Reed's* Mumbo Jumbo

1   Perhaps Du Bois's discussion of "double consciousness," *Souls*, 1–7, is
    the common touchstone for subsequent discussions of African American
    repetition with a difference. For theoretical discussions of repetition and
    difference in black cultural traditions, see Henry Louis Gates, *The Sig-
    nifying Monkey*, and Snead, "Repetition as a Figure of Black Culture."
    For concrete demonstrations of how a wide range of African American
    writers have repeated Western forms with a difference, see Bell, *The Afro-
    American Novel and Its Traditions*.

2   See Harris's *The Jazz Aesthetic:* "It is not an improvement or modification
    of available techniques that the black artist requests; rather, his call is for
    an entirely new grammar" (26).

3   Though note that the vocabulary of the concept changes in Deleuze and
    Guattari's late work *What Is Philosophy?*: what in *Difference and Repe-
    tition* is called a "concept"—the static arresting of a flow—in *What is
    Philosophy?* will be called a "function." In fact, the concept will come
    to name the productive deterritorialization of philosophy: "It is a *con-
    cept* that apprehends the event, its becoming, its inseparable variations;
    whereas a function grasps a state of affairs, a time and variables, with their
    relations depending on time. The concept has a power of repetition that is
    distinct from the discursive power of the function. In its production and
    reproduction, the concept has the reality of a virtual, of an incorporeal, of
    an impassible, in contrast with the functions of an actual state" (159).

4   Most of these differences have to do with a larger discussion about Marx-
    ism. Reed's self-professed individualism makes him suspicious of Marxian
    collectivity. As he writes in a 1974 address to the Afro-American Writers
    Conference, "a good deal of discussion in the last years has been clogged

up with pseudo-Marxist nit-picking, abstract thought. Marx recognized
man's material needs, but he didn't recognize man's psychic needs"
(*Shrovetide*, 58). Or, as he puts it more bluntly in his self-interview: "why
all this antagonism toward individuality?" (140). For Baraka, there's plenty
wrong with individuality: "Recently, the bourgeoisie has been pushing
Ishmael Reed very hard. . . . Reed stumps for individualism, and asserts
ubiquitously that the leadership of Black folks is the Black middle class,
rather than the working class" ("Afro-American," 11). For Baraka, who calls
Reed a "traitor" and "arsehole" (12), Reed belongs among the accommoda-
tionist "*formalists*, for whom form is principal or form is everything, [and
who] generally uphold bourgeois aesthetics. We get offered nothing, really,
except subjectivism, elitism, solipsism—the world-erasing, super 'I' over
everything" (12). I discuss the tension between Reed and Baraka in more
detail below; for now, suffice it to say that I find Baraka's dismissal a bit
hasty.

5 Compare the strategy of the Slovenian punk band Laibach, who in the
1980s deployed alienation as a bulwark against Soviet-style communism.
As Žižek and Salecl write, "In Yugoslavia, it was an extreme form of alienation, a totally non-transparent system that nobody, including those in
the power structure, could comprehend. There were almost two million
laws in operation. No one could master it. This was the paradox: this is
what you get when you want total disalienation or pure transparency. This
was how we experienced Laibach, for example. Their fundamental cry, for
us, was 'We want more alienation'" ("Lacan in Slovenia," 26).

6 Compare Baraka: "The shabbiness, even embarrassment, of Hazel Scott
playing 'concert boogie woogie' before thousands of white middle-class
music lovers, who all assumed that this music was Miss Scott's invention,
is finally no more hideous than the spectacle of an urban, college-trained
Negro musician pretending, perhaps in all sincerity, that he has the same
field of emotional reference as his great grandfather, the Mississippi slave"
(*Blues*, 218).

7 Reed writes, in the context of Berbelang's discussion of Faust in *Mumbo
Jumbo*, "Western man doesn't know the difference between a *houngan* [Vo-
doun priest, healer] and a *bokor* [charlatan]. He once knew this difference
but the knowledge was lost when the Atonists crushed the opposition" (91).

8 See Baraka's assessment from the early '60s in *Black Music:* "The cool
and hard bop/funk movements since the '40's seem pitifully tame, even
decadent, when compared to the music men like Ornette Coleman, Sonny
Rollins, John Coltrane, Cecil Taylor and some others have been making
recently" (16). As I'll argue in more detail later, for Baraka the improvisational force of Coleman makes him—through Coltrane—the legitimate
heir to bebop.

9 See Deleuze and Guattari's *Anti-Oedipus*, 69–70, 76. In "Deterritorial-

izing 'Deterritorialization'" Holland writes, such "connective synthesis produces not the closed binary couple, 'this and that,' but rather an open-ended series 'this and then that and then this . . .'" (55).

10 Reed writes in *Mumbo Jumbo:* "Jazz was a Jes Grew which followed the Jes Grew of Ragtime" (214), and Atonists realize that they will have to "use something up-to-date to curb Jes Grew. To knock it dock it co-opt it swing it or bop it" (64). On that co-opting, see Baraka's "Swing—From Verb to Noun" in *Blues People.*

11 See Baraka's *Black Music:* "Alto saxophonist, Charlie Parker, was one of the two most exciting soloists jazz has seen so far; the other, of course, being Louis Armstrong" (37–38).

12 For more on this question, see Bell, *The Afro-American Novel,* 27.

13 For an example of that challenge, see Johnson, "Hear Me Talkin' to Ya," who argues that the site-specific performative nature of jazz improvisation makes it a form "highly resistant to commodification" (1).

14 On the complexities of improvisation, see Berliner's *Thinking in Jazz,* especially 1–20 and 63–95. See also Gioia's chap. 2, "Jazz and the Primitivist Myth," in *The Imperfect Art.*

15 See Hegel's (in)famous pages on Africa in *Lectures on the Philosophy of World History,* 173–89. For incisive commentary on Hegel and Africa, see Kuykendall, "Hegel and Africa," and Snead, "Repetition."

16 See Hegel's *Phenomenology,* where this movement of chiasmic inversion is thematized as "the simple essence of life, the soul of the world, the universal blood, whose omnipresence is neither disturbed nor interrupted by any difference, but rather is itself every difference, as also their suppression" (100).

17 Compare Deleuze and Guattari's *What Is Philosophy?:* "Philosophy is becoming, not history; it is the coexistence of planes, not the succession of systems" (59).

18 For more on the topic of "minority" in Deleuze and Guattari, see "What Is Minor Literature?," where they argue that Kafka's use of "Prague German" as a minor or "deterritorialized language" "can be compared in another context to what blacks in America today are able to do with the English language" (59).

19 Rap producer Hank Shocklee strikes a similar chord: "music is nothing but organized noise. You can take anything—street sounds, us talking, whatever you want—and make it music by organizing it. That's still our philosophy, to show people that this thing you call music is a lot broader than you think it is" (in Rose, *Black Noise,* 82).

20 And here one clearly reads Deleuze's debt to Nietzschean notions of interpretation as the weighing of forces, as the becoming-active of reactive force. See, for example, *Nietzsche and Philosophy,* 147–94. Compare West on the reactive force self-deployed in the black community as either as-

similationism or nationalism: "one does *not* find this kind of 'reactive' behavior in jazz. Charlie Parker didn't give a damn" what the mainstream thought of him ("Charlie Parker," 63).

21   See Du Bois's "Of the Meaning of Progress" in *Souls:* "Progress, I understand, is necessarily ugly" (43). Du Bois continues, "How shall man measure progress where the dark-faced Josie lies? How many heartfuls of sorrow shall balance a bushel of wheat?" (45). See also Snead, "Repetition," who argues that the tying of repetition to some Hegelian teleological notion of "difference, defined as progress and growth" (214), makes it impossible to understand African Americans' unique culture of repetition.

22   On the deployments of "negative freedom" in poststructualist thought, see McGowan, *Postmodernism and Its Critics,* especially chap. 4.

23   See Holland, "Deterritorializing 'Deterritorialization'": "The best instance of absolutely deterritorialized collective enunciation I know of is still improvisational jazz" (65 n).

24   For Deleuze and Guattari, if we want to follow the paths of improvisatory becoming, finally we cannot talk at all of things becoming-human, things being brought under the sway of human economic control: "Music dispatches molecular flows. Of course . . . music is not the privilege of human beings; the universe, the cosmos, is made of refrains; the question in music is that of a power of deterritorializing permeating nature, animals, the elements, and deserts as much as human beings" (*Thousand,* 309). Compare Reed's telegram in *Mumbo Jumbo:* "THIS JUST IN! OUTBREAKS OF JES GREW 60 MILES FROM NEW YORK CITY. 30,000 CASES REPORTED INCLUDING COWS, CHICKENS, SHEEP AND HORSES, DISPROVING SPECULATIONS THAT ITS EFFECTS ARE CONFINED TO THE HUMAN SPECIES. EVEN THE SAP IN THE MAPLE TREES MOVES NASTY" (105–6).

25   Compare Baraka: "there *is* an Afro-American culture . . . impossible without the American experience, but it is a *specific* culture" ("Afro-American," 9–10; Baraka's ellipsis and italics).

26   See also *Flight to Canada,* where it is tempting to conflate Raven's arch aestheticism with Reed's project: "He was so much against slavery that he had begun to include prose and poetry in the same book, so that there would be no arbitrary boundaries between them. . . . Each man to his own Canada" (88). However, in the end Uncle Robin seems to be Reed's "hero" in *Flight:* while 40's and Leechfield play out the dead-end nationalist versus assimilationist debate and Raven fawns over his writing (bravely mixing genres in the fight against slavery), Uncle Robin—the "house Tom"—arranges to murder Swille and takes over his estate.

7 · White Male Anger: Failure, Resentment, and Performative Political Theory

1   For similarities and differences between Butler and Laclau, see their exchange in *diacritics*.

2   The report was released on 22 July 1997.

3   Recall Limbaugh's self-generated intellectual genealogy, "Kierkegaard, Nietzsche, Limbaugh," and the Nietzschean title of Liddy's autobiography, *Will*. Buchanan, for his part, was a philosophy major at Georgetown (see Crawford, *Thunder on the Right*, 175, 190).

4   See Omi and Winant, "Response to Stanley Aronowitz," for a powerful analysis of white male anger: "These folks are now experiencing an 'identity deficit': formerly, whiteness and maleness constituted cultural norms, and were thus invisible, transparent. Now, this unquestioned identity is being replaced by a kind of 'double consciousness.' Whites and males must now manage their racial and gender identities to some degree, just as nonwhites and women have always done. Does this mean that they must necessarily identify with reactionary racial or gender politics?" (131).

5   Specifically, Modleski is here discussing Deleuze's reading of masochism—the potential for a strategy of renouncing the father by entering into a masochistic relationship with the mother, who symbolically beats the normative law of the father out of the son—and its applicability to men's attempts to join in feminist ethical resistance to the law of the father.

6   *The Turner Diaries* (written by Pierce under the name Andrew Macdonald) is a right-wing fiction about the coming race war in America, and has been taken by many extreme WAMs as a kind of blueprint. Pierce's novel, for example, portrays the destruction of FBI Headquarters by an ammonium nitrate fertilizer bomb packed into a delivery truck, the strategy later used by *Turner* fan McVeigh in Oklahoma City (see Marks, 59). Likewise, extremist group The Order—responsible for the murder of Jewish talk-show host Alan Berg and a $3.6 million armored car heist used to finance Aryan movements—overtly took its inspiration from *Turner's* portrayal of "'the Organization,' a right wing group that starts a race war against the System, including extreme violence to eliminate Jews, blacks and passive whites" (Marks, 86).

7   For suggestions on deploying this anger otherwise, see Ivins, "Lone Star Republic": "Working-class people are getting screwed by their own government. . . . More tax breaks for the rich mean a larger share of the tax burden for everybody else. What we have here is just a little case of misdirected anger" (5). See also Omi and Winant, "Response," and groups like Angry White Guys *for* Affirmative Action (http://www.cts.com/browse/publish/rocka.html).

8   See *The Nation* 265 no. 5 (August 1997):7.

9 See Crawford, *Thunder*, on the new right's politics of resentment; a conservative himself, he traces the right's move from a kind of William F. Buckley model of reasoned argument to the Reaganite model of resentful affect.

10 For Connolly, this absence should be figured as an *excess* rather than *lack* (see *Ethos*, 55), but it seems to me that one cannot so easily play excess off against lack, insofar as both depend on some chimeric notion of normative wholeness.

11 See Butler's *Psychic* on the inevitability of bad conscience in the *Genealogy:* "The internalization of instinct—which takes place when the instinct does not immediately discharge as the deed—is understood to produce the soul or the psyche instead; the pressure exerted from the walls of society forces an internalization which culminates in the production of the soul, this production being understood as a primary artistic accomplishment, the fabrication of an ideal" (74). Although this is certainly true in Nietzsche, there is nevertheless a topology of forces that one can diagnose, and not all of those forces are inherently "reactive."

12 See "Axiomatic," the introduction to Sedgwick's *Epistemology*. As an example of social constructionism used against queers, see conservative columnist Linda Bowles, writing after the "coming-out" episode of TV's *Ellen:* "Homosexuals are made, not born. With our dumb permission, they are using the public-school classrooms to indoctrinate our children. . . . They aren't trying to get into the Boy Scouts because they want to learn to tie knots or into the military because they want to fight wars" ("Ellen Show," 2).

13 Compare Žižek's "critique" of Deleuze and Guattari: "at the level of 'micro-power,' the Khmer-Rouge regime functioned as an 'anti-Oedipal' regime in its purest, i.e., as the 'dictature of adolescents,' instigating them to denounce their parents" (*Tarrying*, 224).

14 Just-in-time delivery, for example, is a new business formation that, though lamentable in most of its effects on working people, nevertheless opens up possibilities for effective interventions. As any number of GM work stoppages have proven in recent years, with the advent of JIT, a strike at a single supply or relay link can cripple an entire company.

Conclusion · *Choosing Ethics, Affirming Alterity*

1 The "choice" that Derrida lays out here seems a reinscription of Nietzsche's distinction between the "rational man" and the "intuitive man" at the end of "On Truth and Lying."

2 But as Bataille shows in "Hegel, Death and Sacrifice," this ability to sacrifice is precisely the *privilege* of the human subject; so it is difficult to thematize sacrifice unproblematically as the disruption of such a privilege.

3   Derrida writes on the metaphorics of birth; "With the birth of a child—
the obvious image of an absolute arrival—you can analyze the causalities,
the genealogical, genetic, and symbolic conditions, and all the wedding
preparations as well, if you like. But even if such an analysis could ever
be complete, you would never be able to eliminate the element of chance
which constitutes the place of this taking-place" ("Deconstruction," 36).

Works Cited

Altieri, Charles. *Canons and Consequences: Reflections on the Ethical Force of Imaginative Ideals*. Evanston, IL: Northwestern University Press, 1990.

Aronowitz, Stanley. "Against the Liberal State: ACT-UP and the Emergence of Postmodern Politics." In *Social Postmodernism: Beyond Identity Politics*, edited by Linda Nicholson and Steven Seidman. Cambridge, UK: Cambridge University Press, 1995. 357–83.

———. "The Situation of the Left in the United States." *Socialist Review* 23, no. 3 (1994): 5–80.

Austin, J. L. *How to Do Things with Words*. Edited by J. O. Urmson and Marina Sbisà. Cambridge, MA: Harvard University Press, 1975.

Bakhtin, M. M. *Art and Answerability: Early Philosophical Essays*. Edited by Michael Holquist and Vadim Liapunov. Translated by Vadim Liapunov. Austin: University of Texas Press, 1990.

———. *The Dialogic Imagination*. Edited by Michael Holquist. Translated by Caryl Emerson and Michael Holquist. Austin: University of Texas Press, 1981.

———. *Problems of Dostoevsky's Poetics*. Edited and translated by Caryl Emerson. Minneapolis: University of Minnesota Press, 1984.

———. *Toward a Philosophy of the Act*. Edited by Michael Holquist and Vadim

Liapunov. Translated by Vadim Liapunov. Austin: University of Texas
Press, 1993.

Baraka, Amiri. "Afro-American Literature and Class Struggle." *Black American Literature Forum* 14, no. 1 (1980): 5–14.

———. "Black Art." In *The LeRoi Jones/Amiri Baraka Reader*, edited by William J. Harris. New York: Thunder's Mouth, 1991. 219–20.

———. *Black Music*. New York: William Morrow, 1969.

———. "The 'Blues Aesthetic' and the 'Black Aesthetic': Aesthetics as the Continuing Political History of a Culture." *Black Music Research Journal* 11, no. 2 (1991): 101–9.

———. *Blues People: Negro Music in White America*. New York: William Morrow, 1963.

———. "Interview with William J. Harris." In *Conversations with Amiri Baraka*, edited by Charlie Reilly. Jackson: University of Mississippi Press, 1994. 174–84.

———. "The Legacy of Malcolm X." In *The LeRoi Jones/Amiri Baraka Reader*, edited by William J. Harris. New York: Thunder's Mouth, 1991. 161–68.

———. "Preface to the Reader." In *The LeRoi Jones/Amiri Baraka Reader*, edited by William J. Harris. New York: Thunder's Mouth, 1991. xi–xiv.

Bataille, Georges. "Hegel, Death and Sacrifice." Translated by Jonathan Strauss. *Yale French Studies* 78 (1990): 9–28.

Baudrillard, Jean. *Simulations*. Translated by Paul Foss et al. New York: Semiotext(e), 1983.

Bauman, Zygmunt. *Postmodern Ethics*. Cambridge, UK: Blackwell, 1993.

Bell, Bernard. *The Afro-American Novel and Its Traditions*. Amherst: University of Massachusetts Press, 1988.

Berliner, Paul F. *Thinking in Jazz: The Infinite Art of Improvisation*. Chicago: University of Chicago Press, 1994.

Bernstein, Charles. *A Poetics*. Cambridge, MA: Harvard University Press, 1992.

Bhabha, Homi K. "DissemiNation: Time, Narrative and the Margins of the Modern Nation." In *Nation and Narration*, edited by Homi K. Bhabha. New York: Routledge, 1990. 291–322.

Bialostosky, Don H. "Dialogics as an Art of Discourse in Literary Criticism." *PMLA* 101, no. 5 (1986): 788–97.

Bordo, Susan. *Unbearable Weight: Feminism, Western Culture and the Body*. Berkeley: University of California Press, 1993.

Bowles, Linda. "The Ellen Show, a Propaganda Triumph." *Grand Rapids Press*, 9 May 1997: 2.

Brown, Wendy. *States of Injury: Power and Freedom in Late Modernity*. Princeton: Princeton University Press, 1995.

———. "Wounded Attachments." *Political Theory* 21, no. 3 (1993): 390–410.

Burroughs, William. "Christ and the Museum of Extinct Species." *Conjunctions* 13 (1989): 264–73.

———. *Junky*. New York: Penguin, 1977.

———. *Naked Lunch*. New York: Grove, 1992.

Butler, Judith. *Bodies That Matter*. New York: Routledge, 1993.

———. "Burning Acts: Injurious Speech." In *Performativity and Performance*, edited by Eve Kosofsky Sedgwick and Andrew Parker. New York: Routledge, 1994. 197-227.

———. "Exchange with Ernesto Laclau." *diacritics* 27, no. 1 (1997): 4-12.

———. *Excitable Speech: A Politics of the Performative*. New York: Routledge, 1997.

———. *Gender Trouble: Feminism and the Subversion of Identity*. New York: Routledge, 1990.

———. "Poststructuralism and Postmarxism." *diacritics* 23, no. 4 (1993): 3-11.

———. *The Psychic Life of Power: Theories in Subjection*. Palo Alto: Stanford University Press, 1997.

———. *Subjects of Desire: Hegelian Reflections in Twentieth-Century France*. New York: Columbia University Press, 1987.

Carroll, David. "The Alterity of Discourse: Form, History, and the Question of the Political in M. M. Bakhtin." *diacritics* 13, no. 2 (1983): 65-83.

Chanter, Tina. "Feminism and the Other." In *The Provocation of Levinas*, edited by Robert Bernasconi and David Wood. London: Routledge, 1988. 32-56.

Cohen, Tom. *Anti-Mimesis: From Plato to Hitchcock*. Cambridge, UK: Cambridge University Press, 1994.

Connolly, William. *The Ethos of Pluralization*. Minneapolis: University of Minnesota Press, 1995.

———. *Identity/Difference*. Ithaca, NY: Cornell University Press, 1991.

Crawford, Alan. *Thunder on the Right: The "New Right" and the Politics of Resentment*. New York: Pantheon, 1980.

Critchley, Simon. *The Ethics of Deconstruction: Derrida and Levinas*. Cambridge, UK: Blackwell, 1992.

———. "*Il y a*—A Dying Stronger than Death (Blanchot with Levinas)." *Oxford Literary Review* 15, nos. 1-2 (1993): 81-131.

Culler, Jonathan. *On Deconstruction*. Ithaca, NY: Cornell University Press, 1982.

Cumming, R. D. "The Odd Couple: Heidegger and Derrida." *Review of Metaphysics* 34 (1981): 487-521.

Currie, Christopher. "Andy Warhol: Enigma, Icon, Master." *Semiotica* 80, nos. 3-4 (1990): 253-63.

Davies, Paul. "A Fine Risk: Reading Blanchot Reading Levinas." In *Re-Reading Levinas*, edited by Robert Bernasconi and Simon Critchley. Bloomington: Indiana University Press, 1991. 201-28.

de Greef, Jan. "Skepticism and Reason." Translated by Dick White. In *Face to Face with Levinas*, edited by Richard A. Cohen. Albany: State University of New York Press, 1986. 159-80.

Deleuze, Gilles. *Difference and Repetition.* Translated by Paul Patton. New York: Columbia University Press, 1994.

———. *Nietzsche and Philosophy.* Translated by Hugh Tomlinson. New York: Columbia University Press, 1983.

———. "Psychoanalysis and Desire." In *The Deleuze Reader,* edited by Constantin V. Boundas. New York: Columbia University Press, 1993. 105–14.

———. "What Is Desire?" In *The Deleuze Reader,* edited by Constantin V. Boundas. New York: Columbia University Press, 1993. 136–44.

Deleuze, Gilles, and Félix Guattari. *Anti-Oedipus.* Vol. 1 of *Capitalism and Schizophrenia.* Translated by Robert Hurley et al. Minneapolis: University of Minnesota Press, 1983.

———. *A Thousand Plateaus.* Vol. 2 of *Capitalism and Schizophrenia.* Translated by Brian Massumi. Minneapolis: University of Minnesota Press, 1987.

———. "What Is Minor Literature?" Translated by Dana Polan. In *Out There: Marginalization and Contemporary Cultures,* edited by Russell Ferguson et al. Cambridge, MA: MIT Press, 1990. 59–69.

———. *What Is Philosophy?* Translated by Hugh Tomlinson and Graham Burchell. New York: Columbia University Press, 1994.

de Man, Paul. *Allegories of Reading.* New Haven: Yale University Press, 1979.

———. *Blindness and Insight.* Minneapolis: University of Minnesota Press, 1983.

———. "Dialogue and Dialogism." In *Rethinking Bakhtin: Extensions and Challenges,* edited by Gary Saul Morson and Caryl Emerson. Evanston, IL: Northwestern University Press, 1989. 105–14.

Derrida, Jacques. "At This Very Moment in This Work Here I Am." Translated by Ruben Berezdivin. In *Re-Reading Levinas,* edited by Robert Bernasconi and Simon Critchley. Bloomington: Indiana University Press, 1991. 11–48.

———. "Declarations of Independence." Translated by Tom Keenan and Tom Pepper. *New Political Science* 15 (1986): 7–15.

———. "The Deconstruction of Actuality." Translated by Jonathan Reé. *Radical Philosophy* 68 (1994): 28–41.

———. "Force of Law: The 'Mystical Foundation of Authority.'" *Cardozo Law Review* 11, nos. 5–6 (1990): 919–1045.

———. *Limited Inc.* Translated by Samuel Weber. Evanston, IL: Northwestern University Press, 1988.

———. "Living On—Border Lines." Translated by James Hulbert. In *Deconstruction and Criticism,* edited by Harold Bloom et al. New York: Seabury Press, 1979. 75–176.

———. *Memoirs of the Blind.* Translated by Pascale-Anne Brault and Michael Naas. Chicago: University of Chicago Press, 1993.

———. *The Other Heading: Reflections on Today's Europe.* Translated by Pascale-Anne Brault and Michael Naas. Bloomington: Indiana University Press, 1992.

————. *Positions.* Translated by Alan Bass. Chicago: University of Chicago Press, 1981.

————. "Restitutions of the Truth in *Pointure.*" In Derrida, *Truth in Painting,* 255–382.

————. "The Rhetoric of Drugs." Translated by Michael Israel. *differences* 5, no. 1 (1993): 1–24.

————. "Signature Event Context." In *Margins of Philosophy,* translated by Alan Bass. Chicago: University of Chicago Press, 1982, 307–30.

————. "Some Statements and Truisms." Translated by Anne Tomiche. In *The States of "Theory,"* edited by David Carroll. New York: Columbia University Press, 1990. 63–94.

————. *Specters of Marx.* Translated by Peggy Kamuf. New York: Routledge, 1994.

————. *Speech and Phenomena.* Translated by David B. Allison. Evanston, IL: Northwestern University Press, 1973.

————. "Structure, Sign and Play in the Discourse of the Human Sciences." In *Writing and Difference,* translated by Alan Bass. Chicago: University of Chicago Press, 1978. 278–93.

————. " 'To Do Justice to Freud': The History of Madness in the Age of Psychoanalysis." Translated by Pascale-Anne Brault and Michael Naas. *Critical Inquiry* 20 (1994): 227–66.

————. *The Truth in Painting.* Translated by Geoff Bennington and Ian McLeod. Chicago: University of Chicago Press, 1987.

————. "Violence and Metaphysics." In *Writing and Difference,* translated by Alan Bass. Chicago: University of Chicago Press, 1978. 79–153.

Dhaliwal, Amarpal. "Response to Stanley Aronowitz." *Socialist Review* 23, no. 3 (1994): 81–97.

Du Bois, W. E. B. *The Souls of Black Folk.* 1903. Reprint, New York: Dover, 1994.

Emerson, Caryl. "Getting Bakhtin, Right and Left." *Comparative Literature* 46, no. 3 (1994): 288–303.

————. "Russian Orthodoxy and the Early Bakhtin." *Religion and Literature* 22, nos. 2–3 (1990): 109–31.

Fanon, Frantz. *Black Skin, White Masks.* Translated by Charles Lam Markmann. New York: Grove Press, 1967.

Foucault, Michel. *The Archaeology of Knowledge* and *The Discourse on Language.* Translated by A. M. Sheridan Smith (New York: Pantheon, 1972). Originally published as *L'archéologie du savoir* (Paris: Gallimard, 1969), and *L'ordre du discours* (Paris: Gallimard, 1971).

————. "My Body, This Paper, This Fire." Translated by Geoff Bennington. *Oxford Literary Review* 4, no. 1 (1979): 9–28.

————. "Nietzsche, Genealogy, History." Translated by Donald Bouchard and Sherry Simon. In *The Foucault Reader,* edited by Paul Rabinow. New York: Pantheon, 1984. 76–100.

———. *Power/Knowledge.* Edited by Colin Gordon. Translated by Colin Gordon et al. New York: Pantheon, 1980.

———. Preface to *Anti-Oedipus*, by Gilles Deleuze and Félix Guattari. Minneapolis: University of Minnesota Press, 1983. xi–xiv.

———. *This Is Not a Pipe.* Translated by James Harkness. Berkeley: University of California Press, 1983.

———. "What Is Enlightenment?" In *The Foucault Reader*, edited and translated by Paul Rabinow. New York: Pantheon Books, 1984. 32–50.

Franklin, Ursula. "A Differant Quest for Truth and Shoes: Derrida on Heidegger and Schapiro on Van Gogh." *Centennial Review* 35, no. 1 (1991): 141–65.

Gardiner, Michael. "Alterity and Ethics: A Dialogical Perspective." *Theory, Culture, and Society* 13, no. 2 (1996): 121–43.

———. *The Dialogics of Critique: M. M. Bakhtin and the Theory of Ideology.* New York: Routledge, 1992.

Gasché, Rodolphe. "God, for Example." In *Phenomenology and the Numinous*, edited by the Simon Silverman Phenomenology Center. Pittsburgh: Duquesne University Press, 1988. 43–66.

———. *Inventions of Difference: On Jacques Derrida.* Cambridge, MA: Harvard University Press, 1994.

Gates, David. "White Male Paranoia." *Newsweek* 29 March 1993, 48–53.

Gates, Henry Louis. *The Signifying Monkey: A Theory of African-American Literary Criticism.* New York: Oxford University Press, 1988.

Gearhart, Suzanne. *The Interrupted Dialectic.* Baltimore: Johns Hopkins University Press, 1992.

Gioia, Ted. *The Imperfect Art: Reflections on Jazz and Modern Culture.* New York: Oxford University Press, 1988.

Giroux, Henry. "Post-Colonial Ruptures and Democratic Possibilities." *Cultural Critique* 21 (1992): 4–39.

———. "Rewriting the Discourse of Racial Identity: Towards a Pedagogy and Politics of Whiteness." *Harvard Educational Review* 67, no. 2 (1997): 285–315.

Goldstein, Jonah, and Jeremy Rayner. "The Politics of Identity in Late Modern Society." *Theory and Society* 23 (1994): 367–84.

Grosz, Elizabeth. *Volatile Bodies.* St. Leonards, UK: Allen and Unwin, 1994.

Guattari, Félix. *Soft Subversions.* Edited by Slyvère Lotringer. Translated by David L. Sweet and Chet Wiener. New York: Semiotext(e), 1996.

Habermas, Jürgen. *The Philosophical Discourse of Modernity.* Translated by Frederick Lawrence. Cambridge, MA: MIT Press, 1990.

Hale, Dorothy. "Bakhtin in African American Literary Theory." *ELH* 61 (1994): 445–71.

Haraway, Donna J. *Simians, Cyborgs, and Women: The Reinvention of Nature.* New York: Routledge, 1991.

Harris, William J. *The Jazz Aesthetic: The Poetry and Poetics of Amiri Baraka.* Columbia: University of Missouri Press, 1985.

Hartman, Charles O. *Jazz Text: Voice and Improvisation in Poetry, Jazz and Song.* Princeton, NJ: Princeton University Press, 1991.

Harvey, Irene. "Derrida and the Issues of Exemplarity." In *Derrida: A Critical Reader,* edited by David Wood. Oxford: Basil Blackwell, 1992. 193–217.

Hegel, G. W. F. *Lectures on the Philosophy of World History.* Translated by H. B. Nisbet. Cambridge, UK: Cambridge University Press, 1975.

———. *Phenomenology of Spirit.* Translated by A. V. Miller. Oxford: Oxford University Press, 1977.

Heidegger, Martin. *Being and Time.* Translated by John Macquarrie and Edward Robinson. New York: Harper & Row, 1962.

———. "The Origin of the Work of Art." Translated by Albert Hofstadter. In *Poetry, Language, Thought.* New York: Harper & Row, 1971. 15–88.

———. "The Question Concerning Technology." Translated by William Lovitt. In *Basic Writings,* edited by David Krell. New York: Harper & Row, 1972. 287–317.

———. "What Is Metaphysics?" Translated by David Krell. In *Basic Writings,* edited by David Krell. New York: Harper & Row, 1977. 91–112.

Holland, Eugene W. "Deterritorializing 'Deterritorialization': From *Anti-Oedipus* to *A Thousand Plateaus.*" *SubStance* 66 (1991): 55–66.

Holquist, Michael. "The Architectonics of Answerability." In *Art and Answer-ability,* by M. M. Bakhtin. Austin: University of Texas Press, 1990. ix–xlix.

———. *Dialogism: Bakhtin and His World.* New York: Routledge, 1990.

Honneth, Axel. "Integrity and Disrespect: Principle of a Conception of Morality Based on the Theory of Recognition." *Political Theory* 20, no. 2 (1992): 187–201.

Horkheimer, Max, and Theodor Adorno. *Dialectic of Enlightenment.* Translated by John Cumming. New York: Continuum, 1972.

Huffer, Lynne. "Luce *et veritas:* Toward an Ethics of Performance." *Yale French Studies* 87 (1995): 20–41.

Irigaray, Luce. "The Fecundity of the Caress." Translated by Carolyn Burke. In *Face to Face with Levinas,* edited by Richard A. Cohen. Albany: State University of New York Press, 1986. 231–56.

———. "Questions to Emmanuel Levinas: On the Divinity of Love." Translated by Margaret Whitford. In *Re-Reading Levinas,* edited by Robert Bernasconi and Simon Critchley. Bloomington: Indiana University Press, 1991. 109–19.

Ivins, Molly. "Lone Star Republic." *The Nation* 264, no. 20 (26 May 1997): 4–5.

Jameson, Fredric. *Postmodernism, or, the Cultural Logic of Late Capitalism.* Durham, NC: Duke University Press, 1991.

Johnson, Bruce. "Hear Me Talkin' to Ya: Problems of Jazz Discourse." *Popular Music* 12, no. 1 (1993): 1–12.

Kelley, Robin D. G. "Identity Politics and Class Struggle." *New Politics* 6, no. 2 (1997): 84–96.

Kojève, Alexandre. *Introduction to the Reading of Hegel.* Edited by Allan Bloom. Translated by James H. Nichols Jr. Ithaca, NY: Cornell University Press, 1980.

Kuykendall, Ronald. "Hegel and Africa: An Evaluation of the Treatment of Africa in *The Philosophy of History.*" *Journal of Black Studies* 23, no. 4 (1993): 571–81.

Lacan, Jacques. *The Seminar of Jacques Lacan.* Translated by Sylvia Tomaselli. Cambridge, UK: Cambridge University Press, 1988.

Laclau, Ernesto. *New Reflections on the Revolution of Our Time.* London: Verso, 1990.

Laclau, Ernesto, and Chantal Mouffe. *Hegemony and Socialist Strategy: Towards a Radical Democratic Politics.* London: Verso, 1985.

Leitch, Vincent. "Postmodern Culture: The Ambivalence of Fredric Jameson." *College Literature* 19, no. 2 (1992): 111–22.

Levinas, Emmanuel. *Ethics and Infinity.* Translated by Richard A. Cohen. Pittsburgh: Duquesne University Press, 1985.

———. *Existence and Existents.* Translated by Alphonso Lingis. The Hague: Martinus Nijhoff, 1978. Originally published as *De l'existence à l'existant* (Paris: Fontaine, 1947).

———. "Meaning and Sense." Translated by Alphonso Lingis. In *Collected Philosophical Papers,* edited by Alphonso Lingis. The Hague: Martinus Nijhoff, 1987. 75–108.

———. *Otherwise than Being, or Beyond Essence.* Translated by Alphonso Lingis. The Hague: Martinus Nijhoff, 1981. Originally published as *Autrement qu'être ou au-delà de l'essence* (The Hague: Martinus Nijhoff, 1978).

———. "The Paradox of Morality." In *The Provocation of Levinas,* edited by Robert Bernasconi and David Wood. London: Routledge, 1988. 168–80.

———. "Philosophy and the Idea of Infinity." Translated by Alphonso Lingis. In *Collected Philosophical Papers,* edited by Alphonso Lingis. The Hague: Martinus Nijhoff, 1987. 47–60.

———. "Reality and Its Shadow." Translated by Alphonso Lingis. In *The Levinas Reader,* edited by Séan Hand. Cambridge, MA: Basil Blackwell, 1989. 129–43.

———. *Sur Maurice Blanchot.* Montpellier, France: Fata Morgana, 1975.

———. "Time and the Other." Translated by Richard Cohen. In *The Levinas Reader,* edited by Séan Hand. Cambridge, MA: Basil Blackwell, 1989. 38–58.

———. *Totality and Infinity.* Translated by Alphonso Lingis. Pittsburgh: Duquesne University Press, 1969.

———. "Wholly Otherwise." Translated by Simon Critchley. In *Re-Reading Levinas,* edited by Robert Bernasconi and Simon Critchley. Bloomington: Indiana University Press, 1991: 3–10.

Libertson, Joseph. *Proximity: Levinas, Blanchot, Bataille and Communication.* The Hague: Martinus Nijhoff, 1983.

Llewelyn, John. *The Middle Voice of Ecological Conscience: A Chiasmic Reading of Responsibility in the Neighbourhood of Levinas, Heidegger, and Others.* London: Macmillan, 1991.

———. "The 'Possibility' of Heidegger's Death." *Journal of the British Society for Phenomenology* 14, no. 2 (1983): 127–38.

Lyotard, Jean-François. "Levinas' Logic." Translated by Ian McLeod. In *Face to Face with Levinas,* edited by Richard A. Cohen. Albany: State University of New York Press, 1986. 117–58.

McGowan, John. *Postmodernism and Its Critics.* Ithaca, NY: Cornell University Press, 1991.

McShine, Kynaston, ed. *Andy Warhol: A Retrospective.* New York: Museum of Modern Art, 1989.

Mackey, Nathaniel. *Discrepant Engagement: Dissonance, Cross-Culturality and Experimental Writing.* Cambridge, UK: Cambridge University Press, 1993.

Manning, R. J. S. *Interpreting Otherwise than Heidegger: Emmanuel Levinas's Ethics as First Philosophy.* Pittsburgh: Duquesne University Press, 1993.

Marks, Kathy. *Faces of Right Wing Extremism.* Boston: Branden Publishing, 1996.

Miller, J. Hillis. *The Ethics of Reading.* New York: Columbia University Press, 1987.

Modleski, Tania. *Feminism without Women: Culture and Criticism in a "Postfeminist" Age.* New York: Routledge, 1991.

Monson, Ingrid. "Doubleness and Jazz: Irony, Parody, and Ethnomusicology." *Critical Inquiry* 20 (1994): 283–313.

Morson, Gary Saul, and Caryl Emerson. "Introduction: Rethinking Bakthin." In *Rethinking Bakhtin: Extensions and Challenges,* edited by Gary Saul Morson and Caryl Emerson. Evanston, IL: Northwestern University Press, 1989. 1–60.

———. *Mikhail Bakhtin: Creation of a Prosiacs.* Stanford: Stanford University Press, 1990.

Mouffe, Chantal. "Radical Democracy: Modern or Postmodern?" Translated by Paul Holdengräber. In *Universal Abandon? The Politics of Postmodernism,* edited by Andrew Ross. Minneapolis: University of Minnesota Press, 1988. 31–45.

Naas, Michael. "Introduction: For Example." In *The Other Heading,* by Jacques Derrida. Bloomington: Indiana University Press, 1992. vii–lix.

Nancy, Jean-Luc. "The Compearance: From the Existence of 'Communism' to the Community of 'Existence.'" Translated by Tracy B. Strong. *Political Theory* 20, no. 3 (1992). 371–98.

Nancy, Jean-Luc, et al., eds. *Who Comes after the Subject?* New York: Routledge, 1991.

Nealon, Jeffrey T. *Double Reading: Postmodernism after Deconstruction.* Ithaca, NY: Cornell University Press, 1993.

Nietzsche, Friedrich. *The Birth of Tragedy* and *The Case of Wagner.* Translated by Walter Kaufmann. New York: Vintage, 1967.

———. *On the Genealogy of Morals.* Translated by Walter Kaufmann. New York: Vintage, 1967.

———. "On Truth and Lying in an Extra-Moral Sense." Translated by Sander Gilman. In *Friedrich Nietzsche on Rhetoric and Language,* edited by Sander Gilman. New York: Oxford University Press, 1989. 246–57.

Omi, Michael, and Howard Winant. "Response to Stanley Aronowitz." *Socialist Review* 23, no. 3 (1994): 127–34.

Patterson, David. "Signification, Responsibility, Spirit: Bakhtin and Levinas." *Cithara* 22, no. 2 (1987): 6–19.

Patton, Cindy. "Refiguring Social Space." In *Social Postmodernism: Beyond Identity Politics,* edited by Linda Nicholson and Steven Seidman. Cambridge, UK: Cambridge University Press, 1995. 216–49.

Payne, Michael. "Derrida, Heidegger, and Van Gogh's 'Old Shoes.'" *Textual Practice* 6, no. 1 (1992): 87–99.

Pechey, Graham. "Boundaries versus Binaries: Bakhtin in/against the History of Ideas." *Radical Philosophy* 54 (1990): 23–31.

Peperzak, Adriaan. *To the Other: An Introduction to the Philosophy of Emmanuel Levinas.* West Lafayette, IN: Purdue University Press, 1993.

Perloff, Marjorie. "Empiricism Once More." *Modern Language Quarterly* 54, no. 1 (1993): 121–31.

Ponzio, Augusto. "The Relation of Otherness in Bakhtin, Blanchot, Levinas." *Semiotic Inquiry* 7, no. 1 (1987): 1–18.

Reed, Ishmael. *Flight to Canada.* New York: Antheneum, 1976.

———. *Mumbo Jumbo.* New York: Antheneum, 1972.

———. *Shrovetide in Old New Orleans.* New York: Doubleday, 1978.

Roberts, Mathew. "Poetics Hermeneutics Dialogics: Bakhtin and Paul de Man." In *Rethinking Bakhtin: Extensions and Challenges,* edited by Gary Saul Morson and Caryl Emerson. Evanston, IL: Northwestern University Press, 1989. 115–34.

Roediger, David. *Towards the Abolition of Whiteness.* London: Verso, 1994.

Ronell, Avital. *Crack Wars: Literature, Addiction, Mania.* Lincoln: University of Nebraska Press, 1992.

Rose, Tricia. *Black Noise: Rap Music and Black Culture in Contemporary America.* Middletown, CT: Wesleyan University Press, 1994.

Ross, Loretta. "White Supremacy in the 1990s." In *Eyes Right! Challenging the Right Wing Backlash,* edited by Chip Berlet. Boston: South End Press, 1995. 166–81.

Saussure, Ferdinand de. *Course in General Linguistics.* Translated by Wade Baskin. New York: McGraw Hill, 1959.

Savran, David. "The Sadomasochist in the Closet: White Masculinity and the Culture of Victimization." *differences* 8, no. 2 (1996): 127–52.

Schapiro, Meyer. "The Still Life as Personal Object: A Note on Heidegger and Van Gogh." In *The Reach of Mind: Essays in Memory of Kurt Goldstein*, edited by Marianne L. Simmel. New York: Springer, 1968. 203–9.

Scott, Charles E. *The Question of Ethics*. Bloomington: Indiana University Press, 1990.

Sedgwick, Eve Kosofsky. *Epistemology of the Closet*. Berkeley: University of California Press, 1990.

Shaviro, Steven. *The Cinematic Body*. Minneapolis: University of Minnesota Press, 1993.

Silverman, Kaja. *Male Subjectivity at the Margins*. New York: Routledge, 1993.

———. *The Subject of Semiotics*. Oxford: Oxford University Press, 1983.

Smith, John H. *The Spirit and Its Letter: Traces of Rhetoric in Hegel's Philosophy of "Bildung."* Ithaca, NY: Cornell University Press, 1988.

Snead, James A. "Repetition as a Figure of Black Culture." In *Out There: Marginalization and Contemporary Cultures*, edited by Russell Ferguson et al. Cambridge, MA: MIT Press, 1990: 213–32.

Taussig, Michael. *Mimesis and Alterity*. New York: Routledge, 1993.

Todorov, Tzvetan. *Mikhail Bakhtin: The Dialogical Principle*. Translated by Wlad Godzich. Minneapolis: University of Minnesota Press, 1984.

Tucker, Bruce. "Black Music after Theory." *Black Music Research Journal* 11, no. 2 (1991): iii–vii.

Ulmer, Gregory. *Applied Grammatology*. Baltimore: Johns Hopkins University Press, 1985.

Warminski, Andrzej. *Readings in Interpretation*. Minneapolis: University of Minnesota Press, 1987.

West, Cornel. "Charlie Parker Didn't Give a Damn." *New Perspectives Quarterly* 8, no. 3 (1991): 60–63.

Wiexlmann, Joe. "African American Deconstruction of the Novel in the Work of Ishmael Reed and Clarence Major." *Melus* 17, no. 4 (1991): 57–79.

Wyschogrod, Edith. "From the Disaster to the Other: Tracing the Name of God in Levinas." In *Phenomenology and the Numinous*, edited by the Simon Silverman Phenomenology Center. Pittsburgh: Duquesne University Press, 1988. 67–86

Yúdice, George. "What's a Straight White Man to Do?" In *Constructing Masculinity*, edited by Maurice Berger, Brian Wallis, and Simon Watson. New York: Routledge, 1995. 267–83.

Ziarek, Krzysztof. "The Language of Praise: Levinas and Marion." *Religion and Literature* 22, nos. 2–3 (1990): 93–107.

Žižek, Slavoj. "Beyond Discourse Analysis." In *New Reflections on the Revolution of our Time*, by Ernesto Laclau. London: Verso, 1990. 249–60.

———. *Enjoy Your Symptom! Jacques Lacan in Hollywood and Out*. New York: Routledge, 1992.

———. *For They Know Not What They Do.* London: Verso, 1991.

———. *Tarrying with the Negative: Kant, Hegel and the Critique of Ideology.* Durham, NC: Duke University Press, 1993.

Žižek, Slavoj, and Renata Salecl. "Interview: Lacan in Slovenia." *Radical Philosophy* 58 (1991): 25–31.

Index

Jeffrey T. Nealon is Associate Professor in the
Department of English at Pennsylvania State
University. He is the author of *Double Reading:
Postmodernism after Deconstruction.*

Library of Congress Cataloging-in-Publication Data
Nealon, Jeffrey T.
Alterity politics : ethics and performative subjectivity /
Jeffrey T. Nealon.
Includes bibliographical references and index.
ISBN 0-8223-2125-4 (alk. cloth).
ISBN 0-8223-2145-9 (pbk. : alk. paper)
1. Group identity—Political aspects.   2. Identity
(Psychology)—Political aspects.   3. Political
psychology.   4. Political sociology.   5. Social ethics.
I. Title.
JA74.5.N43   1998   320.01′1—dc21   98-14403 CIP